# Estonia's Transition to the EU

Two decades on from the start of the 'Singing Revolution', and five years daon from the Baltic States' entry to the European Union, the time is ripe to take stock of Estonia's remarkable transition from Soviet Republic to EU member state and address the challenges – some new, some ongoing – and uncertainties that have arisen following the country's entry to the EU.

This book locates the post-accession period within the broader sweep of post-communist transition and diagnoses the problems facing Estonia as the global economic downturn takes hold and a new mood of pessimism reigns in Central and Eastern Europe. Until recently, Estonia enjoyed an international reputation as an emerging high-growth 'tiger economy' and reform pioneer, not least in the sphere of IT. This economic success story, however, masked the continued problematic political and social legacies of the Soviet period, including the issue of ethnic integration, which again hit the headlines following riots in Tallinn in April 2007. In 2008, after fabulous economic growth of the last eight years, the deep economic recession had awakened society from consumerist dreams and pushed Estonia to find a new paradigm of development.

This fully up-to-date appraisal – the first in English – covers all of the key issues, and will appeal to specialists in Baltic and Central and Eastern European politics and society, as well as to anyone with an interest in European integration more generally.

This book was previously published as a special issue of the *Journal of Baltic Studies*.

**Marju Lauristin** is Professor Emeritus at the University of Tartu and works as Professor of Social Communication in the Institute of Journalism and Communication. Her research interests are related to the social, cultural and political conditions and implications of the Estonian post-communist transition.

**Peeter Vihalemm** is Professor of Media Studies at the Institute of Journalism and Communication, University of Tartu, Estonia. His work has been focused on political and cultural aspects of postcommunist transformation, especially on development of media system and media use, and changing spatial relations in the Baltic Sea region.

# Estonia's Transition to the EU

Twenty Years On

Edited by Marju Lauristin
and Peeter Vihalemm

LONDON AND NEW YORK

First published 2010 by Routledge

2 Park Square, Milton Park, Abingdon, Oxon OX14 4RN
711 Third Avenue, New York, NY 10017, USA

*Routledge is an imprint of the Taylor & Francis Group, an informa business*

First issued in paperback 2016

Copyright © 2010 The Association for the Advancement of Baltic Studies

Typeset in Perpetua by Value Chain, India

All rights reserved. No part of this book may be reprinted or reproduced or utilised in any form or by any electronic, mechanical, or other means, now known or hereafter invented, including photocopying and recording, or in any information storage or retrieval system, without permission in writing from the publishers.

Notice:
Product or corporate names may be trademarks or registered trademarks, and are used only for identification and explanation without intent to infringe.

The AABS would like to make it known that it is subsidizing the price of this book by waiving its entitlement to receive royalties.

*British Library Cataloguing in Publication Data*
A catalogue record for this book is available from the British Library

ISBN 978-0-415-55732-0 (hbk)
ISBN 978-1-138-96898-1 (pbk)

# Contents

*Notes on Contributors*   vi

1. The Political Agenda During Different Periods of Estonian Transformation: External and Internal Factors   1
   *Marju Lauristin and Peeter Vihalemm*

2. The Estonian Tiger Leap from Post-Communism to the Information Society: From Policy to Practice   28
   *Pille Runnel, Pille Pruulmann-Vengerfeldt and Kristina Reinsalu*

3. Emerging Consumer Types in a Transition Culture: Consumption Patterns of Generational and Ethnic Groups in Estonia   51
   *Veronika Kalmus, Margit Keller and Maie Kiisel*

4. The Patterns of Cultural Attitudes and Preferences in Estonia   73
   *Maarja Lõhmus, Marju Lauristin and Eneli Siirman*

5. Cultural Differentiation of the Russian Minority   92
   *Triin Vihalemm and Veronika Kalmus*

6. Inter-Ethnic Attitudes and Contacts Between Ethnic Groups in Estonia   116
   *Külliki Korts*

7. The Bronze Soldier: Identity Threat and Maintenance in Estonia   133
   *Martin Ehala*

*Index*   153

# Notes on Contributors

**Martin Ehala** is a senior researcher at the University of Tartu. His main research interests are the development of the Estonian linguistic environment, language maintenance and ethno linguistic vitality. He has also published on topics related to language and identity, and contact induced changes in Estonian.

**Margit Keller** (PhD) is Senior Researcher at the Institute of Journalism and Communication, University of Tartu. Her research interests include consumer culture and consumer socialization. She has published on these topics in *European Journal of Cultural Studies, Journal of Consumer Culture, Childhood and Young*.

**Maie Kiisel** (MA) is Assistant Lecturer and doctoral student at the Institute of Journalism and Communication, University of Tartu. Her research focuses on changes in environmental consciousness, participation processes and risk society.

**Veronika Kalmus** (PhD) is Associate Professor at the Institute of Journalism and Communication, University of Tartu. Her current research interests are socialization in the informatizing society and transition culture. She has published in *Discourse & Society, Journal of Baltic Studies, Journal of Curriculum Studies, Young and Cyberpsychology*.

**Külliki Korts** is a Research Fellow of Media Studies in the Institute of Journalism and Communication at the University of Tartu. Her research interests include nationbuilding and inter-ethnic relations in post-communist societies.

**Veronika Kalmus** (PhD) is Associate Professor at the Institute of Journalism and Communication, University of Tartu. Her current research interests are socialization in the informatizing society and transition culture. She has published in *Discourse & Society, Journal of Baltic Studies, Journal of Curriculum Studies, Cyberpsychology and Young*.

**Marju Lauristin** is Professor Emeritus at the University of Tartu and works as Professor of Social Communication in the Institute of Journalism and Communication. Her research interests are related to the social, cultural and political conditions and implications of the Estonian post-communist transition.

**Maarja Lõhmus** works as Associated Professor in the Institute of Journalism and Communication at the University of Tartu. She is involved with various socio-semiotic research projects dealing with socio-cultural practices in Estonian society and teaches theoretical, semiotic and cultural studies courses at the University of Tartu.

**Marju Lauristin** is Professor Emeritus at the University of Tartu and works as Professor of Social Communication in the Institute of Journalism and Communication. Her research interests are related to the social, cultural and political conditions and implications of the Estonian post-communist transition.

**Pille Pruulmann-Vengerfeldt** is a Research Fellow in Media Studies at the University of Tartu's Institute of Journalism and Communication. Her research interests include people and practices in the information society. She is the Head of Young Scholars' section at the European Communication Research and Education Association, and is organizer of the European Media and Communication Doctoral Summer School.

**Pille Runnel** is the Estonian National Museum's Research Director and Research Fellow in Media Studies at the University of Tartu's Institute of Journalism and Communication. She is involved with various research projects dealing with sociocultural practices in the Estonian information society.

**Kristina Reinsalu** is the Estonian e-Governance Academy's Program Director and a Research Fellow of Communication Management at the University of Tartu's Institute of Journalism and Communication. Her research focuses on the application of ICTs in the development of democratic governance at the local level.

**Eneli Siirman** is a doctoral student in Sociology at the University of Tartu. Her research interests include social differentiation of cultural practices.

**Triin Vihalemm** (PhD) is Associate Professor at the Institute of Journalism and Communication, University of Tartu. Her current research interests focus on the transformation of ethnic, linguistic, regional and other identities in media and consumer culture. She has published in *Nationalities Papers, Journal of Baltic Studies, Journal of Borderlands Studies, Diasporas* and *Young*.

**Peeter Vihalemm** is Professor of Media Studies at the Institute of Journalism and Communication, University of Tartu, Estonia. His work has been focused on political and cultural aspects of postcommunist transformation, especially on the development of media system and media use, and changing spatial relations in the Baltic Sea region.

# THE POLITICAL AGENDA DURING DIFFERENT PERIODS OF ESTONIAN TRANSFORMATION: EXTERNAL AND INTERNAL FACTORS

## Marju Lauristin and Peeter Vihalemm

### Introduction

In 2009 the majority of Europe's post-communist countries are members of the EU and may now consider themselves to be modern capitalist societies. Yet, the mood of optimism and appraisal of post-communist achievements prevalent in the 1990s has turned into caution and criticism during the post-accession years. The well-known analyst of post-communist transformation, Jacques Rupnik, has even characterized the post-accession backlash in the Central and Eastern European countries as a 'return to post-communism' in which 'the moral and political vacuum left by communism was fully exposed' (Rupnik 2006). In the Baltic states, too, the years since EU and NATO accession have revealed that beneath the surface of extraordinarily high economic growth, society is tormented by unsolved political, economic and social problems. Despite having the fastest growing economies among the new EU members, the three countries still lag behind in the level and efficiency of social spending, and have the highest rates of 'social diseases', such as crime, drugs, HIV and suicides (*Europe in figures* 2008; Heidmets 2007b; Lauristin 2003).

The controversies surrounding Estonia's development can be well illustrated with reference to the divergent assessments of change held by the international community on the one hand, and by domestic media and public opinion on the other. Indeed, the political agenda of change, as well as its outcomes could be 'read' completely differently from the perspectives of external observers *vis-à-vis* internal, local participants (Lauristin & Heidmets 2002, pp. 23–4). For example, whereas from the external perspective, the issue of the Russian minority belongs to the area of human rights, the domestic political agenda has placed the accent on historical justice and the preservation of the majority language and culture (Ruutsoo 2002, pp. 41–52). External agencies and experts have highlighted the successful economic development and growing international competitiveness of Estonia, whose post-communist transformation has been assessed as one of the most successful amongst the 2004 accession states (Bertelsmann 2006, 2008; *Nations in Transit 2008*, available at: www.freedomhouse.hu/index.php?option=com_content&task=view&id=196, accessed 13 December 2008).

The domestic view, however, has focused on the dark side of the changes shadowing this success story (Heidmets 2007a; Lauristin 2003). Evaluations of Estonian development by influential domestic experts sound rather critical:

> When measured against Europe, Estonian society seems contradictory. On the one hand, we have fast economic growth, excellent employment levels, and a thriving digitalisation process; on the other hand we are characterized by poor health, xenophobia, incompetence in battling HIV, and overcrowded prisons. ... Our human development has taken us towards freedom, but not enough responsibility and common values. The result is a fragmented and individualistic Estonia that finds it difficult to fit conventional notions and way of life of Europe. (Heidmets 2007b, p. 115)

Has this imbalance emerged as a result of the external pressures exercised by strong monetary institutions headed by the IMF and EU? Or could it be better explained by stressing internal factors, such as the domination of right-wing parties on the political scene or the rapid shift from national development goals to individualistic values and consumerist orientations?

## The Nature of External and Internal Factors in Social Change

The role of external and internal factors has been one of the key topics within analyses of Estonia's development (see Clemens 2001; Raik 2003; Smith 1999, pp. 176–82). When speaking of 'external factors', we mean those influences emanating from the presence of international, intersocietal and intercultural forces in a given society, whereas 'internal factors' refers to the mutual interrelations of values and social structure (social classes, ethnic groups, generations, gender groups, etc.) as they are institutionalized in a given society (Smelser 1992, p. 370). The model for the analysis of external and internal conditions of transition has been developed by Norgaard (2000), who highlighted several factors specific to Estonia: closeness to the Nordic countries, and specifically Finland (including access to alternative information channels in the Finnish language); the greater readiness of the Estonian managerial elite for the economic reforms; and lower involvement in the Soviet military–industrial complex (compared to Latvia) (Norgaard 2000, pp. 174–8). In several studies the analysis is focused on the factors behind Estonia's success during the early stages of transition (Buchen 2006; Feldmann 2007; Feldmann & Sally 2002; Norkus 2007; Panagiotou 2001). However, in the field of democratic consolidation, more critique than praise has been voiced: a common theme for all post-communist societies is the weakness of civil society (Howard 2003) and the specificity of the post-communist culture (Kennedy 2002; Sztompka 2004; Vogt 2005). Low trust and political instability is seen as characteristic of the reform process (Mishler & Rose 2001; Rose et al. 1998).

In the vast literature analyzing the changes in Central and Eastern Europe over the past two decades, the role of international agencies in promoting non-violent and successful re-integration of the so called 'new democracies' (including the Baltic countries) with Europe has merited particular attention (Löfgren & Herd 2000; Raik 1998, 2003; Schimmelfennig & Sedelmeyer 2005; Vachudova 2005). The focus here is on the impact of the EU and international monetary institutions (IMF, World Bank, WTO) on the decisions and choices made by the governments of the post-communist countries, the influence of financial and knowledge flows from the West to the East, and the effects of regional and bilateral cooperation. Swedish economist Anders Aslund, summarizing the experience of 'building capitalism', has suggested that successful examples in the European post-communist countries are mostly related to extensive foreign input, whereas in those areas where the West has lacked sufficient willingness and/or resources for comprehensive involvement, the outcomes of transition have not been good enough. Witness, for instance, Aslund's claim that 'no international organization focused on democracy building or the building the rule of law, and little progress occurred' (Aslund 2007, p. 313). On the other extreme are those authors who accuse external agencies of imposing liberal reforms and enhancing social inequalities. We, however, cannot accept this kind of black and white assessment of external input as a reason for the success or failure in certain areas of the transformation agenda. We rather agree with Smelser that the interaction between internal and external factors is one of the most interesting issues. The question is: 'how the distinction sometimes breaks down as the two kinds of forces fuse to generate or block the change' (Smelser 1992, p. 370).

The field of minority protection has provided good examples of the interplay between international and domestic agencies in framing the political agenda. Looking at the influence of the EU, the OSCE and the COE on policy concerning minority education in Estonia, Elena Jurado has discovered that the effects of certain modes of external influence differed in the early 1990s, compared to later periods (Jurado 2003, p. 420). At the present time, we can speak about a turn from an external to an internal focus in the Estonian policy of minority integration after the shock produced in society by the so called 'Bronze soldier' crisis in April 2007 (see Petersoo & Tamm 2008).

Competition between parties is one of the most visible internal factors in the process of transformation (Grzymala-Busse 2007; Orenstein 2001; Vachudova 2005). As regards social agencies, the 'winners' and 'losers' of transition (Rychard 1996) and the role played by the various interest groups, especially the inhibiting role of so-called rent seekers and 'old *nomenklatura*' (Aslund 2002, 2007; Szelenyi 1999), have deserved some attention. The role of the initial leaders in setting the agenda of transition has been also stressed. For example, the composition of the first Estonian government after 1991, formed mostly by young radicals who lacked the burden of

Soviet-era 'competence', has been mentioned as a factor facilitating the implementation of liberal reforms (Arias King 2003).

Authors who have critically analyzed political developments in the post-communist countries have pointed to the difficulty of establishing stable party systems, and fighting corruption and clientelism, as well as to the rise of populist conservative–nationalist political forces (Arter 1996; Berglund *et al.* 2004; Rupnik 2006). Estonia has not escaped any of these problems, although it has been formally recognized as a full and stable democratic system since the late 1990s and, comparatively speaking, has been deemed successful in many areas of democratic reform, displaying: a low level of corruption, stabilization of the party-system, consistency and predictability of economic policy, transparency in decision making, and the development of e-democracy (Johannsen 2006). The main areas of concern continue to be minority integration, public health and social protection policies. However, accession to the EU has played a positive role in terms of the supply of resources and opportunities for international networking in these fields.

One cannot underestimate the significance of cultural values, ideological visions, and popular beliefs as internal factors in post-communist development. The cultural and social background of political choices made in different post-communist countries deserve much more attention than is often acknowledged. Among cultural factors historical memories play a special role. As an explanation of the differences in the pace of post-communist developments in the three Baltic countries Zenonas Norkus has highlighted the stronger influence of the pietist 'protestant scarcity' tradition in Estonia, compared to the other Baltic countries (2007). Cultural aspects are also especially important in the formation of minority policies in Estonia and Latvia [see, for example, the comparison of the value structures of Estonia and Latvia's majority and minority groups presented in Vihalemm and Kalmus (2009)]. Changing very slowly and carrying cultural memory and traditions formed through centuries, values and identities of people belong to the core of internal factors influencing policy formation. However, within a context of fundamental systemic change, even these values could alter under the pressure of external factors. In his analysis of post-communist transition culture, Michael Kennedy differentiates between the transition agendas 'exported' by two kinds of external agents: the liberalist economic agenda pursued by international financial bodies like the World Bank, and the human rights and human development agenda created by institutions related to the United Nations (Kennedy 2002, pp. 98–116). Referring to the results of qualitative studies conducted in Estonia and Ukraine, Kennedy argues that in the former, the specific 'transition culture' stressing competitiveness, 'Westerness' and orientation to success have fostered support for the liberalist agenda even among those who have found themselves on the 'losing side' (Kennedy 2002, pp. 272–4). Here we would add that the 'transition culture' is itself an ideological formation that has taken the perspectives of the most successful social actors and framed these as 'self evident' aims for the whole society. In so doing, it has legitimized approaches that prioritize the economic dimensions of reform while downplaying their social implications and reducing these to 'individual failures' (Kennedy 2002). The leading role in the formation of the 'transition culture' has been performed by political, economic and cultural elites, who participate in the construction of the new social order, producing and institutionalizing their 'ontological visions' of society (Eisenstadt 1992, p. 412). The visions of political elites have been verbalized in concepts such as 'Westernization', 'marketization', 'liberalization', 'building of the nation state', 'democratization', but also 'social justice', 'sustainable development', etc. These concepts have not been produced in isolation, but have mostly been a product of 'discursive learning' in the process of interaction between domestic elites and their international partners (Raik 2003). Some of these concepts are prioritized and privileged in the political agenda and/or in popular beliefs; others are not. Some of them were widely supported during the transition years and became contested only recently; some of them were pushed to the margins or even completely neglected, only to reappear and create extensive public debate and even crises. These concepts have in turn informed public perceptions of the aims, conditions, standards and criteria of development. They have created criteria of success or failure, and defined the nature of challenges and problems for society.

The distinction between the internal and external dimensions of the political agenda is summarized in Table 1.

An analysis of the interaction between the internal and external agenda within concrete policy fields would require extensive research of documents and public texts and qualitative interviews with participants in the decision-making process. At this stage we shall limit ourselves to the more modest task of tracking the changing role of internally or externally prioritized policy agendas through the different stages of Estonian transition. Through this internal *vs.* external perspective the essay tries to envisage the turning points in the country's transformation. Our interest lies in the differences between periods as a whole, rather than differences between policies in concrete fields.

## Periodization of Transition and Changing Priorities in Political Agenda

As discussed above, the role of external *vs.* internal factors in the post-communist transformation of Estonian society has been changing over time. In order to follow these changes, we have further developed the periodization of the Estonian transition (Lauristin & Vihalemm 2002), making distinctions between five different stages and introducing for the present analysis some novel aspects, especially concerning the last period:

1. 1988–1991: breaking with the old system, the 'Singing Revolution';
2. 1991–1994: radical reforms, constituting a new political, economic and social order; a time of 'extraordinary politics';
3. 1995–1998: economic stabilization, start of the period of integration with the EU and NATO;
4. 1999–2004: preparations for EU accession, growing inner tensions;
5. 2005–2008: new challenges of the post EU accession period, identity crisis, the turn from economic growth to slowdown.

**TABLE 1** Differentiation of the external and internal perspectives in formation of the transformation agenda

| | External | Internal |
|---|---|---|
| Leading actors | EU, NATO, IMF and other international organizations, transnational corporations, international NGO networks, USA, Russia, Nordic and other countries, global media | Economic, political and cultural elites, social and ethnic groups, political parties and governmental agencies, NGOs, social movements, national media |
| The goals of reforms | Global geopolitical restructuring, international security and stability, financial sustainability, expansion of the Western economic and political system, European integration, human rights, minority protection | National independence, strong nation state, national security, historical justice, economic growth and national competitiveness, representative political system, preservation of Estonian language and culture, integration with the EU and NATO |
| Leading concepts and values | Modernization, Westernization, democratization, marketization, integration, globalization | National identity, success, freedom, democracy, growth of individual opportunities and wealth, social equality, stability and security, breaking with the communist past |
| Criteria of evaluation, indicators of success or failure | Standardized international indicators of economic growth, political freedom, democracy and human development | Life satisfaction, trust in institutions, level of incomes, political participation, public health, personal security, living conditions, social (in)equality |
| Main problems and challenges | Lack of expected progress in the areas monitored by the international agencies, 'lagging behind' in international economic competition, failure in fulfillment of EU accession criteria or Eurozone conditions, etc. | Social and ethnic tensions, low trust and alienation, de-population, economic instability, threats to national security, poverty and inequality, corruption, weakness of civil society, pertinence of the communist legacy |
| Steering mechanisms | Conditionalities in receiving international funding, monitoring and ratings by international agencies, conditionalities set in EU and NATO accession, compliance with EU directives and international conventions | Political competition between parties, free elections, legislation, governmental actions and administrative control, Tripartite et al. social agreements, lobbying, media, public opinion, protest actions |

## Breakthrough: the 'Singing Revolution' (1988–1991)

It is sometimes argued that external factors played the decisive role in the liberation of Central and Eastern Europe from the communist regime (and the Baltic countries from Soviet occupation) – namely, the reforms initiated by Gorbachev, which ended the Cold War and ultimately led to the collapse of the Soviet Union (Fischer-Galati 2005, p. 167). However, if one looks at the different ways in which various parts of the dissolved Soviet Union had been developing, there is justification for the claim that pressure from the Baltic mass movements and their coordinated activities on the international level were crucial in bringing about the independence and further successful development of the Baltic countries (Judt 2005, pp. 644–7; Norgaard & Johannsen 1999, pp. 24–30, 54–5; Smith 2001, p. xxiv). It is important to remember that initially neither the governments of the USA and other Western states, nor Gorbachev, Yeltsin or other democratic leaders in the former USSR supported the agenda of Baltic independence. The same could be said of the mainstream Western media. Consequently, one can say that during the period of the 'Singing Revolution' it was the internal agenda that prevailed, while national movements sought to enlist the support of international agencies for their objectives.

The period in question was characterized by the highest possible level of civic participation: overwhelming involvement of the people in mass rallies, nationwide participation in public debates concerning the future of the Baltic countries as independent states (for example, the 'Baltic Way' conference, organized by the Popular Fronts of Estonia, Latvia and Lithuania in May 1989), heated discussions about the content of strategic documents (for example, the IME program in Estonia, concerning how to achieve economic independence). It is widely acknowledged that the leading role during this period was played by social movements, which mobilized approximately 70% of the Estonian population.

The main importance of the external dimension at this time was in providing the arguments used by different movements: whereas Popular Fronts in all Baltic countries took their cue from the democratic changes in the Soviet Union, the civic movements focused on international law and the politics of non-recognition practiced by the USA, the UK and some other Western governments throughout the 'Cold War'. The latter explains why the citizens' movement prioritized the concept of restitution, based on the legal continuity of the pre-war Baltic states.

Thus, a difference in focus becomes apparent when looking at the agenda of the main actors. Within the Popular Front, the dominant idea was to pursue 'step-by-step' changes to the Soviet Union, with a view to bringing about its complete dissolution. This would bring freedom to all of its inhabitants, and create opportunities for the Baltic states to gain independence. With increasing experience of collective self-expression through participation in mass rallies and public meetings, the courage of people to openly pursue their ultimate political goal – independence from Soviet rule – grew rapidly.

In the more radical Citizens' Committees movement the leading positions were held by people who were not satisfied with the 'step-by-step' approach. These discerned an historical 'window of opportunity' that allowed for an immediate break with the hated regime. Their core value was full 'restitution' not just in a material (as in the return of properties), but also (and most importantly) in a moral and cultural sense, as a restoration of the social order destroyed by the communist regime. As the movement was perceived in the first place as a moral step toward the realization of historical justice, it defined its task as overcoming the cleavage between the past and the future. This could not be done by moving cautiously 'step-by-step'. The people who joined the citizens' movement and elected the Estonian Congress had this great leap forward in mind and collected the strength to accomplish this decisive move at just the right moment.

Consent regarding the national agenda was achieved as part of a dramatic process of discursive contestation between the two movements and their representative institutions, whereas the majority of rank and file members were participating in the activities of both.

The most influential external factor during this period was the permanent threat from Soviet troops and the reluctance of the Soviet leadership (including Gorbachev) to acknowledge the rights of the Baltic people to restore their independence. The fight with Moscow was locally represented by the Interfront movement. Support from the West, which was very important in terms of asserting the legal and moral claims of the Baltic people, was in practice patchy and inconsistent. Publicly, at least, most Western politicians maintained a stance of diplomatic detachment right up until the last moments of the decisive events of August 1991.

The social agencies and ideological discourses which were formed during this period influenced the structure of the political field in Estonia (as in the other Baltic countries) during the entire period of transition.

## 'Extraordinary politics' and radical economic reforms (1992–1994)

Almost immediately after the restoration of Estonian independence in August 1991 the positive role of external factors started to grow. During the intermediate year of 1991 the internally defined agenda still prevailed: the formation of the Constitutional Assembly and the project for the immediate introduction of the convertible national currency were strategic decisions made by the consensus of all national political actors, even if the external advice was completely different. However, the process of drafting the new constitution drew heavily on the expertise of the Council of Europe. During the years 1991–1993 Estonia was actively preparing for membership of the Council of Europe, which was perceived as the first step in European integration. Monitoring the anticipated (but never realized) outburst of ethnic conflict was performed by the OSCE. After the successful introduction of the national currency in June 1992 (mainly pushed by internal actors – see Kallas 1998; Laar 2002, pp. 45–50; Sank 2001, pp. 94–101), the further development of the Estonian economy was guided by the IMF, the EBRD and the World Bank (Aslund 2002, pp. 210–1). The power of the international monitoring agencies was realized through the implementation of a standardized set of 'transition indicators'. In the economic field these indicators supported the liberal paradigm of transition, based on the principles of the 'Washington consensus' (see Aslund 2002, pp. 72–8; Sachs 1994; Williamson 1993). A number of indexes of structural reform and economic freedom have been elaborated by the World Bank, the EBRD, the Heritage Foundation and the Fraser Institute (Aslund 2002, pp. 160–3).

The first free parliamentary elections in September 1992 were won by those political forces that supported the radical marketization and Westernization of Estonia's economy. The right-of-center coalition, led by the national-conservative *Pro Patria* party, implemented one of the most radical agendas for post-communist reform: liberal 'shock therapy'. The eagerness of the new government to implement the radical reform agenda was stimulated by economic difficulties, and by the need to replace the Soviet administrative legacy with new institutions and legal structures. Despite strife among the political leaders, this agenda initially enjoyed broad national consent, which was encouraged by the 'negative external pressure' arising from the continued presence of the Soviet (now Russian) army on Estonian soil. At the same time, the know-how and resources provided by international organizations and cooperation with the Nordic countries was important in terms of sustaining the national will to overcome the difficulties associated with the reform process. Foreign policy was aimed at international recognition and creating an attractive reputation for foreign investors, thus breaking economic and political dependence on Russia. As Lagerspetz and Vogt have pointed out in their overview of Estonian politics, the 'Russian factor' played a very important role in shaping Estonian reform policies:

> Although the Estonians were able to break away from the Soviet Empire, history has taught them not to take for granted their national independence, or indeed, their very existence as a people. This attitude serves as a strong incentive for overcoming internal social divisions – people are simply postponing their demands for better living standards because of the perceived Russian threat. This attitude has until recently given the governments a free hand to implement radical economic reform policies, without having to fear protests from the social groups most negatively affected. In short, the Estonians' emphasis on identity politics has made it possible to pursue consensual policies. This is what we consider the key factor explaining the radical nature of Estonia's post-socialist economic reforms. (Lagerspetz & Vogt 2004, pp. 80–1)

Western countries and international agencies provided significant material resources and the technical assistance that were needed to cope with the severe problems emerging after the break – political, social and cultural/symbolic – with the previous system. In the early 1990s, Estonia – like other post-communist societies – was frequently characterized in terms of the 'weakness' of its young political parties, its civic society, and its capacity to collect taxes or administer privatization. Complaints about the 'dictatorship' of international agencies, be it the IMF, World Bank, OSCE, EU Commission or Soros Foundation, often exposed the lack of preparedness of the authorities or NGOs in the post-communist countries which were not well-placed to maintain their own agenda when dealing with international partners. Estonia became in this sense 'a model pupil', quickly developing the capacity to absorb external input and adjust to the new rules.

According to a World Bank analysis, Estonia in 1994 belonged to a group of countries that had made a 'clear break with the previous regime' and reached high levels of political freedom and economic stabilization (De Melo et al. 1996, p. 420).

It was during this period – when the vast majority of important decisions had to be made despite a deficit of money, information, know-how and human resources – that the role of external aid and technical assistance was most significant. Knowledge transfer (supplemented by financial resources for implementation from the EBRD, World Bank, IMF and the EU) was especially fruitful in those areas where the remnants of the Soviet system needed to be replaced as quickly as possible with effective new structures: *inter alia* taxation, customs, banking, social insurance, public health, labor market, etc. However, there were some areas in which the young Estonian government insisted on the realization of national visions, even if they contradicted the schemes proposed by foreign experts and international institutions. The policy of restitution was certainly one of them. In all European post-communist countries debates over the different privatization schemes were informed by the conflict between economic efficiency (supported by international financial agencies), social equality (based on post-communist cultural schemes recognizing the right of all people to the fruits of their labor), and historical justice (compensation for the losses and restitution of the property rights of the pre-Soviet owners and their descendants). Some analysts pointed to the hidden social agenda behind the choice of privatization schemes:

> While privatization and the opening of economies to foreign direct investment were often combined, post-communist governments had other motives for transferring state assets to private owners. Though they certainly believed that private ownership would transform bureaucratically run state enterprises into efficient profit making companies, privatization was also conceived as a tool of post-communist social engineering that would lead to the creation of a new capitalist class. With this intention, early post-communist governments pursued a wide range of privatization strategies from the sale of businesses to foreign multinationals to restitution to former owners. (Pittaway 2007, p. 35)

The Estonian solution was a combination of all three of the above-mentioned schemes, matching the interests of the different social actors. Economic efficiency was the leading argument for using international open bids in selling large state-owned companies, while social justice was implemented in the privatization of apartments in exchange for vouchers based on the length of the working years. Socially most controversial was the scheme supporting full restitution of pre-war property rights for all real estate owners as of June 1940 and their descendants. Despite the quite extensive critique of the social consequences of restitution, our survey from 2005 proves that 50% of present-day Estonians find the restitution principles fair, against 31% who find that it was a mistake which caused a lot of new injustices (Kalmus *et al.* 2004).

Issues of ethnic policy, including citizenship, were at this time strongly in focus. Their internationally criticized solutions were embedded in the overwhelming longing of Estonians for 'historical justice' after 50 years of forcible Russification. Nevertheless, international vigilance did help to prevent the implementation of the most extreme proposals, such as the radical suggestion that 'Soviet occupants' be left without social guarantees. At this time the liberalization of citizenship regulations, advocated by many Western experts, was opposed by the majority of the

Estonian people. This opposition expressed by a majority of ordinary Estonians could not be overruled without creating serious instability in society. Dealing with this complicated situation required a policy of compromise between national and international agencies, which supported a patient step-by-step evolution of the interethnic relations towards integration (see Jurado 2003; Lauristin & Heidmets 2002; Lauristin & Kallas 2008).[1]

Compared to other post-Soviet republics, including Latvia and Lithuania, Estonian public opinion remained the most supportive of reform policies throughout the entire period of transition (Ehin 2007). Despite the positive results of opinion polls and international recognition of Estonia's liberal economic policy, its consequences were difficult to bear for many people. After the first year of reforms, the readiness of the population to make sacrifices for the common good rapidly decreased. As Estonian sociologist Anu Narusk noted, 'for most of the population the reforms have meant the end of the customary way of life' (1996, p. 13). From the viewpoint of participatory democracy, the initial period of radical reforms did not offer a bright perspective. After the almost 100% level of participation in mass movements during the 'Singing Revolution', the people suddenly seemed to have lost interest in politics. We can speak about a 'spiral of silence' surrounding opposition to reforms. The majority accepted shock therapy as the only safe way to get out of Russia's economic influence and achieve economic sustainability. Even if protests were voiced (from those who were hit by the consequences of privatization and restitution, from the Russian speakers who did not accept their new status as 'aliens', and from the pensioners and farmers who were deprived of their subsistence means), they were not heard. Government and politicians spoke with these groups in the voice of international authorities and 'higher' national interests. By the end of the period, this style of policy making started to have a negative impact on the credibility and legitimacy of the government and contributed to feelings of disillusionment and alienation (Vogt 2005).

*Economic stabilization (1995–1998)*

The growing protest against the 'shock therapy' policy of the first government coalition helped the left-of-center bloc of the Coalition Party (*Koonderakond*) and Country People's Union (*Maarahva Ühendus*) win the parliamentary elections in 1995; however, the governments formed by the Coalition Party and its partners were not stable. Due to various political scandals they changed four times in two years from April 1995 to March 1997.

The situation after the elections in 1995 demonstrates the continuing strength of the external frame in the domestic policy formation. Forgetting their own severe attacks on the radical reforms during the election campaign, the new coalition formed by center-right and center-left 'post-communist' parties, continued after the elections with practically the same agenda. The constant presence of international monitoring agencies helped to keep Estonian policy on a stable track. The economic results, which supported confidence in the positive effects of liberalization and de-Sovietization, started to reveal themselves. After several years of decrease, Estonia's GDP increased by 4.5% in 1995, by 5% in 1996 and by 10.8% in 1997. In 1995, following the first signs of success in the Estonian economy, the Association

Agreement between the EU and Estonia was signed. Two years later, Estonia was included in the first group of candidate countries invited by the EU to enter into pre-accession negotiations. The effects of the pre-accession process on the institutional developments of candidate countries have been extensively analyzed (Pettai & Zielonka 2003; Raik 2003; Vachudova 2005) and do not need further exploration. At the same time, it is important to see how the pre-accession atmosphere contributed to the marginalization of socially oriented political choices. The focus of the Maastricht criteria on market liberalization had much stronger effects on domestic policy than the comparatively weak and patchy 'social dimension' of the Copenhagen criteria. The high bureaucratic pressure supported technocratic elitism, and weakened even further the democratic mechanisms of social accountability.

Positive effects of international pressure for the stabilization of society have been found in the area of minority policy. In this field the defensive position of the national political elite was effectively counterbalanced by external agencies, stressing the universal principles of minority rights (Jurado 2003). The first draft of the minority integration program was created with the help of experts from UNDP in 1997, and supported financially by the Nordic countries. Its primary goal was to find a compromise between three agencies: the ethnic Estonian majority who mostly desired to preserve the mono-ethnic nation state; the Russian minority who wanted to receive recognition as a legitimate part of Estonian society and to improve its own social and economic standing in Estonia; and the Nordic countries together with the UNDP and the OSCE who desired to reduce the risks of ethnic conflict and exercise 'soft pressure' in order to force Estonian politicians to take steps for the protection of minority rights. International NGOs and foundations, most notably the Soros Foundation and different Nordic networks, including trade unions, also had strong effects on the revitalization of civic society.

The prospective membership of the EU and NATO inspired optimistic self-confident visions of Estonia's future. One of the most prominent promoters of these was the first post-communist president, the writer, film director and historian Lennart Meri. His inspiring role, often compared to the impact of Vaclav Havel, is a good example confirming the need for visionary leaders during transition times. One of his ideas, the creation of the national program for rapid and full computerization of Estonia,[2] had the most profound influence on Estonian society, not only in terms of facilitating technological modernization, but also as far as changing cultural and social perspectives was concerned.

*Preparations for EU-accession (1999–2004)*

After the 1999 elections, developments in Estonian society reached a new stage characterized by intense preparations to achieve EU accession and integration with NATO. While the EU and NATO took the leading role, some international organizations, which had been very active in the previous periods, started to withdraw their activities from Estonia (UNDP, OSCE). Nevertheless, despite the active preparations for accession to the EU and NATO, this period could be characterized by the strengthening of the influence of domestic agencies.

The same right-of-center pro-reform coalition of the conservative *Pro Patria* party, liberal Reform party and the social democratic Moderates, which together had formed the first government in 1992, regained a majority in parliament and formed the coalition government. As one of its main tasks, the new government announced the need to bridge the widening gap of alienation between people and the government. Expectations towards the new government were high. Responding to them, the government promised to speed up reforms in several areas: public administration, health care, pension insurance, family policy and higher education. Due to the pre-accession logic defined by the 'chapters' of the EU agreement, several policies came out of the shadows, like agriculture, environment, social protection and minority policy (not only including the Russian minority, but also gender equality). Social protection schemes now began to be discussed by domestic decision makers rather than simply social policy professionals and international experts. A dramatically decreased birth rate, high unemployment and an ageing population informed the internal agenda of reforms. The introduction of a new pension scheme, with the 'second pension pillar' based on individual contributions, was the major achievement of the coalition government in the area of social policy.

However, the expected change from the libertarian paradigm of 'minimal state' to the socially responsible state did not succeed. The main reason for the popularity of market liberalism as the dominating ideology not only in Estonia, but in many post-communist societies could be found in the above mentioned success-oriented 'transition culture'. These societies are characterized by the social dichotomy between 'winners' and 'losers'. In ethnically divided societies like Estonia or Latvia, the 'losers' were not only socially marginalized, but also often identified with the 'ethnic others'. This left very little ground for social solidarity. Even if the majority of people, according to our survey data from 2002, supported the social responsibility of the state and the abstract idea of social justice, they were not ready to implement these ideas through more effective taxation or more generous social policy. Growing individualism and consumerism[3] coupled with the success-oriented and market-driven 'transition culture' created good grounds for the hegemony of right-wing ideology, supported by the new political class, business community, and the young generation of media professionals. At the same time organizations and movements that could give a 'voice' to the 'losers' (elderly, disabled people, industrial and agricultural workers, unemployed, lonely mothers, ethnic minorities) were still underdeveloped.

At the same time, the pre-accession situation supported tendencies towards the bureaucratization and professionalization of politics, and raised the influence of professional managers and bureaucrats. Intensive institutional learning was needed in order to raise administrative capacity. As the younger generation occupied more and more posts, one could speak about the rise in Estonia of a new political class, uniting the new capitalist elite, party politicians and a new generation of Western-oriented bureaucrats.

This new elite prioritized rapid integration with European structures and full and effective implementation of the national ICT policy (the 'Tiger Leap' program). In the strategy of research and development, adopted by the Estonian parliament in 2001, an information society was proclaimed to be the official goal of Estonian development (see Runnel *et al.* 2009). The empowerment of civic organizations was envisaged in the 'Strategy for the development of civic society in Estonia' adopted by the Estonian parliament in 2002, but like many good strategies, this one also remained unimplemented for years. A number of other strategies were created in various fields (energy, regional development, culture etc.), but without the allocation of sufficient resources for their implementation, the majority of them remained on paper only.

Looking back at the reasons why these kinds of political promises failed, we have to point to a growing democratic deficit and lack of public accountability. The center-right coalition which returned to power after the elections in 1999 tried to continue with the methods of governance practiced during the period of 'emergency politics' of the early 1990s. The conflict between the interests of the new social agencies (national business circles, the academic community, unions of medical professionals and teachers, new farmers, local municipalities) and the political agenda pursued by the government, referring to the external demands shaped by the EU pre-accession *aquis communotaire*, was growing at the beginning of the new millennium. When the government decided to privatize the Estonian railways and energy systems on international markets, a group of local business leaders demanded that the government change this policy in favor of the 'national interests' of domestic capitalists. The new Estonian economic elite did not approve of Western investors, who had already taken over the Estonian banking system, having the leading role in other key branches of the national economy. At the same time, dissatisfaction with the social consequences of the liberal reforms started to grow. Those who had expected that after elections the new government would focus on measures which could increase incomes and provide everyday security and stability felt cheated. The socially driven crisis emerged in the summer of 2000.

In the atmosphere of rising dissatisfaction, the media was amplifying distrust in public institutions, in the parliament and in the government. The gloomy picture of failures in domestic policy created in the media was in strong contrast with the external image of Estonia's success story.

In April 2001, the media published a memorandum signed by leading social scientists, blaming politicians for the marginalization of ordinary people and for neglecting urgent social problems. Social scientists coined the concept of 'two Estonias', expressing the widening gap between the political elite and the masses. The memorandum called for a new participatory and balanced policy (Vetik 2002). The debate on 'two Estonias' aimed to take on board ethnic and social issues and form a new domestic agenda as an alternative to the liberal market-driven one created under external influence and prioritizing the interests of the economic elite and political class. The externally defined agenda of 'Westernization and marketization', set as a common goal at the beginning of the post-communist transition, was openly challenged. There were public demands that reduction of social inequality and poverty be recognized as a priority for the government.

These demands found their unexpected and ironic resolution during the presidential elections of September 2001, when the former Chairman of the Supreme Soviet, Arnold Rüütel, representing the Rural Union, became the new president. He was expected to become a 'peacemaker' between 'winners' and 'losers', urban and rural, advanced and lagging parts of Estonian society. Fears that the post-communist figure of the new president would damage the international image of Estonia were not confirmed. However, this event raised into the focus of public debate the re-established position of 'former communists' in Estonian society.

The Estonian crisis of 2000–2001 was not exceptional. Almost all successfully reformed countries have gone through similar backlashes. Although the vast majority of people did not support a return to the socialist past, surveys made in Central European countries demonstrate a large degree of dissatisfaction amongst the population at the turn of the century (see Munro 2001, pp. 18–23). Trust in political institutions was in many other post-communist countries even lower than in Estonia (see Rose 2006). On the back of growing popular disappointment with the policies of the first decade of transition, in many East and Central European countries populist parties took power. The same happened in Estonia. The elections of 2003 brought to the fore the new populist neo-conservative party *Res Publica* (see Haughton 2007, pp. 67–8). The leading core of this party was formed by a new generation of state bureaucrats, young lawyers and business people, who wanted to distance themselves from the image of compromises made in the early 1990s. However, their political failure came very soon, exactly as Jaques Rupnik has described: 'Populists come to power promising "to clean house", but once they move in and become identified with the house and all its flaws, they fall back on clientelism and state capture by the ruling parties (as we are now seeing in Poland) rather than becoming more radical' (Rupnik 2006). Already on the eve of national elections in 2007, *Res Publica* merged with the conservative nationalist *Pro Patria* party, whose politics (as the leading party in the first coalition after the 1992 elections and one of the main forces behind the 'old politics' of radical marketization) the leaders of *Res Publica* had earlier fiercely criticized.

In conclusion, we could say that by the time Estonia joined the EU, the main task of the post-communist reforms – the break with the communist political and economic order and establishment of the new (capitalist) one – seemed to have been completed. Estonia had stepped into the new millennium as a 'normal' free-market society. To the foreground now came problems neglected during the years of rapid economic and political changes: public morals, democratic participation, development of an innovative knowledge-based economy, and coping with global risks.

## *New challenges after EU-accession 2005–2008*

In characterizing the post-accession atmosphere in Central and Eastern Europe, many authors expressed their concern about the 'post-EU malaise'.

> Some spoke of a post-EU malaise following the period in which so much elite energy had been expended on the demands of membership. Certainly relations with Brussels were no longer the major focus of government concern. 'Transition issues' remained, particularly in Hungary and Poland. Along with the policy battles of 'normal politics' these dimensions continued to make Central Europe rather different from its West European neighbours. (Millard 2007, p. 37)

Among the 'new versions of old themes' identified by authors, Tim Haughton (2007, pp. 62–70) mentions the following: debates over the communist past, policies towards minorities, the lack of moral values in post-communist societies, corruption, disillusionment with politicians and the fluidity of party politics, global and regional challenges (energy security and terrorism).

As Haughton concludes, despite these 'old themes' the position of the new members in relations with the EU had changed: from objects of EU policies they had become political subjects, influencing EU policy from inside. In this new role they have to be prepared for new challenges:

> Now the challenge is not to create a market economy or conform to the demands of EU conditionality, the states of CEE are faced with the need to prepare themselves for the demands of competing in the twenty-first century global market place. (Haughton 2007, p. 70)

Some of those topics (the communist past, minorities, the fluidity of party politics, energy security) have special importance for Estonia. Once accession had been achieved, suppressed social and ethnic controversies concerning the evaluation of the Estonian past, present and future began to manifest themselves. Intense preparations for NATO and EU membership had kept these conflicting issues hidden; subsequently, however, the inner conflict behind the peaceful façade grew. Since fall 2004, controversial attitudes and images concerning the participation of Estonians in World War II, previous membership of the Communist Party, Estonian–Russian official relations etc., moved to the center of public debate. Many intellectuals expressed their dissatisfaction with the deepening moral vacuum in the country. Fifteen years after the 'Singing Revolution', the presidential election campaign in the fall of 2006 once again mobilized masses of people. The incumbent President Rüütel was perceived to be a symbol of continuing 'post-communism'. Newly elected president, former chairman of the Estonian Social Democratic Party, Swedish-born Toomas Hendrik Ilves envisaged his political program to be the 'return of the state to citizens', promising in his inauguration speech to concentrate on the future instead of the past (Ilves 2006). However, one of the first new institutions established by him was an 'Institute of Memory'.

The controversy between past and future orientation is encompassing two important fields of Estonian policy: minority issues and the search for the new paradigm of economic development. After the emergence of the global financial crisis, the whole paradigm of further Estonian economic development has been questioned.

## Changing focus in minority policy

The field of minority protection has provided good examples of the interplay between the international and domestic agencies in framing the content of policies. The issues related to the integration of the large Russian-speaking minority continued to influence the internal agenda in Estonia (and in Latvia) throughout all the stages of transition. As mentioned above, the first attempts to solve the problems of minority integration were initiated by international agencies. Looking at the influence of the EU, OSCE and COE on the policy concerning minority education in Estonia, Elena Jurado has described in detail the different modes of international influence on the domestic decision-making process: rational (introducing conditionalities, sanctions and incentives, calculating cost efficiency); cognitive (informing, learning ways of solution); social constructivist (creating norms, changing meanings, giving interpretations and moral judgments). Analyzing the arguments given by Estonian politicians in favor of or against certain provisions of legislation, she has discovered that the effects of certain modes of external influence differed in the early 1990s compared to the later periods (Jurado 2003, p. 420). The minorities themselves were not involved as active participants, but rather as passive target groups in the process of integration policy formation.

As a compromise between international authorities and a quite reluctant national elite, the public image of integration policy was rather negative. Within both ethnic groups it was considered to be nothing more than a formal adaptation by the government to 'European' conditionalities. Surveys conducted in 2005, 2006 and in June 2007 revealed that despite more than seven years of integration efforts, the gap between the Estonian majority and the Russian-speaking minority was not closing, but increasing in terms of social equality and mutual contacts, and concerning values and attitudes.[4] But after the shocking experience of the 'Russian riot' in April 2007, ignited by the removal of the Soviet military monument from the center of Tallinn, the internal priority given to minority issues has increased remarkably. The people started worrying about the effectiveness of the integration policy for the future stability of society and became more interested in the positive development of this field. A new agency had emerged, wanting more opportunities to influence Estonian politics: a generation of young and well adapted naturalized citizens with a Russian background sought their legitimate role in Estonian society and were prepared to be partners, not targets of the minority policy. The new integration strategy for the years 2008–2013, adopted by the government in April 2007, for the first time prioritized equal social and economic opportunities and effective participation as the aim of integration policy, and interpreted language learning and naturalization as the means for achieving these goals, not as the end in itself. This is an important shift to the 'ownership' of integration policy by new internal actors, including employers' organizations, trade unions and other NGOs, where members of minorities are invited to play a more active role.[5]

*Economic development: the need for a new paradigm*

Comparative analysis of world economies has shown that Estonia is amongst those post-communist countries which have reached the stage of transition to innovation-driven economies (Lopez-Claros *et al.* 2006, p. 12; Sala-i-Martin *et al.* 2007, pp. 8–9). Until recent years the ideas of the 'Lisbon strategy' stressing the central role of R&D in economic development, sounded to Estonians like an abstract part of 'Europolitics':

> Future orientations that should direct the development of the Estonian economy and society tend to remain non-specific and declarative. They are often based on external sources, for instance, having been rewritten from the materials of the European Union or some other international organizations. Moreover, the threats and opportunities for the long-term future of Estonia are either not properly analyzed – or at least relevant decisions are not made. (Terk *et al.* 2008, pp. 88–9)

Instead of the long-term policies, which could prepare Estonia for entering the Eurozone, post-accession Estonia was experiencing a boom of consumerism, especially among the younger population.[6] In the fall of 2007, after the sustained economic growth of the previous five years, the signs of economic slowdown awakened society from consumerist dreams fed by the promises of populist politicians. Pushed to find a way out of the coming economic decline, experts in economics, bankers, and industrialists became more involved in the search for new approaches, including strategic planning, which has so far been neglected by Estonian politicians. Criticism was raised against the *laissez faire* attitude of the governing Reform Party. This party, representing extreme market liberalism, dominated the Estonian political scene for almost all of the periods of transition, surfing on the waves of consumerism and economic optimism (see Table 2). The low priority given by the ruling political elite to strategic development and research, coupled with the undermining of industrial policy during the post-communist transition, was named among the main reasons for slow economic reorientation (Tiits *et al.* 2003, 2005). The difficulties that Estonia is experiencing in transition to innovation-based policy are related not only to the smallness of the country, but to unsolved internal problems, such as stacked reforms in education, big inequalities and low capacity for networking and cooperation (Linnas 2007). One of Estonia's leading experts, Erik Terk, has compared the scale of changes that will be needed in order to bring about a transition to innovation-driven development with the shock experienced by Estonians in the early 1990s during the transition to a market economy (Terk 2007). The experience of the deepening global and domestic economic difficulties in the fall of 2008 proved this forecast to be true.

In 2007 the Estonian Development Fund was launched in order to intensify and consolidate efforts in the field of development planning. The first major strategic project of this fund was targeted at the analysis of the Estonian economic structure and the elaboration of alternative development scenarios for the coming decades. The main conclusion from this analysis stressed that internal factors – the capacity of enterprises and individuals to change and to cooperate, and the active or passive role of the governmental sector in economic development – would play the decisive role in future development. External factors, while very important for Estonia's macroeconomic situation, can nevertheless only play a background role, which may influence the process but does not change it in essence (Terk & Varblane 2008; Varblane *et al.* 2008).

## Concluding Discussion

The picture presented here has demonstrated that the role of external and internal factors in the formation of the Estonian post-communist transition agenda has changed, and that the influence of internal social actors has grown over time. During the early stages of transition, when the political field in Estonia was still in the making and different political cleavages were not clearly distinguishable (Arter 1996), the dominance of external factors supported the quite narrow political priorities of institution-building and the liberalization of the economy. From the beginning of the

**TABLE 2** Participation of the right-wing and left-wing political parties in the Estonian government 1992–2007 (+ indicates participation in government, ++ indicates leading of the government, post of the prime minister)

| Year | | | 1992 | 1993 | 1994 | 1995 | 1996 | 1997 | 1998 | 1999 | 2000 | 2001 | 2002 | 2003 | 2004 | 2005 | 2006 | 2007 I–III | 2007 IV–XII |
|---|---|---|---|---|---|---|---|---|---|---|---|---|---|---|---|---|---|---|---|
| Party | | %* | | | | | | | | | | | | | | | | | |
| | | | | | | | | **Right-wing** | | | | | | | | | | | |
| Reform Party and its predecessor Liberal Democrats | Neo-liberal | 22.5 | (+) | (+) | (+) | + | + | | | + | + | + | ++ | ++ | + | ++ | ++ | ++ | ++ |
| Pro Patria** | Conservative | 18.1 | ++ | ++ | ++ | + | | | | ++ | ++ | ++ | | | | | | | + |
| Res Publica*** | Neo-Conservative | 12.5 | | | | | | | | | | | | ++ | ++ | ++ | | | |
| Coalition Party | Post-communist center-right | 6.6 | | | | ++ | ++ | ++ | ++ | ++ | | | | | | | | | |
| | | | | | | | | **Left-wing** | | | | | | | | | | | |
| Center Party | Post-communist center-left | 10.6 | | | | + | | | | | | + | + | | + | + | + | + | |
| Development Party | | 1.0 | + | + | | ++ | | + | + | | | | | | | | | | |
| Moderates/SDE | Social democratic center-left | 11.2 | + | + | ++ | ++ | | | + | + | + | + | | | | | | | + |
| People's Union and its predecessors | Post-communist rural | 9.3 | | + | + | + | + | + | + | + | | | | + | + | + | + | + | |
| Non-party members of the government | | 8.2 | + | + | + | + | + | + | + | | | | | | | | | | |

Notes: *% is calculated from the period October 1992–December 2007, in months. ** Since April 2007 Pro Patria and Res Publica Union. *** Until merger with Pro Patria new millennium, when the resourcefulness of the internal agents (their economic, social and cultural capital) increased, they started to play a more decisive and independent role in setting priorities and learned how to use external conditions as tools for developing their own policies. Whereas in countries with a slower pace of reform, the 'rent-seekers' from the socialist managerial class tried to inhibit the pace of reform (Aslund 2002, 2007), in Estonia the high pace of reform was profitable first and foremost for the new, young entrepreneurial groups. Surfing on the wave of reforms, these 'winners of transition', together with representatives of the middle-aged managerial class, formed the new capitalist elite. This elite became one of the strongest agencies supporting the domination of the liberal market-oriented paradigm throughout two decades of Estonian post-communist history. Political parties representing the interests of this new business community won the majority of seats in all parliamentary elections, and were in the leading position in all coalition governments (see Table 2).

As in most post-communist countries, Estonian right-wing parties combined liberal market orientations with a populist nationalist appeal, which enabled them to secure their hegemonic position. It is important to add that throughout the two decades of post-communism, political competition has not followed 'right'–'left' lines, but has rather followed a logic of 'national/reformist' *vs.* 'Soviet/anti-reform', the latter combining nostalgic attitudes concerning the Soviet past with protest against liberal reforms and a reticence concerning 'Westernization' (including also anti-EU orientations) (Lauristin 2007). This was one of the reasons why groups with the weaker social and economic positions were politically marginalized: their claims for social justice and solidarity sounded 'too socialist' in the context of the dominating transition culture, which favored individualistic values, economic success and competitiveness. An additional factor weakening the impact of the left-wing political forces lay in the fact that their electorate, especially concerning the Centre Party (*Eesti Keskerakond*), represented an ethnically heterogeneous population (a big part of which consists of naturalized citizens of Russian origin). The issues of their social exclusion and their social and economic needs were included in the political agenda only in 2008 by the adoption of the new national integration program.

The changing balance between internal and external factors during different stages of the Estonian transformation can be better understood if one keeps in mind the model of post-communist 'triple transition' (Offe 1991, 1996), which called attention to the uneven pace of changes on different layers of society.

During the first half of the 1990s, changes happened in the most rapid and dramatic way at the institutional level: the break with the old political regime and the formation of the new constitutional order was coupled with the re-building of state institutions from scratch. In a situation of extreme lack of domestic competence, the contribution of external resources and know-how was decisive. The new and ambitious political and economic elite was able to launch radical liberal reforms, which helped Estonia become one of the leaders of transition.

Starting from the end of the 1990s, unsolved or neglected social issues became more important and visible. The intellectual opposition raised its voice, supported by the emerging civic society, and called attention to the second layer of transition: social problems created by the restructuring of society. At the same time, ethnic heterogeneity and the social marginalization of the 'losers' in the context of success-oriented transition culture had inhibited the consolidation of the more socially oriented opposition. Redistribution of resources and opportunities between different groups in society, changes in political culture, and inter-ethnic integration are all long-running and complicated social processes. They could not be steered by international organizations, organized from the top of society by political elites or implemented with the help of the external donors.

While during the early stages of transition the differentiation between external and internal factors was more or less clearly distinguishable, the internal and external became more difficult to disentangle as Estonia became increasingly integrated into the regional and international community. We can rather speak about the interplay between domestic factors and international influence. The most interesting question here concerns mutual mediation: when and why internal agencies could effectively use external support for promoting their own agenda and *vice versa*; why in some cases, does even very strong international pressure have no effect on domestic policies? Many analysts have pointed to the fact that politicians or various pressure groups were using international factors (for example, EU directives) in order to mediate their own agenda (or sometimes to legitimize their reluctance to introduce certain changes). For example, when the World Bank set conditionalities concerning public health with the provision of credit for Estonian health care reform, this supported and legitimized the efforts of NGOs, medical professionals and academics to change the paradigm of hospital-centered health care inherited from the Soviet system. The international media and transnational professional, political, economic and civic networks and associations played an important role in the mediation process between East and West which helped in the formation of Estonia's international credibility, and *vice versa*, as well as serving as a source of legitimation and symbolic power for the domestic policy makers (presidents, leading politicians, new financial institutions, etc.).

In looking at Estonian politics during the EU accession process, we agree with Kristi Raik (2003) who has demonstrated the difficulty in evaluating the respective role of external *vs.* internal factors. This derives from the fact that external factors were often mediated by the domestic environment, and the distinction between external and internal was often blurred. Instead of separating internal and external factors of accession-related changes in politics, she found it more productive to use the synthetic concept of 'integration/enlargement discourses' as a set of key elements (called 'the logic of enlargement/integration' in this work), which 'provide a significant framework for democratic politics in the candidate countries – a framework that conditions, constrains and at the same time enables democratic practices' (Raik 2003, p. 112). The main factor that creates external or internal bias in the 'integration/enlargement discourse' is political interest or pressure from the various agencies involved in the process of change.

In this context, we can interpret the whole phenomenon of 'transition culture' as a field of mediation, in which external demands from powerful international agencies are turned through a specific 'learning process' into value preferences and codes of behavior of internal actors. Where the social differentiation in society started to be interpreted in terms of 'winners' and 'losers' of transition (Rychard 1996), and the formation of transition culture was reflected in the beliefs and expectations of the people and in the hopes and needs of the various groups in society, the border between external and internal factors was constantly blurring: external definitions of 'success' and 'failure' were 'naturalized' in the values and practices of people. During the 1990s the fusion between the internal and external agenda in the post-communist transition was the strongest (this was the period when the success-oriented 'transition culture' was the most influential cultural formation). The conflicts between politicians and different pressure groups (new business elites, cultural and academic circles, trade unions, minority activists, etc.) before and after EU accession indicate the growing pressure of internal agents on the formation of the political agenda. However, even the deepening economic crisis has not (yet) profoundly altered the priorities set at the beginning of the Estonian transition: economic competitiveness coupled with national security. The 'Bronze soldier' crisis has resulted in further 'securitization' of minority issues and has produced a return to the strong identity politics which characterized the first period of transition. As Offe predicted at the very beginning of transition (1991), the formation of new identities and values when the previous 'socialist nations' become free European societies will be a most profound and complicated process. According to Inglehart (1997), the shift from survival values to self-expression values in post-communist countries is taking place very slowly. The global economic backlash is inhibiting this process even more.

At present, Estonia, like many other countries is suffering from a serious financial crisis. The extreme openness of the Estonian market and the political vulnerability of this small country to external pressures have made the international influence on Estonian development clearly visible. In this critical situation, the need for a strategic vision of future economic and social development in order to create a new political agenda has been made a focus of public debate (see Heidmets 2007a, 2008). It is self-evident that this new vision must be informed by the strategic choices made by the international community, or in the first place, by the EU. Nevertheless, questions about the specific choices of Estonia (or Latvia, Lithuania, Poland, etc.) and the opportunities for more sustainable development could be asked and answered separately in each and every country, taking into account internal and external constraints and resources.

## Acknowledgements

The research was supported by grants from the Estonian Ministry of Education and Science (0180017s07) and the Estonian Science Foundation (6526).

## Notes

1. We shall return to problems of inter-ethnic integration later on in this essay. These problems are in the focus of three other essays published in the current volume (Ehala 2009; Korts 2009; Vihalemm & Kalmus 2009).
2. The 'Tiger Leap' program has been a priority for all governments since 1997, and has brought Estonia into the group of the leading ICT countries in Europe. A detailed elaboration of the development of information society in Estonia is

provided in the essay of Pille Runnel, Pille Pruulmann-Vengerfeldt and Kristina Reinsalu, published in the current volume.
3   See the essay in the current volume by Veronika Kalmus, Margit Keller and Maie Kiisel on the rising consumer culture and environmentalism in Estonia.
4   See the other essays in the current volume where Triin Vihalemm and Veronika Kalmus focus on the differences in value structures (Vihalemm & Kalmus 2009), Külliki Korts elaborates on the issue of contacts and tolerance (Korts 2009), and Martin Ehala explores the political crisis related to the replacement of a Soviet military monument in the context of Estonian and Russian identity changes (Ehala 2009).
5   *Integration Strategy 2008–2013*, available at: www.rahvastikuminister.ee/?id=11104, accessed 20 April 2008.
6   Details illuminating spread of consumerist attitudes in Estonia are presented in the essay by Veronika Kalmus, Margit Keller and Maie Kiisel in the current volume (Kalmus *et al.* 2009).

## References

Alexander, J., Eyerman, R., Giesen, B., Smelser, N. & Sztompka, P. (2004) *Cultural Trauma and Collective Identity* (Berkeley, Los Angeles & London, University of California Press).
Ant, J. (ed.) (1998) *Kaks algust: Eesti Vabariik–1920.ja 1990. aastad* (Talinn, Eesti Riigiarhiiv).
Arias King, F. (2003) 'The Centrality of Elites', *Democratizatsiya*, 11, 1, pp. 150–60.
Arter, D. (1996) *Parties and Democracy in Contemporary Europe: The Case of Estonia* (Aldershot, Dartmouth).
Aslund, A. (2002) *Building Capitalism: The Transformation of the Former Soviet Bloc* (Cambridge, Cambridge University Press).
Aslund, A. (2007) *How Capitalism was Built: The Transformation of Central and Eastern Europe, Russia, and Central Asia* (Cambridge & New York, Cambridge University Press).
Berglund, S., Ekman, J. & Aarebrot, F. (eds) (2004) *The Handbook of Political Change in Eastern Europe*, 2nd edn (Cheltenham & Northampton, Edward Elgar).
Bertelsmann (2006) *Bertelsmann Transformation Index 2006: Auf dem Weg zur marktwirschaftlichen Demokratie* (Gütersloh, Bertelsmann Stiftung), partly available at: www.bertelsmann-transformation-index.de, accessed 13 December 2008.
Bertelsmann (2008) *Bertelsmann Transformation Index 2008: Political Management in International Comparison* (Gütersloh, Bertelsmann Stiftung), partly available at: www.bertelsmann-transformation-index.de, accessed 13 December 2008.
Boje, T., Steenbergen, B. van & Walby, S. (eds) (1999) *European Societies: Fusion or Fission?* (London & New York, Routledge).
Buchen, C. (2006) 'Estonia and Slovenia as Antipodes', in Lane, D. & Myant, M. (eds) (2006).
Clemens Jr, W. C. (2001) *The Baltic Transformed: Complexity Theory and European Security* (Lanham, Boulder, New York & Oxford, Rowman & Littlefield).
De Melo, M., Denizer, C. & Gelb, A. (1996) 'Patterns of Transition from Plan to Market', *World Bank Economic Review*, 10, 3, pp. 397–424.

Ehala, M. (2009) 'The Bronze Soldier: Identity Threat and Maintenance in Estonia', *Journal of Baltic Studies*, 40, 1.

Ehin, P. (2007) 'Political Support in the Baltic States 1993–2004', *Journal of Baltic Studies*, 38, 1, pp. 1–20.

Eisenstadt, S. N. (1992) 'A Reappraisal of Theories of Social Change and Modernization', in Haferkamp, H. & Smelser, N. J. (eds) (1992).

*Europe in Figures – Eurostat Yearbook 2008*, available at: http://epp.eurostat.ec.europa.eu/cache/ITY_OFFPUB/KS-CD-07-001/EN/KS-CD-07-001-EN.PDF, accessed 22 October 2008.

Feldmann, M. (2007) 'The Origins of Varieties of Capitalism: Lessons from Post-Socialist Transition in Estonia and Slovenia', in Hancke, B., Rhodes, M. & Thatcher, M. (eds) (2007).

Feldmann, M. & Sally, R. (2002) 'From the Soviet Union to the European Union: Estonian Trade Policy, 1991–2000', *World Economy*, 25, 1, pp. 79–106.

Fisher-Galati, S. (2005) 'A Changing Political Culture? East-Central Europe in the 1990s', in Kersting N. & Cronquist, L. (eds) (2005).

Grzymala-Busse, A. (2007) *Rebuilding Leviathan: Party Competition and State Exploitation in Post-Communist Democracies* (Cambridge & New York, Cambridge University Press).

Haferkamp, H. & Smelser, N. J. (eds) (1992) *Social Change and Modernity* (Berkeley, Los Angeles & Oxford, University of California Press).

Hancke, B., Rhodes, M. & Thatcher, M. (2007) *Beyond Varieties of Capitalism: Conflict, Contradictions, and Complementaries in the European Economy* (Oxford & New York, Oxford University Press).

Haughton, T. (2007) 'The Other New Europeans', in White, S., Batt, J. & Lewis, P. (eds) (2007).

Heidmets, M. (ed.) (2007a) *Estonian Human Development Report 2006* (Tallinn, Public Understanding Foundation), available at: www.kogu.ee/public/trykised/EIA06_eng.pdf, accessed 22 October 2008.

Heidmets, M. (2007b) 'Where is Estonia?', in Heidmets, M. (ed.) (2007a).

Heidmets, M. (ed.) (2008) *Estonian Human Development Report 2007* (Tallinn, Eesti Koostöö Kogu), available at: www.kogu.ee/public/trykised/EIA07_eng.pdf, accessed 22 October 2008.

Howard, M. (2003) *The Weakness of Civil Society in Post-Communist Europe* (Cambridge, New York, Melbourne, Madrid & Cape Town, Cambridge University Press).

Ilves, T. H. (2006) 'President of the Republic at the Inauguration Ceremony', available at: www.president.ee/en/duties/speeches.php?gid=82273, accessed 20 April 2008.

Inglehart, R. (1997) *Modernization and Postmodernization: Cultural, Economic and Political Change in 43 Societies* (Princeton, Princeton University Press).

Johannsen, L. (2006) 'The Baltic States: A Miracle?', in Rakowska-Harmstone, T. & Dutkewicz, P. with Orzelska, A. (eds) (2006).

Judt, T. (2005) *Postwar: A History of Europe since 1945* (New York, Penguin).

Jurado, E. (2003) 'Complying with European Standards of Minority Education: Estonia's Relations with the European Union, OSCE and Council of Europe', *Journal of Baltic Studies*, 34, 4, pp. 399–431.

Kallas, S. (1998) '1992. aasta rahareform ja selle mõju Eesti arengule', in Ant, J. (ed.) (1998).

Kalmus, V., Keller, M. & Kiisel, M. (2009) 'Emerging Consumer Types in Transition Culture: Consumption Patterns of Generational Ethnic Groups in Estonia', *Journal of Baltic Studies*, 40, 1.
Kalmus, V., Lauristin, M. & Pruulmann-Vengerfeldt, P. (eds) (2004) *Eesti elavik 21. sajandi algul: ülevaade uurimuse Mina. Maailm. Meedia tulemustest* [*Estonian Lifeworld in the Beginning of the 21st Century: Overview of Results from Research Project Me. The World. The Media*] (Tartu, Tartu Ülikooli Kirjastus).
Kennedy, M. (2002) *Cultural Formations of Post-Communism: Emancipation, Transition, Nation, and War* (Minneapolis & London, University of Minnesota Press).
Kersting, N. & Cronquist, L. (eds) (2005) *Democratization and Political Culture in Comparative Perspective* (Wiesbaden, Verlag Für Sozialwissenschaften).
Korts, K. (2009) 'Inter-Ethnic Attitudes and Contacts between Ethnic Groups in Estonia', *Journal of Baltic Studies*, 40, 1.
Laar, M. (2002) *Das Estnische Wirtschaftswunder* (Tallinn, Konrad Adenauer Stiftung).
Lagerspetz, M. & Vogt, H. (2004) 'Estonia', in Berglund, S., Ekman, J. & Aarebrot, F. (eds) (2004).
Lane, D. & Myant, M. (eds) (2006) *Varieties of Capitalism in Post-Communist Countries* (London, Palgrave Macmillan).
Lauristin, M. (2003) 'Social Contradictions Shadowing Estonia's "Success Story"', *Democratizatsiya*, 11, 4, pp. 601–16.
Lauristin, M. (2007) 'World-view and Support for Political Parties', in Heidmets, M. (ed.) (2007a), available at: www.kogu.ee/public/trykised/EIA06_eng.pdf, accessed 22 October 2008.
Lauristin, M. & Heidmets, M. (2002) 'Introduction: The Russian Minority in Estonia as a Theoretical and Political Issue', in Lauristin, M. & Heidmets, M. (eds) (2002).
Lauristin, M. & Heidmets, M. (eds) (2002) *The Challenge of the Russian Minority: Emerging Multicultural Democracy in Estonia* (Tartu, Tartu University Press).
Lauristin, M. & Kallas, K. (2008) 'The Participation of Non-Estonians in the Estonian Social Life and Politics', in Heidmets, M. (ed.) (2008).
Lauristin, M. & Vihalemm, P. (2002) 'The Transformation of Estonian Society and Media: 1987–2001', in Vihalemm, P. (ed.) (2002).
Linnas, R. (2007) 'Innovatsioonipoliitika kavandamisest Eestis', *Riigikogu Toimetised*, 15, pp. 65–72.
Löfgren, J. & Herd, G. (2000) *Estonia and the EU: Integration and Societal Security in the Baltic Context*, Tampere Peace Research Institute, Research Report No. 91 (Tampere, University of Tampere).
Lopez-Claros, A., Altinger, L., Blanke, J., Drzeniek, M. & Mia, I. (2006) 'The Global Competitiveness Index: Identifying the Key Elements of Sustainable Growth', in Lopez-Claros, A., Porter, M. & Schwab, K. (eds) (2006).
Lopez-Claros, A., Porter, M. & Schwab, K. (eds) (2006) *The Global Competitiveness Report 2006–2007* (New York, Palgrave Macmillan), partly available at: www.weforum.org, accessed 13 December 2008.
Millard, F. (2007) 'The Czech Republic, Hungary and Poland', in White, S., Batt, J. & Lewis, P. (eds) (2007).
Mishler, W. & Rose, R. (2001) 'What Are the Origins of Political Trust?', *Comparative Political Studies*, 34, 1, pp 30–62.

Munro, N. (2001) *National Context or Individual Differences? Influences on Regime Support in Post-Communist Societies*, Studies in Public Policy Number 347 (Glasgow, University of Strathclyde).

Narusk, A. (1996) 'Gendered Outcomes of the Transition in Estonia', *Idäntutkimus*, 3, 3–4, pp. 12–39.

Norgaard, O. (2000) *Economic Institutions and Democratic Reform* (Cheltenham & Northampton, Edward Elgar).

Norgaard, O., Johannsen, L. with Skak, M. & Sorensen, R. H. (1999) *The Baltic States after Independence*, 2nd edn (Cheltenham & Northampton, Edward Elgar).

Norkus, Z. (2007) 'Why did Estonia Perform Best? The North–South Gap in the Post-Socialist Economic Transition of the Baltic States', *Journal of Baltic Studies*, 38, 1, pp. 21–42.

Offe, C. (1991) 'Capitalism by Democratic Design? Democratic Theory Facing the Triple Transition in East Central Europe', *Social Research*, 58, 4, pp. 865–902.

Offe, C. (1996) *Varieties of Transition* (Cambridge, Polity Press).

Orenstein, M. (2001) *Out of the Red: Building Capitalism and Democracy in Postcommunist Europe* (Ann Arbor, University of Michigan Press).

Panagiotou, R. A. (2001) 'Estonia's Success: Prescription or Legacy?', *Communist and Post-Communist Studies*, 34, 3, pp 261–77.

Petersoo, P. & Tamm, M. (eds) (2008) *Monumentaalne konflikt: mälu, poliitika ja identiteet tänapäeva Eestis* (Tallinn, Varrak).

Pettai, V. & Zielonka, J. (2003) *The Road to the European Union. Volume 2: Estonia, Latvia and Lithuania* (Manchester & New York, Manchester University Press).

Pittaway, M. (2007) 'From Communist to Post-Communist Politics', in White, S., Batt, J. & Lewis, P. (eds) (2007).

Porter, M., Sala-i-Martin, X. & Schwab, K. (eds) (2007) *The Global Competitiveness Report 2007–2008* (New York, Palgrave Macmillan), partly available at: www.weforum.org, accessed 13 December 2008.

Raik, K. (1998) *Towards Substantive Democracy? The Role of the European Union in the Democratisation of Estonia and the Other Eastern Member Candidates*, Tampere Peace Research Institute, Research Report No. 84 (Tampere, University of Tampere).

Raik, K. (2003) *Democratic Politics or the Implementation of Inevitables? Estonia's Democracy and Integration into the European Union* (Tartu, Tartu University Press).

Rakowska-Harmstone, T. & Dutkewicz, P. with Orzelska, A. (eds) (2006) *New Europe: The Impact of the First Decade. Vol. 2. Variations on the Patterns* (Warsaw, Institute of Political Studies, Polish Academy of Science and Collegium Civitas Press).

Rose, R. (2006) *Diverging Paths of Post-Communist Countries: New Europe Barometer Trends since 1991*, Studies in Public Policy Number 418 (Aberdeen, University of Aberdeen).

Rose, R., Mishler, W. & Haerpfer, C. (1998) *Democracy and Its Alternatives: Understanding Post-Communist Societies* (Oxford, Polity & Baltimore, Johns Hopkins University Press).

Runnel, P., Pruulmann-Vengerfeldt, P. & Reinsalu, K. (2009) 'Estonian Tiger Leap from Post-Communism to the Information Society: From Policy to Practices', *Journal of Baltic Studies*, 40, 1.

Rupnik, J. (2006) 'The Return of Post-Communism', available at: www.project-syndicate.org/commentary/rupnik5/English, accessed 30 March 2008.

Ruutsoo, R. (2002) 'Discursive Conflict and Estonian Post-Communist Nation-Building', in Lauristin, M. & Heidmets, M. (eds) (2002).

Rychard, A. (1996) 'Beyond Gains and Losses. In Search of Winning Losers', *Social Research*, 63, 2, pp. 465–85.
Sachs, J. (1994) 'Life in the Economic Emergency Room', in Williamson, J. (ed.) (1994).
Sala-i-Martin, X., Blanke, J., Drzeniek Hanouz, M., Geiger, T., Mia, I. & Paua, F. (2007) 'The Global Competitiveness Index: Measuring the Productive Potential of Nations', in Porter, M., Sala-i-Martin, X. & Schwab, K. (eds) (2007).
Šank, E. (2001) *Peategelane: Siim Kallase rollid* (Tallinn, Lejula).
Schimmelfennig, F. & Sedelmeyer, U. (2005) *The Europeanization of Central and Eastern Europe* (Ithaca, Cornell University Press).
Smelser, N. J. (1992) 'External and Internal Factors in Theories of Social Change', in Haferkamp, H. & Smelser, N. J. (eds) (1992).
Smith, D. (2001) *Estonia: Independence and European Integration* (London & New York, Routledge).
Smith, G. (1999) *The Post-Soviet States: Mapping the Politics of Transition* (London, Arnold).
Szelenyi, I. (1999) 'The Rise of Managerialism: The "New" Class after the Fall of Communism', in Boje, T., Steenbergen, B. van & Walby, S. (eds) (1999).
Sztompka, P. (2004) 'The Trauma of Social Change: A Case of Postcommunist Societies', in Alexander, J., Eyerman, R., Giesen, B., Smelser, N. & Sztompka, P. (2004).
Terk, E. (2007) 'Eesti Arengufond – teel järgmisse majandusse', *Riigikogu Toimetised*, 15, pp. 49–53.
Terk, E., Sepp, J. & Murulauk, A. (2008) 'Foresight for Estonia: What and Why', in Heidmets, M. (ed.) (2008).
Terk, E. & Varblane, U. (2008) 'Future Scenarios', in Heidmets, M. (ed.) (2008).
Tiits, M., Kattel, R. & Kalvet, T. (2005) *Made in Estonia* (Tartu, Balti Uuringute Instituut).
Tiits, M., Kattel, R., Kalvet, T. & Kaarli, R. (2003) *The Estonian Economy Competitiveness and Future Outlooks*, available at: www.praxis.ee/?lang=en&act=show_book&book_id=32&menu_id=135, accessed 30 March 2008.
Vachudova, M. A. (2005) *Europe Undivided: Democracy, Leverage, and Integration after Communism* (Oxford & New York, Oxford University Press).
Varblane, U., Eamets, R., Haldna, T., Kaldaru, H., Masso, J., Mets, T., Paas, T., Reiljan, J., Sepp, J., Türk, K., Ukrainski, K., Vadi, M. & Vissak, T. (2008) *Eesti majanduse konkurentsivõime hetkeseis ja tulevikuväljavaated. Aruande lühiversioon* (Tallinn, Eesti Arengufond).
Vetik, R. (ed.) (2002) *Kaks Eestit. Artiklite, ettekannete ja analüüside kogumik* (Tallinn, TPÜ Kirjastus).
Vihalemm, P. (ed.) (2002) *Baltic Media in Transition* (Tartu, Tartu University Press).
Vihalemm, T. & Kalmus, V. (2009) 'Cultural Differentiation of the Russian Minority', *Journal of Baltic Studies*, 40, 1.
Vogt, H. (2005) *Between Utopia and Disillusionment: A Narrative of the Political Transformation in Eastern Europe* (New York & Oxford, Berghahn Books).
White, S., Batt, J. & Lewis, P. (eds) (2007) *Developments in Central and East European Politics 4* (Durham, NC, Duke University Press).
Williamson, J. (1993) 'Democracy and the "Washington Consensus"', *World Development*, 21, 8, pp. 1329–36.
Williamson, J. (ed.) (1994) *The Political Economy of Policy Reform* (Washington, DC, Institute for International Economics).

# THE ESTONIAN TIGER LEAP FROM POST-COMMUNISM TO THE INFORMATION SOCIETY: FROM POLICY TO PRACTICE

## Pille Runnel, Pille Pruulmann-Vengerfeldt and Kristina Reinsalu

Estonia's post-communist transformation has been marked by several parallel processes, such as democratization, economic liberalization and the rise of consumerism. Another crucial component has been technological change – most notably the emergence of the personal computer and the Internet. The rapid transition to the information society began with governmental initiatives to develop various areas of societal life through the introduction of new technologies, but soon made its presence felt in people's everyday lives. As the initial phase of transformational euphoria began to subside, technological 'revolution' was mooted as one possible means of reducing citizens' growing alienation from the state and revitalizing Estonia's democracy. The latter approach has previously been discussed in other academic and political contexts, both in Europe and the US. Distinguishing technological and democratic developments from one another is next to impossible, therefore analyzing them in context and with reference to each other is important.

Information and communication technologies have been part of the development processes of the Estonian state since the 1990s. The Tiger Leap Program was officially launched in 1997 in order to provide Estonian schools with information and communication technology (ICT) infrastructure, and to support content creation and the acquisition of usage skills. It is largely on the basis of this that 'Internetization' has come to be viewed as one of the central symbols of Estonia's rapidly changing society (Runnel 2001). A few years after these efforts to merge ICTs with the education system, success stories in the areas of e-governance and services gained both domestic and international recognition, leading to a widely held perception of Estonia as a leading e-state.

Recent analyses of changing Eastern European societies have for the most part been concerned with institutional and structural change: the effects of economic and political reforms and their social environment. The focus has been on the 'space of possibilities' rather than on individuals as active agents within these environments. Individuals are rather dealt with as decision makers representing politics, and their administrative capacities are interpreted as one of the prerequisites for change (Nørgaard 2000, p. 9). In the particular framework of EU accession, EU models in various spheres of life have been central (Kalvet 2007; Siil 1997) and thus provide a necessary context when attempting to understand ongoing processes of change. Transition studies have generally followed people in order to estimate the ability and readiness of the population to go along with change, including the study of change by means of the public opinion poll, i.e. from the perspective of agreeing or not agreeing and coping or not coping with ongoing changes. The role of people as interpreters or co-producers of the meaning of change has often been underestimated in such studies. Similarly, ICT-related change – like other areas of transformation – has been dealt with primarily at the macro level and has often been interpreted from the perspective of Eastern Europe 'catching up' with the West (Lass 1999; Lauristin & P. Vihalemm 1997; Vogt 2005, p. 9; Wormald 2005). Even now, micro-level studies of what people do on a daily basis are poorly integrated with the macro level context of the information society (Pruulmann-Vengerfeldt 2006b).

When one looks at Information Society (IS) policies developed throughout the last decade, it becomes clear that they carry ideas visible in public discourse from the early days of IS policies, according to which providing access to ICTs is important in order to: (1) increase competitiveness; (2) reduce division within society; and (3) foster state–individual relationships (Principles of Estonian Information Policy 1998). In the case of Estonia we are dealing with a unique example in which civic participatory culture also started developing in parallel with, and was strongly influenced by, ICT development. At the same time ICTs have strongly influenced democracy and e-participation and are therefore probably much more integrated into Estonia's concept of democracy and political participation (Reinsalu & Winsvold 2008). This concept goes side by side with general social development, which expects the growth of civic society in Estonia and puts public participation very much on the political agenda (Pruulmann-Vengerfeldt 2007).

Departing from this context, our essay will look at the place of informatization within the political agenda and analyze how expectations have been realized (or not). It aims to combine both textual analysis of 1990s political and public texts concerning the information society in Estonia with quantitative survey data from a nationally representative survey of the Estonian speaking population conducted in February 2007. These will be used to analyze what kind of usage practices can be identified and how much participation in online democratic environments is part of the usage.

In what follows, we first briefly locate Estonian developments within the Baltic ICT sector and internationally. We then present the position of ICTs in the early political agenda of Estonia, before focusing on the different Internet user types to identify the diversity of online practices. We then use theoretical material together with empirical examples to analyze the conditions that exist for digital democracy in Estonia, and then finally return to our survey data to focus on actual participatory activities.

## Estonia's Position in Baltic and European Comparison of ICT Indicators

The rapid pace of Estonian ICT development could already be seen in the late 1990s in parallel with information policy processes. An analysis of computer ownership in the three Baltic states during the 1990s shows that between 1997 and 1999 Estonia 'took off' and left the two other Baltic countries behind. In 1995 and 1997, home computer ownership grew equally (steadily increasing by around 1% in two years in all countries). By 1999, however, Estonian computer ownership had grown from 5% to 14%, whereas in Latvia and Lithuania it was still only 6%. The successful dissemination of ICTs is also evidenced by high Internet use in recent years – a total of 64% of Estonians had used the Internet in the past three months when surveyed in 2004, which is 9% higher than in Latvia and 15% higher than in Lithuania (Vengerfeldt & Runnel 2004, p. 250) (see Figure 1).

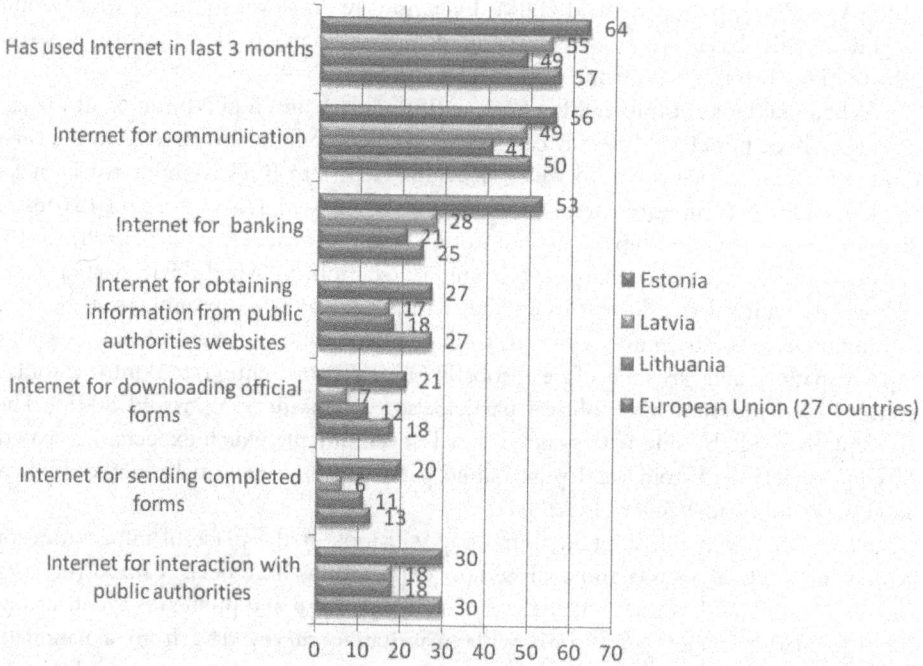

**FIGURE 1** Percentage of the population which has used the Internet in the three past months and the percentage of the population which has used the Internet for the listed activities.
Source: Eurostat (2007), data retrieved from the online database available at: http://epp.eurostat.ec.europa.eu/pls/portal/portal.home, accessed April 2008.

Today, more than ten years after the initial documents were launched, Estonia can indeed be proud of its achievements in ICT-related development as the country has quickly positioned itself ahead of many larger Western economies. The use of complex measures also indicates Estonia's relative success in achieving its aims of distributing access to information, while enjoying the competitive edge that ICTs have brought to Estonia. The Lisbon Review (of the competitiveness of EU member states) lists Estonia in 12th place. This is the highest of the ten member states that joined in 2004, a position that Estonia has since maintained. Lithuania is in 20th position, rising from 21st position, while Latvia is in 22nd position having fallen from 16th position in 2004 (World Economic Forum 2006).[1]

While the Lisbon Review could be seen as showing the success of Estonian ICT policies as measured by social dissemination and by competitiveness, the Global Competitiveness Report (2007) adopts a broader perspective, using a sample group of 131 countries. Here Estonia ranks 27th, with Lithuania 38th and Latvia 45th. In the technological readiness category Estonia is 19th, Lithuania 38th and Latvia 40th. This shows that Estonia has fairly successfully managed to integrate ICTs in terms of economic competitiveness, and also in terms of social inclusion.

However, it is one thing to measure the prerequisites, in the form of technical infrastructure; another question is how much of this Internet usage is for participation in public life? As can be seen from Eurostat data (see Figure 1), the percentage of Estonians using the Internet for communication is close to the average across the Internet, while the percentages using Internet banking are also equally similar. Yet when it comes to using the Internet to obtain information from public websites, or to interact with the government or other public authorities, Estonia is ahead of its Baltic neighbors, although only average among the EU27 countries.

The Internet is now well integrated into the personal lives of Estonians – even Internet banking, which requires skill and trust.[2] However, although it is often claimed that once people start using and trusting online banking, use of all other Internet applications will follow, the data here suggest otherwise. Despite being ahead in the field of Internet banking, Estonians still have a lot to learn about participatory online activities. This can be explained at least partially by the fact that the government focused on investments in infrastructure, encouraging an increase in competitiveness but leaving local Internet users somewhat empty-handed – a void that was quickly filled by activities in the private sphere. The task of explaining the use and functionality of ICTs was quickly taken over by banks, which saw an immediate return on their revenues, rather than the state.

One of the reasons for this situation could be that the measurement of competitiveness, as it relates to Estonia's information society, follows the internationally much criticized path (Barzilai-Nahon 2006; Menou & Taylor 2006; Servaes 2003) of quantitative and technology centered measures: number of Internet users, number of computers and number of Internet connections. This in itself proposes a normative barrier – it becomes more important to achieve target numbers than to focus on the activities individuals perform within online environments. These formal measures helped Estonia gain the international image of an advanced e-state. The successful implementation of information technologies became a spectacular characteristic that was used to sell Estonia to international audiences. Estonia also became a yardstick, a comparison that was eagerly used by the international media when describing a rapidly changing country. Estonian newspapers carefully quoted stories in the foreign media that portrayed Estonia's success, thus helping in their turn to bring this particular form of hype back to Estonia (Driessen 1999).

## ICTs in the Political Agenda of Estonian Transition Society

The first strategic document discussing the information society in Estonia, *The Estonian Way to the Information Society*, was published in 1994 (Eesti Informaatikanõukogu 1994). As Kalvet (2007) and Siil (1997) point out, the document demonstrated an aspiration to follow similar processes then occurring in the EU, the joining of which was Estonia's main national goal at the time. The development of information technology, and its implementation into different spheres of life, was discussed extensively in general policy reports like the Estonian Human Development Report (1996, 1997), in more focused policy plans like the Tiger Leap Program,[3] which aimed to bring computers and Internet connections to Estonian schools (1997), and in Estonian Information Policy (1998); similar aspirations also appeared in the speeches of visionaries (for example IT activist Linnar Viik, former foreign minister Toomas Hendrik Ilves, former prime minister Mart Laar, etc.), forming ways of understanding the concept of the information society.

According to these documents, the rationale behind the ICT-related change in society lay in its benefit to society: the ability of technology to increase Estonian competitiveness, reduce social divisions, and foster state–individual relationships. Special emphasis was placed on introducing ICTs to the education system in order to prepare future citizens and entrepreneurs.

The development of ICTs and the Internet, and their integration into everyday life in Estonia, occurred at a time when many of the most far-reaching changes had already been made, during a period characterized first by relative stability (1995–1998), and subsequently, by the euphoria of success. At that time ICTs became part of the political agenda and policy overviews and development plans were drafted discussing the role of ICTs in general social change, with the aim of incorporating technology into the changes. At that time, administrative, academic, technological and industrial groups made successful efforts to boost Estonian economic development through strong ICT policy (Lauristin & P. Vihalemm 1997) and conscious investment in technology and ICT infrastructure. This was to be followed by initiatives designed to acquaint the population with the new technological infrastructure.

Despite strong reservations, including claims by some social scientists that ICTs possibly add to the strong stratification of society, generally very optimistic and even uncritical statements can be found across all of the documents. Estonia is seen as having the necessary prerequisites for the implementation of ICT-related change, for example flexibility and a relatively high level of education (Human Development Report 1996). The Tiger Leap Program, which became the metaphor for the whole success story of rapid reforms during the pre-accession period, was notably based on rather strong ideological beliefs. For example, Enel Mägi, general manager of the

Tiger Leap Foundation, stressed that the information age gives Estonia great opportunities:

> The Tiger Leap Program is a step toward ensuring our success in competing with larger nations in the 21st century, when the world is evolving into a society in which information is the main commodity. Estonia is willing to invest in the future of its people. (Mägi 1999, p. 31, quoted in Runnel 2001, p. 59)

Ideologically, the notion of the 'Tiger Leap' embodied many aspects other than merely providing access to the Internet. The Tiger Leap Program became the metaphor for a general computerization of society that was not limited to the field of education.

Among other aims, the Principles of Estonian Information Policy (1998) also promised to provide a forum enabling every individual to join the discussion on shaping the information society. This forum never came into being, although one can see early ideas relating to it at the web portal TOM (*Täna Otsustan Mina* – Today I Decide[4]), which was established in order to facilitate participation. The tone of the document, however, was one of providing information for citizens in order to guarantee a successful realization of the 'opportunities [that moving into the Information Society] gives them' (Siil 1997).

The policy documents were inspired not only by strategic decisions, but also by the general technology-friendly culture in Estonia, including a general awareness of technology and a readiness to use it. Although the importance of technology diminished in comparison to other values during the 1990s (Lauristin & T. Vihalemm 1997), the understanding of technology as a modernist value and the idealized view of progress so characteristic of the Soviet period still lingered on, creating a favorable environment for technological change.[5]

It can therefore be said that ICT friendliness, represented in policy documents, was as much a cultural model as it was an economical tool. In his study of the Hungarian information society, anthropologist Tom Wormald refers to technological change as an integral part of applying EU models of statehood (Wormald 2005). Vogt (2005) also states that the technological utopia, or rather the information society, was in many ways an essential driver for widespread change in Eastern Europe: people wanted to achieve the technological level and possibilities of the West as soon as possible. Today the feeling of the 'grand narrative of ICTs' (Servaes & Heindercykx 2002) has diminished and Estonia has in many respects 'caught up with and overtaken' 'old Europe'; as there are no good examples of, or statements about, continuous improvement, there is now less ambition regarding the participation of citizens in online environments. Here one can also see conflicting ideas about individual well-being as achievable through the use of technology. State success is proclaimed through aspirational speeches on the future. Many individuals have achieved basic well-being and the use of technologies is now put towards personal goals rather than participation in public life.

## Conditions for Democratic Practices – Theoretical Considerations and Actual Online Participation

When, in 1998, the Principles of Estonian Information Policy were adopted by the Estonian government, the transition process had reached the alienation, or post-revolutionary phase (see Lauristin & Vihalemm 2008). As in other countries, academic and political circles regarded the technological 'revolution' as a remedy for the shortcomings of democracy. For this reason, citizens' participation was highlighted as one of the main principles in IT policy documents. Although the development of institutional democracy in Estonia had been impressively rapid, the decreasing numbers of voters and increasing public discussion about the alienation of the state (Ehin 2007) showed that people had become more focused on their individual needs.

The expectation that ICTs would quickly foster new hybrid forms of participatory and representative democracy, however, betrayed a lack of critical engagement. As has been the case in other countries, Estonia adopted a very top-down approach to implementation: rather than introducing the proposed online discussion forum dealing with what kind of information society citizens would like (Principles of Estonian Information Policy 1998), the emphasis was instead given to several state-initiated projects. Although this was looked upon highly favorably in the international political scene, it is not that appreciated by individuals. As Hague and Loader (1999, p. 10) describe:

> The underlying logic would appear to run along the following lines: ICTs are a good thing *per se*; those who can access and have the skills to utilize these ICTs will gain obvious advantages (primarily economic) for themselves and will be more useful (primarily economically) to society (...).
>
> What is missing here is any attempt to ground awareness raising and training regarding ICTs in the everyday experience of individuals and communities and to allow them to decide for themselves what use ICTs may be for them.

Estonian ICT policy documents and state initiated projects follow a similar top-down logic. This leaves very little space to understand that the use of ICTs does not necessarily lead to individuals seeking 'valuable' information, or making 'valuable' deliberations, etc.; rather these functions and practices come when space is provided for them, while at the same time leaving the possibility for social shaping. For instance, the large scale public campaign to train 100,000 Estonians to use computers (Look at the World[6]) can also be considered for the most part to have been a public relations exercise, as the four–eight hours of training available was enough to raise curiosity rather than increase skill levels, particularly the skills required to search and participate (Pruulmann-Vengerfeldt & Kalvet 2008). From the point of view of the social shaping of technology, there is an inherent political similarity to law and policy, although unlike the latter, technology policy is often designed without public debate (Docter & Dutton 1999).

The concept of participation plays a crucial role in theoretical models proposing that the Internet will open a new public sphere, with the possibility of a more direct and/or deliberative democracy. But this raises new questions. 'Quick-fix' Internet solutions for democratic crises have been both celebrated and criticized, and while the Internet is seen as a mobilizing tool to bring the young and underrepresented into politics, it also appears to some to be just another way of reinforcing existing social divisions (Hibberd 2003; Norris 2001; Scheufele & Nisbet 2002).

In the Estonian context there is some confusion and ambiguity about the terms that express participation within the theoretical debate. In current political rhetoric more emphasis is put on the word *kaasamine* (engagement), whereas the concept of participation is more explicitly expressed in Estonian using the word *osalemine*. Lagerspetz (2006) explains the two key concepts *osalus* and *kaasamine* in the context of Estonian civic society, as follows: *Kaasamine* is (a) an inward-oriented 'mobility' of a target group or constituency; or (b) activities of the public or private sector aimed at giving citizens or citizens' organizations the chance to participate in decisions that are related to them, including legislative processes. *Osalus* is the individual's possibility to have a say in decisions that are related to him/her.

'Engagement', with its top-down nature, in which people are engaged or involved when it is deemed suitable by the groups in power, has become a new catchword in the wider public vocabulary. Marju Lauristin has noted the improper replacement of 'participation' (*osalus*) by 'engagement' (*kaasamine*) noting that:

> Engagement is a one-sided (the dominant, governing), group activity towards another (dominated, governed) group; the one who engages is a subject while the one who is being engaged is more of an object whose possibilities to influence final decisions are limited. (Lauristin 2007)

Despite the criticism expressed above, the e-state as well as some well-known examples of online participation have supported the success-story idea of the 'Tiger Leap' in Estonia. Three key initiatives from within the Estonian Internet sphere (Internet based voting and two e-participation/consultation websites) have become symbols of Internet participation: they are often used in public discussions about Estonian Internet initiatives and are often considered to be trademarks of Estonian online participatory democracy.

Regardless of the above-mentioned idea that technology might bring new and hybrid forms of democracy, the best-known Estonian application of the Internet within the democratic process is online voting. E-voting has already been used twice in Estonia, in local elections in 2005 and in the parliamentary elections of 2007. E-voting enables people to vote from anywhere using their identity card and a smart-card reader to select their favored candidate from lists held on the relevant website. About 9,000 people used this option in 2005 and more than 30,000 people (5.4% of the population) in 2007 (VVK 2007). It can be said that having the option to vote via the Internet has helped to increase citizen involvement. As Vassil's (2007) analysis of e-voters shows, the number of people whose participation depended on e-technologies is small but significant: 10% of e-voters in the analysis claimed that they would not have voted if Internet voting was not an option, while 95% of e-voters were convinced that they would not like to vote in the traditional way if e-voting continues as an option. This indicates relative techno-friendliness in some groups. However, it should be kept in mind that e-voting can be viewed as the preparation of citizens and institutions to trust and accept online activities, rather than an adequate model of e-participation.

Although internationally less well known or discussed than e-voting, we consider e-participation and consultation website initiatives to be more significant achievements from the point of view of participatory democracy, even though one of the websites is a relatively low-traffic environment and the other is still in the stages of implementation and development. In the following passages we will give a more thorough overview of them and analyze the possible reasons for their relatively low visibility and usage.

When seeking a more participatory model of the democratic process, Estonia has found ways to support hybrid democratic forms and has tried to set up a deliberative democratic space to foster participation in policy making. *Täna Otsustan Mina* – (Today I Decide, TOM) – was set up in 2001 and received a great deal of media attention as the ideal democratic forum. It is a state-initiated forum website where registered users can propose legislative changes. According to a recent study, only 9% of the 6,000 registered users have ever presented an idea, and only 1% of them have presented more than two ideas (Tallo et al. 2007). TOM appears to be a good example of what the OECD (2001) calls participatory democracy, namely an initiative where people have the opportunity to co-decide on policy agendas and to influence other (political) agendas. However, in TOM, the problem of power imbalance negates any democratic potential: not only have administrations more time and flexibility in their reactions to citizens' comments, but practice also shows the hesitancy of the administration to respond in a non-protective and stimulating way. In its ideal version, TOM could facilitate what the OECD (2001, p. 12) calls 'active participation and [an] effort to engage citizens in policy making on a partnership basis', but the lack of dialogue and severe power imbalances evident in practice make it seem more like what Verba calls 'pseudo-participation, in which the emphasis is not on creating the situation in which participation is possible, but on creating the feeling that participation is possible' (Verba 1961, pp. 220–1, quoted in Carpentier 2007, p. 215).

Arnstein (1969) defines a ladder of participation in local life, similar to the OECD's classification of participation, in order to separate activities that are inclusive of citizens (partnership, delegated power and citizen control) from those that only appear so (for example, informing, consulting and placating citizens) and are in fact 'tokenisms'. Estonia is doing well in terms of informing its citizens and excellent attempts have been made on the consultation front, but according to the model, there is still progress to be made towards using the Internet to form partnerships and to provide tools for citizen control. Currently the available participatory models online have changed from being state originated public discussions, to relatively closed and small-scale civic society initiatives. One of the latest state initiatives aimed at using the Internet for improved consultation purposes is the newly founded participation web Osale.ee,[7] which defines itself using ideas of community engagement. There are several forms of opinion expression at Osale.ee: non-formal 'comments' and more formal 'opinions'. Some of the consultations also include a survey, where open-ended questions are added to the consultation process to structure the positions. By the end of summer 2008, 31 consultations had been carried out, with a few or no comments on each, which makes this a very low-traffic participatory website. Although the word *osale* means to participate in Estonia, as previously explained, the page aims to offer the possibility of community engagement (*kaasamine*) and does not reach the level of participation. In order to become a tool facilitating genuine participation, it not only needs the additional functionalities of TOM (which are in fact in the process of being implemented), but also legislative recognition of its mandate and the proposals it generates (Pruulmann-Vengerfeldt 2007).

Another way of analyzing the (dis-)engagement of the Estonian population in the online sphere is to look at user practices and see if and how those practices reflect the variety of democratic and participatory activities.

## Individual Practices

This essay has previously pointed out that many transition studies focus only on macro processes, taking individuals only as obedient recipients of these processes. In the next section, we analyze Estonian Internet users and their participatory practices in order to focus on the diversity of online practices and compare different Internet users and non-users. In addition to the textual analysis above and the secondary analysis of the usage of participatory initiatives, we also use survey data to highlight some of the participatory practices undertaken by individuals. We use the data to illustrate the variety of Internet user types and their practices in various fields of online activities. In order to evaluate the fulfillment of the democratic potential of Internetization, we also compare Internet users and non-users using two participation indices – online and offline participation at the local level.

### Methodology

In analyzing how the democratic potential of ICTs is realized, we use two important measures: Internet user typologies, and an index for local participation. We draw these data from a nationwide survey conducted in February 2007. A total of 803 Estonians between the ages of 18 and 74 participated in the survey. Respondents were recruited using the source address method, and in rural areas an age and gender based quota was used. A self-completed survey with in total 305 variables was used. An additional weight variable was used to match the data with census information.

We used statistics analysis software SPSS to analyze the data both by cross-tabulation of different variables and by conducting cluster analyses in order to formulate Internet user typologies and index calculations for participatory activities. In total 70% of the people participating in this survey were Internet users. First, we will look at the Internet user types. Through illustration of these types we can see that the Internet user practices differ greatly, and thus if some groups have grasped more of the variety of options available, this cannot be said of everyone. Internet user typology is composed using participants' self-evaluation as to how well they consider themselves to be able to perform each named Internet activity (in total 13 activities[8]). The value of these ratings on a scale of 1 (not at all) to 7 (very well) was used as a basis for a two-step cluster analysis with a preset number of clusters – in this case six. Several numbers of clusters were tested, but finally six was preferred as it held the best explanatory power. This also supports previous findings, which used similar survey data to analyze Internet user typologies (de Almeida Alves 2007; Pruulmann-Vengerfeldt 2006b; Vengerfeldt & Runnel 2004). In addition, six clusters were best distributed composition-wise among the groups. An additional cluster was created by analyzing missing values and redefining them as Internet non-users as non-users did not answer those questions on the survey and thus could not play a role in cluster analysis.

*Internet usage practices*

Next we will give a short overview of the Internet users based on their Internet use and socio-demographic characteristics.

(1) The Versatile user's Internet use is characterized by versatility and above-average active participation in all listed activities. This group is generally aged between 18 and 44; there are more people with higher incomes in this group.

(2) Work, communication and e-services oriented users are relatively active Internet users who feel that their usage is generally characterized by communicating with friends and family, seeking information related to work, using e-services and seeking advice and help. Least characteristic of this group is online participation and seeking exciting information. This pragmatic user type is 72% female, and one third of this group is aged between 25 and 34.

(3) Entertainment and exciting information oriented users feel that their usage is first and foremost characterized by seeking entertainment and exciting information. Searching for information from state, Intranet and Internet services is least likely to characterize their use. An average age of between 18 and 34 makes this type characteristic of the younger population.

(4) The Work and information oriented user is positively characterized by Intranet use, seeking information from state and work, and searching for study related information. People in this category consider using Internet services, and using the Internet for practical information and reading online journalism is also characteristic to their Internet use. At the same time seeking entertainment and participation in forums has, for them, significant negative association with their Internet use. These Internet users are generally aged between 35 and 64, and this group is the one with the greatest proportion of people with higher education. Their income is average or above average.

(5) E-services oriented users feel that their Internet use is most clearly characterized by the use of e-services like banking, the tax office and use of other form filling websites. They are fairly passive Internet users and they could be seen as single application users (Pruulmann-Vengerfeldt & Kalvet 2008). Seeking information from the state and using job search facilities are slightly above average, but can still be considered characteristic. In comparison, participating in forums, seeking entertainment, and seeking advice and help can all be considered activities that are significantly less characteristic than average. One third of Internet users in this type are aged 45–54 and nearly half of this group has higher education.

(6) Small-scale users are not characterized by any of the listed activities and are the most passive group. Of the listed activities, they feel most associated with Internet services (banking, tax office and form filling), but still on a much smaller scale than other Internet users. This is the oldest user group, with nearly one quarter over 55 years of age.

The seventh type is Internet non-users – those who said that they have not used the Internet or did not list any characteristic activities, leaving all variables blank. There are very few of them among 18–34 year olds and there are more in this group with only primary education.

Table 1 gives an overview of the socio-demographic background of the six Internet user types used in this analysis.

*Local participation through traditional and new media*

In this essay we use our survey in order to identify how active our Internet users and non-users are in local life. For that we analyze two activism indices: traditional forms of activism in local life and new media forms of local participation. Participants were asked whether they had undertaken listed activities in the last four–five years, and based on this an index was prepared in which people were placed in one of three groups: (1) those who have participated in none of the activities; (2) those who have participated in one; and (3) those who have participated in two or more of the activities. Traditional participation was composed using three criteria: (1) those who have participated in a local community problem-oriented meeting, action or demonstration, or given their signature to a joint letter to local government; (2) those who have contacted local government or council members in relation to a local problem or issue; and (3) those who have contacted a local newspaper or radio, or spoken in the local media on an issue relating to a local problem. The new media participation index consisted of four activities: (1) following a debate in the Internet relating to local life or politics; (2) expressing an opinion about local politics or the local community in a debate or survey on the Internet; (3) calling, or sending an e-mail or SMS to a radio or TV show dealing with local life; and (4) participating in a local newspaper's online forum, or writing commentaries on the online edition of a local newspaper. Based on the results, we compared Internet user types and non-users using their activism scale both through traditional and new media forms.

The following indices were analyzed using mean results in both participation categories. Figure 2 shows the average means: 0.39 for traditional participation and 0.29 for new media participation (maximum 2 for both indices) as well as the differences within the Internet user and non-user groups. Versatile Internet users, and Work and information oriented users, are the most active in both methods of participation, while the former group is more active in online participation and the latter more active in traditional participation. Non-users and Small-scale users are equally very passive on the new media participation scale, although Small-scale users at least have had some contact with the Internet. After Entertainment and exciting information users, they are the most passive in terms of traditional participation.

We have drawn a two-dimensional matrix of scales based on average results from the traditional and new media participation scales: active–passive in traditional participation and active–passive in new media participation. Figure 3 gives an overview of the relative placements of Internet users and non-users on these scales. The relative center point is taken from the average result on both scales.

Here one can see that in the first quartile are Versatile Internet users, Work and information oriented Internet users and Work, communication and e-services

**TABLE 1** Socio-demographic profiles of whole population, Internet user types and Internet non-users based on gender, age, education and income

| | N (%) | Versatile Internet users | Work, communication and e-services oriented users | Entertainment and exciting information user | Work and information oriented user | E-services oriented user | Small-scale user | Non-user |
|---|---|---|---|---|---|---|---|---|
| N | 799 | 143 | 75 | 94 | 70 | 89 | 95 | 233 |
| % of total population | 100 | 18 | 9 | 12 | 9 | 11 | 12 | 29 |
| Male | 374 (47) | 50 | 28 | 62 | 50 | 45 | 42 | 46 |
| Female | 425 (53) | 50 | 72 | 38 | 50 | 55 | 58 | 54 |
| 18–24 | 125 (16) | 35 | 22 | 43 | 1 | 7 | 4 | 3 |
| 25–34 | 157 (20) | 36 | 34 | 31 | 17 | 17 | 18 | 3 |
| 35–44 | 152 (19) | 22 | 23 | 13 | 34 | 25 | 17 | 13 |
| 45–54 | 138 (17) | 4 | 15 | 13 | 20 | 36 | 24 | 17 |
| 55–64 | 122 (15) | 2 | 5 | 0 | 21 | 13 | 25 | 28 |
| 65–74 | 102 (13) | 1 | 1 | 1 | 7 | 2 | 12 | 35 |
| Primary education | 136 (17) | 8 | 1 | 31 | 1 | 3 | 12 | 35 |
| Secondary education | 423 (54) | 62 | 57 | 57 | 34 | 47 | 53 | 53 |
| Higher education | 235 (30) | 30 | 42 | 13 | 65 | 49 | 35 | 12 |
| Income up to 1,500 kr | 66 (9) | 5 | 8 | 12 | 3 | 4 | 10 | 11 |
| 1,501–2,500 | 90 (12) | 7 | 11 | 11 | 13 | 11 | 10 | 16 |
| 2,501–4,000 | 223 (30) | 26 | 16 | 21 | 14 | 31 | 24 | 44 |
| 4,001–6,000 | 184 (24) | 20 | 27 | 26 | 30 | 24 | 35 | 18 |
| 6,001–8,000 | 95 (12) | 18 | 16 | 9 | 17 | 21 | 11 | 5 |
| over 8,000 kr | 109 (14) | 24 | 21 | 21 | 22 | 10 | 7 | 6 |

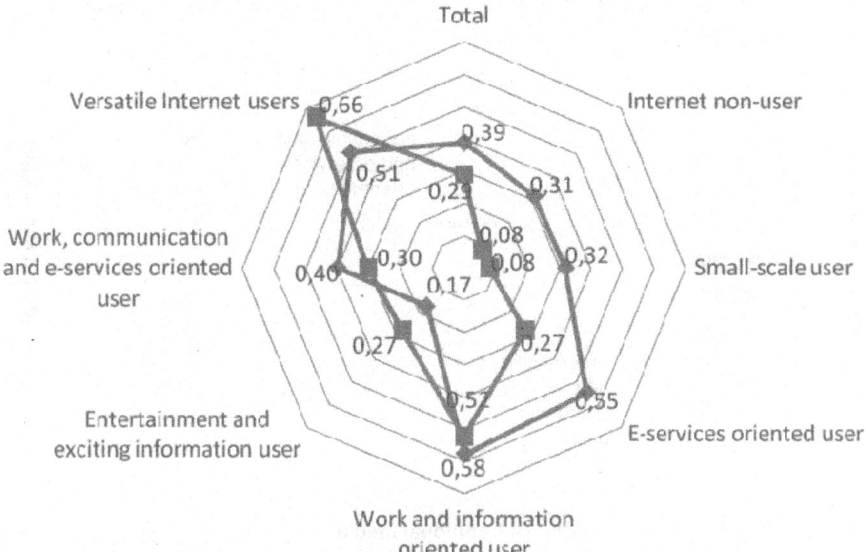

**FIGURE 2** Participation in local life through traditional and new media is measured through indices (max value 3). Means of those indices are calculated for total population, Internet user types and Internet non-users.

oriented users. Members of these groups are more active than average on both participation scales. E-services users, who are relatively passive Internet users, are also passive in terms of e-participation, while being active users of the traditional means of participation. Entertainment and exciting information users are marginally more active when it comes to e-participation, although overall they are still in the third quartile together with Internet non-users and Small-scale users. The latter two are nearly average when it comes to traditional participation. The corner of the matrix where there should be users active in the Internet and passive in traditional participation is empty. On the one hand, this indicates that the Internet is, at the moment, not taken seriously as the sole participatory medium and also that it has not replaced other means of participation. On the other hand, it also shows that those active in the area of participation, seek online channels complementary to their existing practices – the Internet has not created purely online participants.

## Conclusions and Discussion

This essay aimed to look at the state's wish to encourage the implementation of ICTs in society in order to advance Estonia in three major ways: competitiveness, education and democracy, with special emphasis on the latter. Of the three initial aims set out in

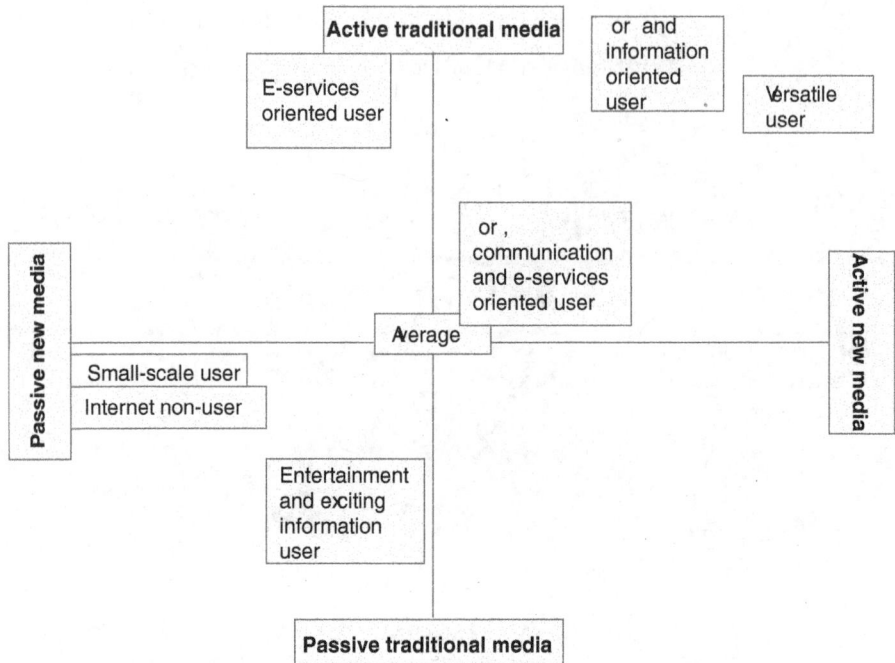

**FIGURE 3** Internet user types and non-users on activity–passivity scales for participation in traditional and new media. The placement is based on mean values (Figure 2) and the relative position is in relation to the average for the total population.

the first policy documents – strengthen competitiveness, increase coherence in society and improve democracy – the first two are better fulfilled. However, serious restructuring of the economy to become more knowledge-based is still underway, with one of the major obstacles being the relative failure to restructure education. The third aim, that of strengthening democracy, has been relatively less successful and it might therefore be assumed that despite the infrastructure and openness to new developments, the lack of the necessary political culture and weakness in civic practices have been important barriers.

In the current study we looked at the relationship between democratic developments and IT, and how this has been reflected in policy documents, major government initiated-projects and individual usage practices. We started by identifying certain patterns and policy aims present in early IS policies in the mid-1990s, which treated ICTs as significant agents in reinforcing democracy, then we went on to look at online environments, reflecting certain understandings about democratic online participation as implemented by the government. Lastly, survey data enabled us to track the current situation from the point of view of the usage practices of individual Internet users, including online activities as well as their local online and offline participation.

It is important to try to view these different aspects together, as policy documents set the basic aims of, and define the bodies responsible for, different sectors, and only in this way does the entire population become subject to these policies. An individual's success very much depends on which of the state's regulative, legislative or opportunity frameworks they act within – the question is how much does what they do reflect or shape the strategic aims set out in policy documents.

Developments in this field are framed by public understanding of the information society and the opportunities it offers. As Leah Lievrouw argues (2000), the whole notion of the information society is based upon an ideological belief in the positive and socially integrative power of technology alongside a prevailing ethic of instrumental rationality and strategically practiced self-interest towards accruing such benefits.

Policy documents in Estonia that dealt with the information society held a more or less technologically deterministic viewpoint, which is not surprising as in the political and economic world technological determinism still appears as a prevailing ideology in debates concerning general technological change and the information society. The dominance of this discourse probably also depends on the small number of academic analyses dealing with the questions of how various social and cultural practices influence the development and distribution of information technologies (Vengerfeldt & Runnel 2004).

In the vein of such technologically deterministic approaches, the policy documents show that Estonia adopted a very top-down approach to the implementation of ICTs as part of its information society policies, and that in doing this it was acting in a similar way to other countries. In the policy texts of the 1990s, people were considered important actors in the diffusion and acceptance of new technologies, but they were viewed mostly as passive recipients, who were expected to adopt infrastructure step by step.

In implementing policies, the supporting actions for better acquisition of technologies were often missing. In the field of democratic development, policy documents did emphasize the importance of participation and Internet democracy, but in reality activities and projects were focused mainly on the development of technology.

However, state initiated projects, following the aims set out in the earlier documents and generally executed in the international political spotlight, are often not that widely used or even recognized by individuals. Providing citizens with tools with which to express their opinions has been accompanied neither by education nor by a willingness to listen.

Although Estonia possesses one excellent example of a service where offer and demand balance (the Estonian electronic tax office, where about 90% of individual income declarations and 94% of value added tax declarations were made in 2008), most e-services cater to government and are intended to make life easier for officials. For instance, online forums launched by central or local governments are mainly in a question and answer format and are not aimed at facilitating discussion (Reinsalu 2006). The rhetoric accompanying the services that have been launched has been generally technical, not motivational: advancement of e-voting, digital signatures, ID cards.

The top-down approach of policy, in which technology itself was the main focus, was probably a useful tactic in the earlier phases of the transition when the focus of attention was on implementing infrastructural change and supporting the development of the private sector. The strong structural reforms that occurred in Estonia came after a series of remarkable years in the country's development – the so-called national awakening period. The 'soft', and perhaps more idealistic, values from the period immediately before and after the regaining of independence which triggered the reforms were quickly replaced by a more pragmatic approach. The period of national awakening, based on an extraordinary mobilization of citizen power, might have offered conditions in which further services for the facilitation of participation could have been developed. Yet, at that time the penetration and understanding of the democratic potential of ICTs was insufficient, although here again Estonia reflected the contemporary international situation. And neither did developments in ICT encourage the development of participatory Internet democracy. In the first phases of Estonia's transition, when people would more eagerly have taken advantage of opportunities for participation, only a representative Internet democracy was developed. By the time the more coherent ICT-related participatory democracy projects were launched, Estonian society had entered the post-revolutionary phase of alienation (Lauristin & Vihalemm 2008). Subsequent years of radical change diminished the potential of participatory democracy, while the rapid development of ICT infrastructure tended to answer, in the majority, the expectations of increasing general competitiveness.

The analysis of the actual user practices online indicates that the number of active and versatile users is increasing in comparison to earlier studies. Despite overall passivity in the fields of participation, active and pragmatic Internet users have also developed ways to participate in online environments. However, the majority of Internet users are still focused on activities within the private sphere. Increasing numbers of forums, semi-public social networking sites and increasing amounts of user generated content is fragmenting the public sphere, while at the same time directing online communication and discussion in different areas of private life. The youngest user groups, generally representing the entertainment and exciting information user type, are among the most passive in both traditional and electronic participation, which perhaps refers to a lack of civic understanding among them. At the same time, this age group is very active in social networking. The most popular Estonian social networking site Rate.ee is used by about 70% of 12–17 year olds and has a total of 300,000 users (one fifth of the country's population).[9] It can be argued that civic participation, in terms of voting or other statutory rights or responsibilities, begins when a person comes of age, but the culture of participation should be part of the socialization processes.

Alienation and institutional development in the public sector, which brought along the consumerist approach of handling citizens as clients, supported the development of consumerist democracy (Bellamy & Taylor 1998; Ridell 2002). At the same time, these developments hindered the participatory democracy, based on real mutual communication.

As part of the reforms, Estonia made several efforts to promote participatory democracy and facilitate governance, among them launching TOM and Osale.ee, as mentioned above. Still it seems that particular services developed by the state to promote participation do reflect the general approach identified in policy documents, which were influenced by techno-determinist interpretations of the ICT-facilitated participatory democracy. Online participation environments do not focus on equal dialogue, and when their usage side is analyzed they turn out to be fairly marginal.

It can however be claimed that this form of Internet democracy also has the potential to develop into a participatory democracy, since it helps to fulfill a significant precondition – enhancing trust in technology, and also indirectly trust in the local authorities that offer services which correspond to the particular needs of the citizen. For example, the most widely used system of e-voting can be viewed as simply one aspect of representative politics that is now in the online sphere. Or it can also be seen as a tool that holds the key to the future introduction of other aspects of direct democracy, which would complement and enrich the existing representative democratic model and make it more inclusive. Despite the fact that the step made by the election system was solely technical, it could be important in encouraging young people to move closer to participation in democratic society.

When looking at the current state of web portals such as TOM and Osale.ee, token participation currently still seems to outweigh real participation. Although those channels do not function well, there is no initiative to find new formats and no investment goes into addressing the weak points of the existing system. The most recently created, state-initiated, participatory environment Osale.ee is rather similar to TOM and attracts fairly low attention. Low user numbers means a lack of credible input, thus the state officials involved have developed skeptical and negative attitudes towards participatory environments like TOM, which in turn discourages new users. Many potential participants move away to the private and third-sector participatory initiatives that have emerged recently, fulfilling their potential there instead.

However, in 2008, Estonia seemed to be entering a new phase regarding participatory activities online. More recently, regular instances of petition signing online have attracted the attention of the traditional media, and thus wider visibility and significance is achieved for online participatory practices. In political rhetoric, these initiatives are still held in low regard. It can be said that Estonia is still searching for recognition of online participatory acts from ordinary citizens, and is in search of users for its state-provided environments. Researchers and practitioners have to analyze more closely the existing participatory environments and user practices in order to support the state in its attempts to engage citizens in the democratic process. At the same time there is a need to help the state understand how it can best take advantage of the participatory initiatives born online but outside its regulated web-space.

## Acknowledgments

The research was partly supported by grants from the Estonian Ministry of Education and Science (0180017s07) and a grant from the Estonian Science Foundation (6526).

## Notes

1   The Information Society sub-index measures how well ICTs are harnessed by various stakeholders through 'variables such as the prioritization of ICT by the

government, ICT penetration rates (Internet, PCs), Internet usage by business and the extent to which students have Internet access in school' (World Economic Forum 2006, p. 2). In this sub-index Estonia is ranked fifth among European countries, quite noticeably outperforming its Baltic neighbors (Latvia ranks 22nd and Lithuania 18th in this index).

2   The success of Internet banking in Estonia has been explained by the fact that banking in general is only some five years younger than electronic banking and so there has not been enough time for customers to get used to branch services (Kerem 2003).

3   The Tiger Leap Program was launched in February 1996 to adjust the Estonian education system to the needs of the information society by equipping schools with information and communication technology, linking them to the Internet and providing ICT education for teachers. The program was called 'Tiger Leap' in order to symbolize rapid changes and technological change as Estonia's main agenda, referring also metaphorically to the example of Asian economic growth. In order to achieve this goal, a special foundation was created in 1997 by the Ministry of Education and private sector ICT firms.

4   TOM (*Täna Otsustan Mina* – Today I Decide) is a key Estonian initiative aimed at fostering participatory online activities (http://www.eesti.ee/tom/). It is a state-initiated forum website where registered users can propose legislative changes, which, after the selection process, are sent to the appropriate administrative unit. In Estonia, laws can be initiated by MPs, by the government or by the president, making this the only possibility for individuals to initiate legislation. The site was launched in 2001. Today, TOM has almost 7,000 users and more than 1,000 ideas have been discussed (TOM 2007).

5   According to a more recent study dealing with values in different population groups, technological development is still rather important, ranking more highly than, for example, 'value' categories like wealth, interesting life, or public recognition (Kalmus & Vihalemm 2004). Pruulmann-Vengerfeldt (2006a) also shows that very favorable attitudes towards computers and the Internet could also be perceived in 2003 and 2005.

6   The Foundation Look@the World (http://www.vaatamaailma.ee) was initiated by ten Estonian private companies with the aim of greatly increasing the number of Internet users and through this the quality of life of Estonians and the state's competitiveness in Europe. Some of this foundation's projects included training in basic computer skills for more than 100,000 people, starting the e-school environment and establishing roughly 500 Public Internet Access Points.

7   The Osale.ee portal (www.osale.ee, opened in July 2007) is managed by the state chancellery in order to facilitate the wider participation of citizens, and citizens' organizations, in politics, and to create legislation through discussions and consultation according to development plans. In the future it will also allow user-generated content. Currently, participation web Osale.ee brings together the legislative domains of all ministries and is an attempt to consolidate different opinion seeking environments under one roof – there has been similar online initiatives in the Ministry of Economic Affairs and Communications and Ministry of Justice.

8   On the 1–7 scale people were asked to mark how well the following activities characterized their Internet use: (1) seeking information from public institutions,

courts, local governments, political parties and other official homepages; (2) seeking practical information (weather, timetables, etc.); (3) using Internet services (bank, tax office, forms, etc.); (4) seeking entertainment (games, music, movies); (5) seeking work and studies related information; (6) seeking interesting and exiting information; (7) seeking information and advice on relationships, family, children, health and other matters related to their personal lives; (8) shopping and gathering information about purchases; (9) seeking information about work, places to live, tourism, new acquaintances, etc.; (10) participating in forums, blogs, surveys, writing commentaries; (11) reading online newspapers and information portals; (12) communicating with friends and acquaintances; and (13) communicating within an organization (Intranet, mailing lists, etc.).

9   Data from www.rate.ee and the survey data gathered in the framework of Estonian Science Foundation Grant no 6526, autumn 2007.

## References

Arnstein, S. R. (1969) 'A Ladder of Citizen Participation', *JAIP*, 35, 4, available at: http://lithgow-schmidt.dk/sherry-arnstein/ladder-of-citizen-participation.html, accessed April 2008.

Barzilai-Nahon, K. (2006) 'Gaps and Bits: Conceptualizing Measurements for Digital Divide/s', *The Information Society*, 22, 5.

Bekkers, V., Duivenboden, van H. & Thaens, M. (eds) (1999) *Information and Communication Technology and Public Communication* (Amsterdam, IOS Press).

Bellamy, C. & Taylor, J. A. (1998) *Governing in the Information Age* (Buckingham, Open University Press).

Berleur, J., Nurminen, M. I. & Impagliazzo, J. (eds) (2006) *Social Informatics: An Information Society for All? In Remembrance of Rob Kling* (Boston, Springer).

Buraway, M. & Verdery, K. (eds) (1999) *Uncertain Transition. Ethnographies of Change in the Postsocialist World* (Lanham, Rowman & Littlefield Publishers).

Carpentier, N. (2007) 'Participation and Interactivity: Changing Perspectives. The Construction of an Integrated Model on Access, Interaction and Participation', in Nightingale, V. & Dwyer, T. (eds) (2007).

Carpentier, N., Pruulmann-Vengerfeldt, P., Nordenstreng, K., Hartmann, M., Vihalemm, P., Nieminen, H. & Cammaerts, B. (eds) (2007) *Media Technologies for Democracy in an Enlarged Europe: The Intellectual Work of the 2007 European Media and Communication Doctoral Summer School* (Tartu, Tartu University Press).

de Almeida Alves, N. (2007) 'Profiles of Internet Users', paper presented at *8th European Sociology Association Conference: Conflict, Citizenship and Civil Society*, Glasgow, 3–6 September 2007 (UK, Glasgow).

Docter, S. & Dutton, W. H. (1999) 'The Social Shaping of the Democracy Network (DNet)', in Hague, B. N. & Loader, B. D. (eds) (1999).

Driessen, H. (1999) 'Public Service Innovation in Europe', in Bekkers, V., Duivenboden, van H. & Thaens, M. (eds) (1999).

Ehin, P. (2007) 'Political Support in the Baltic States, 1993–2004', *Journal of Baltic Studies*, 38, 1.

Estonian Human Development Report (1996) (Tallinn, UNDP), available at: http://web.archive.org/web/19980110191652/www.ciesin.ee/undp/nhdr96/est/index.html, accessed April 2008.

Estonian Human Development Report (1997) (Tallinn, UNDP), available at: http://web.archive.org/web/19980110191337/www.ciesin.ee/undp/nhdr97/est/index.html, accessed April 2008.

Global Competitiveness Report (2007) *The Lisbon Review 2006: Measuring Europe's Progress in Reform, World Economic Forum, Cologny/Geneva*, available at: http://www.weforum.org/pdf/gcr/lisbonreview/report2006.pdf, accessed April 2008.

Hague, B. N. & Loader, B. D. (1999) 'Digital Democracy: An Introduction', in Hague, B. N. & Loader, B. D. (eds) (1999).

Hague, B. N. & Loader, B. D. (eds) (1999) *Digital Democracy: Discourse and Decision Making in the Information Age* (London & New York, Routledge).

Hague, B. N. & Loader, B. D. (eds) (2001) *Digital Democracy: Discourse and Decision Making in the Information Age* (London & New York, Routledge).

Hibberd, L. (2003) 'E-Participation, Broadcasting and Democracy in the UK', *Convergence*, 9, 1.

Kalmus, V., Lauristin, M. & Pruulmann-Vengerfeldt, P. (eds) (2004) *Eesti elavik 21. sajandi algul: ülevaade uurimuse Mina. Maailm. Meedia tulemustest* [*Estonian Lifeworld in the Beginning of the 21st Century: Overview of Results from Research Project Me. The World. The Media*] (Tartu, Tartu Ülikooli Kirjastus).

Kalmus, V. & Vihalemm, T. (2004) 'Eesti siirdekultuuri väärtused' ['Estonian Values of Transition Cultures'], in Kalmus, V., Lauristin, M. & Pruulmann-Vengerfeldt, P. (eds) (2004).

Kalvet, T. (2007) *The Estonian Information Society Developments since the 1990s*, Praxis working paper 29 (Tallinn, Praxis).

Kerem, K. (2003) *Internet Banking in Estonia*, available at: http://www.efmn.info/index.php?option=com_docman&task=doc_view&gid=182, (European Foresight Monitoring network), accessed April 2008.

Lagerspetz, M. (2006) *Kodanikuühiskonna Lühisõnastik* [*Short Dictionary of Civic Society*], available at: http://www.siseministeerium.ee/failid/KYsonaraamatWEB.pdf, accessed April 2008.

Lass, A. (1999) 'Portable Worlds: On the Limits of Replication in the Czech and Slovak Republics', in Buraway, M. & Verdery, K. (eds) (1999), pp. 273–300.

Lauristin, M. (2007) 'Teistsuguse Eesti ootuses' ['Awaiting different Estonia'], *Postimees*, 13 January.

Lauristin, M. & Vihalemm, P. (1997) 'Recent Historical Developments in Estonia: Three Stages of Transition (1987–1997)', in Lauristin, M., Vihalemm, P., Rosengren, K.-E. & Weibull, L. (eds) (1997), pp. 73–126.

Lauristin, M. & Vihalemm, P. (2008) Eesti siirdeaeg tagasivaates: periodiseering ja arengutegurid. Konverentsi kogumik: Eesti Vabariik 90. EV Haridus- ja Teadusministeerium Pärnu 27.–28 aug 2008, lk 97.–101.

Lauristin, M., Vihalemm, P., Rosengren, K.-E. & Weibull, L. (eds) (1997) *Return to the Western World: Cultural and Political Perspectives on the Estonian Post-Communist Transition* (Tartu, Tartu University Press).

Lauristin, M. & Vihalemm, T. (1997) 'Changing Value Systems: Civilizational Shift and Local Differences', in Lauristin, M., Vihalemm, P., Rosengren, K.-E. & Weibull, L. (eds) (1997).

Lievrouw, L. (2000) 'The Information Environment and Universal Service', *The Information Society*, 16, 2.
Mägi, E. (1999) 'Tiger Leap Program', *Global Estonian*, Summer, pp. 28–31.
Menou, M. & Taylor, R. (2006) 'A "Grand Challenge": Measuring Information Societies', *The Information Society*, 22, 5.
Nightingale, V. & Dwyer, T. (eds) (2007) *New Media Worlds: Challenges for Convergence* (Oxford, Oxford University Press).
Nørgaard, O. (2000) *Economic Institutions and Democratic Reform: A Comparative Analysis of Post-communist Countries* (Cheltenham, Edward Elgar).
Norris, P. (2001) 'Digital Divide: Civic Engagement, Information Poverty and the Internet Worldwide', in Hague, B. N. & Loader, B. D. (eds) (2001).
OECD (2001) *Citizens as Partners: Information, Consultation and Public Participation in Policymaking*, PUMA, OECD, available at: http://www.govx.org.uk/communities/spaces/citizenservice/knowledge/entries/engaging-citizens-in-policy-making—an-oecd-handbook/Citizens%20as%20Partners.pdf, accessed April 2008.
Principles of Estonian Information Policy (1998) available at: http://www.riso.ee/en/files/Principles_of_Estonian_Information_Policy_1998.pdf, accessed April 2008.
Pruulmann-Vengerfeldt, P. (2006a) 'Computers and Internet Related Beliefs among Estonian Computer Users and Non-users', in Berleur, J., Nurminen, M. I. & Impagliazzo, J. (eds) (2006).
Pruulmann-Vengerfeldt, P. (2006b) *Information Technology Users and Uses within the Different Layers of the Information Environment in Estonia*, Doctoral Thesis (Tartu, Tartu University Press), available at: http://hdl.handle.net/10062/173, accessed April 2008.
Pruulmann-Vengerfeldt, P. (2007) 'Participating in a Representative Democracy: Three Case Studies of Estonian Participatory Online Initiatives', in Carpentier, N., Pruulmann-Vengerfeldt, P., Nordenstreng, K., Hartmann, M., Vihalemm, P., Nieminen, H. & Cammaerts, B. (eds) (2007).
Pruulmann-Vengerfeldt, P. & Kalvet, T. (2008) *Infokihistumine: Interneti mittekasutajad, vähekasutajad ning hiljuti kasutama hakanud [Information Stratification: Non-users, Small-scale Users and Recent Starters]*, Praxis working paper 41 (Tallinn, Praxis).
Reinsalu, K. (2006) 'Is Estonian Local E-government Responsive to Citizens' Needs? The Case Study of Tartu, Estonia', *Information Polity: An International Journal of Government and Democracy in the Information Age*, 11, 3–4, pp. 255–72.
Reinsalu, K. & Winsvold, M. (2008) 'Does Civic Culture Influence the Use of Online Forums? A Comparative Study of Local Online Participation in Estonia and Norway', *Journal of Public Administration and Public Policy*, 1, 1, pp. 51–67.
Ridell, S. (2002) 'The Web as a Space for Local Agency', *Communications*, 27, 2, pp. 147–69.
Runnel, P. (2001) 'The Tiger Leap Project and the Toilet Wall. Development of the Internet and IT Consciousness in Estonia', *Nord Nytt*, 82, August.
Scheufele, D. A. & Nisbet, M. C. (2002) 'Being a Citizen Online: New Opportunities and Dead Ends', *Press/Politics*, 7, 3.
Servaes, J. (eds) (2003) *The European Information Society: A Reality Check* (Bristol & Portland, Intellect).
Servaes, J. & Heinderyckx, F. (2002) 'The "New" ICTs Environment in Europe: Closing or Widening Gaps?', *Telematics and Informatics*, 19, 2.

Siil, I. (1997) 'The First Year of the Estonian Informatics Centre', in *IT in Public Administration of Estonia 1997*, available at: http://www.riso.ee/en/pub/1997it/, accessed April 2008.

Tallo, I., Ott, A., Leosk, N., Marvet, P., Segaert, S., Trechsel, A. H., Glencross, A. & Rebane, E. (2007) *TOM Analysis Report*, available at: http://tidywork.pbwiki.com/ TOM+analysis+report, accessed April 2008.

TOM (2008) available at: http://www.eesti.ee/tom/, accessed April 2008.

Vassil, K. (2007) *e-Valimistest osavõtmise tegurid ja kogemus: E-valijate võrdlev analüüs 2005. aasta kohalike valimiste ja 2007. aasta riigikogu valimiste põhjal* [Participation Factors and Experience in E-voting: Comparative Analysis Based on Local Government Elections in 2005 and Parliament Elections in 2007], unpublished Masters Thesis, University of Tartu, Department of Journalism and Communications, available at: http://www.jrnl. ut.ee/loputood/2007magistritood/vassil_kristjan.pdf, accessed April 2008.

Vengerfeldt, P. & Runnel, P. (2004) 'Uus meedia Eestis' ['New Media in Estonia'], in Vihalemm, P. (ed.) (2004).

Verba, S. (1961) *Small Groups and Political Behaviour* (Princeton, Princeton University Press).

Vihalemm, P. (ed.) (2004) *Meediasüsteem ja meediakasutus Eestis 1965–2004* [*Media System and Media Use in Estonia 1965–2004*] (Tartu, Tartu University Press).

Vogt, H. (2005) *Between Utopia and Disillusionment: A Narrative of the Political Transformation in Eastern Europe* (New York & Oxford, Berghahn Books).

VVK (2007) *Main Statistics of E-Voting*, available at: http://www.vvk.ee/english/ Ivoting%20comparison%202005_2007.pdf, accessed April 2008.

World Economic Forum (2006) *Global Competitiveness Report 2007–2008*, available at: http://www.gcr.weforum.org/, accessed April 2008.

Wormald, T. (2005) 'Visions of the Future: Technology and Imagination in Hungarian Civil Society', *Anthropology Matters Journal*, 7, 1, available at: http://www. anthropologymatters.com/journal/2005-1/wormald_2005_visions.pdf, accessed April 2008.

# EMERGING CONSUMER TYPES IN A TRANSITION CULTURE: CONSUMPTION PATTERNS OF GENERATIONAL AND ETHNIC GROUPS IN ESTONIA

## Veronika Kalmus, Margit Keller and Maie Kiisel

### Introduction

The transition of East European societies from socialism to capitalism has inspired several sociological and philosophical analyses of post-Soviet cultural conditions (for example, Kalmus & Vihalemm 2006; Kennedy 2002; Outhwaite & Ray 2004; Sztompka 2004; Vogt 2005). Among them, studies of the emerging consumer culture and the discourse and practices of sustainable consumption (SC) are still scarcely represented (for example, Keller 2005; Keller & Vihalemm 2005). This essay offers an insight into the transitional cultural condition from the point of view of consumption and the environment. The aim of our study is to analyze how different socio-demographic groups in Estonia, particularly people of different age groups and ethnicities, vary in terms of their attitudes and practices in these areas. We also investigate if and how Estonian people can be divided into types of consumers based on indices of consumerism and sustainable consumption. Our analysis is based on data from the representative population survey *Me. The World. The Media (Mina. Maailm. Meedia)*, carried out in Estonia in November 2005.

The broadest concept informing our study is the notion of 'transition culture' developed by Kennedy, meaning a framework of values, beliefs, symbols, etc. through which actors interpret the transformation of political and economic systems and undertake actions under new circumstances (Kennedy 2002, pp. 8–9). Our focus, however, is on analyzing the life-world and mentality of people representing different social groups of the Estonian population. Therefore, we also rely on the concepts elaborated by Sztompka (2004), who argues that the cultural context of transition is ambivalent: the symbols, values and identities brought about by new cultural flows exist in parallel with old traditions, narratives and values. Members of society who are faced with the challenge of coping with the ambivalence of a new situation may refer both to old and new cultural resources (Sztompka 2004, pp. 176–7). Furthermore, Sztompka notes that different social groups may 'pick up' diverse symbols and narratives. In particular, Sztompka emphasizes differences between generations in a transition culture (p. 193).

Secondly, we draw on earlier studies of post-socialist consumer culture (Keller 2004) in which today's 'Western' consumer culture is contrasted with its Soviet counterpart of forced homogeneity and 'dictatorship over needs' (Feher *et al.* 1984). Thirdly, and without discussing further the definitions of sustainable consumption – this is beyond the scope of this essay – we give an overview of how SC is contextualized in the practices of post-Socialist Estonia. The emphasis is on the interrelationships between the Soviet legacy and the 'translation' of Western sustainable practices and policies into the Estonian context. Our theoretical section concludes with a brief overview of the specificities of consumption related to age and ethnicity.

After the theoretical section, we describe our data, method and techniques of analysis, followed by a presentation of empirical findings. The latter mostly offers a presentation of data without extensive interpretation, and is divided into three subsections: first we look at different age groups, then at the two major ethnic groups, ethnic Estonians and Estonian Russians, and finally we present an analysis of the consumer typology. Explanation and discussion of the results, in the light of theoretical approaches and earlier studies, is given in the conclusions and discussion.

## Consumer Culture in Transformational Society

### *The Soviet heritage*

Consumer culture in today's transformational Estonia must be analyzed against the background of the Soviet heritage. It still powerfully occupies the memories of the older generations (see Keller & Vihalemm 2005) and its disappearance explains, at times, the contrasting values, practices and orientations of the younger generations. The Soviet time was characterized by a shortage of goods and a forced homogeneity of lifestyle. However, the scarcity was, to a large extent, experienced collectively. The inability to consume like people did on Finnish TV, regularly watched in northern Estonia, was not a private failure; instead, the state was to blame. Many current portrayals of the consumer culture of the 1960s–1980s show it through the prism of a desire for freedom and consumer sovereignty, which embodied a mundane form of civic freedom.

In spite of all its deficiencies, the Soviet consumer culture is often represented in the accounts of the elderly as a time of solidarity and a more respectful relationship between consumers and things, subjects and objects. Since there was no market economy-based cycle of fashions and quick obsolescence of things, there was less waste and 'colorful cheap trash' (see Keller & Vihalemm 2005). Thus, people were, either consciously or unconsciously, 'sustainable' in their everyday consumption practices.

*'Western' consumerism and transformation*

A Western consumer culture started to develop in Estonia at the end of the 1980s. The 1990s saw a rapid influx of new cultural forms, such as advertising, branding and recreational shopping. Volumes of consumption increased, and by 2006 the Estonian Eurostat Index of Actual Individual Consumption had reached the level of 65, compared to an EU27 average of 100 (Svennebye 2008).[1]

Today's consumer culture in Estonia has reached a certain stage of maturity; it is no longer eagerly aspiring to re-Westernization as it was in the early 1990s. By the mid-1990s, a turn towards aestheticization, post-materialism and an increasing sophistication of consumer culture could be observed (Keller 2004). On the one hand, consumers are offered a range of possibilities of symbolic consumption oriented at lifestyle and identity-building that may result in the successful re-appropriation of objects by subjects, and genuine self-actualization and self-expression through material culture, as described by Miller (1987). On the other hand, consumers face many different scarcities today – based on a lack of money, specialty goods or quality of service or on a breadth of choice – which are primarily perceived as private matters. This, in turn, may at times cause strong disappointment and dissatisfaction, which results in indifference and estrangement.

Proceeding from the above, one of the central building blocks of our study is consumerism as a phenomenon. We have operationalized it in our study by drawing on Bauman (1992, p. 223), who claims that consumerism means 'manipulation of signs for various ends' and 'production, desire and consumption of "symbolic goods"'. The determination of which consumption practices are more symbolic than others is of course arbitrary. However, our index of consumerism (for details see Data and Method), which is comprised of practices that we consider more meaningful and revealing in the Estonian context, has proved to have a considerable explanatory force, as our earlier research has demonstrated (Keller & Kalmus 2004, forthcoming). Also, Lauristin (2004) has shown that the Estonian people's subjective self-positioning on the social ladder is directly associated with their levels of consumerism.

## Consumerism and Sustainability

*The turn to the individual*

The 'sustainable development' approach, which gained ground at the end of the 1980s in the 'developed West', shifted the emphasis of the responsibility for the environment from the system level to the local and individual level. The concept of SC emerges from the understanding that sustainability no longer belongs to a counterculture type of environmentalism: ecological discourse is normalized and belongs to everybody (Eder 1996). This new development-centered environmentalism is a matter of individual interpretation. Beck (1995) has even called this tendency 'organized irresponsibility', as instrumentalization of life-worlds has exhausted familiar meanings of the environment and environmental protection, shifting the burden of defining and executing sustainability from the system to individuals. Individualized environmentalism is mainly rationalized as a certain mode of consumer-behavior. Sustainable consumption, which initially was meant to challenge expanding consumerism (see WSSD 2002), has become an object of it, and environmental identities develop within the framework of consumer culture. This is also a reason to take a closer look at the relations between consumerism and sustainable consumption, as both opposing and interlacing phenomena.

## Environmentalism and transition

It is interesting to note that in the Soviet era, the importance of environmental problems was de-emphasized, or referred to as something peculiar to the 'degraded' West (Kiisel 2005). The discursive trend towards individualized environmentalism found no remarkable reflection in the Soviet environmental protection discourse. During the Soviet period, environmental problems received little criticism and analysis due to controlled information and the censored media. This legitimized environmental problems as a normal part of the life-world (Kiisel 2005). Individual responsibility was basically limited to 'no littering or dumping'. Practices such as the collection of used glass containers and paper were not actualized as pro-environmental behavior, but as complex practices with different motives (economic incentives, traditions of the natural economy, scarcity, etc.). The configuration of the latter, however, fell apart at the beginning of the transition.

The transition society inherited the environmental problems and risks created by the totalitarian system, which were initially perceived as nobody's responsibility as there were neither appropriate institutions nor practices at that time. As the Estonian freedom movement of the 1980s developed out of opposition to Soviet proposals for extensive mining of phosphorite, environmental problems were directly associated with the Soviet system. Therefore, in the early years of independence, individuals were left with the impression that threats to the environment had vanished along with the wasteful industrialism of the Soviet era, and a natural vacuum of environmental concern was created. At a time when environmentalism was becoming instrumentalized in the Western world, Estonia (in fact, the whole of the Eastern bloc) was 'plunged into modernity', which destroyed previously existing social norms and frames of reference (Beck & Beck-Gernsheim 2002). An ongoing silence on environmental problems and an extensive growth in consumption (which was not associated with environmental issues at that time) from the start of the 1990s onwards was accompanied by an overall aspiration for a Western-style consumer society. In Estonia, remnants of the traditional nature-related lifestyle are still interwoven with traces of the Soviet mentality – which denies individual responsibility – and modern pro-environmental practices acquired during the transition years, once more referring to the existence of parallel 'old' and 'new' symbols and value orientations theorized by Sztompka (2004).

A remarkable change towards individualized environmentalism has occurred since 2004, when Estonia joined the EU [see Lauristin and Vihalemm (2009) for an analysis of the external and internal agenda in Estonia after accession]. Since 2005, SC (mainly the topic of recycling) has actively occupied the public agenda. Sustainable practices still struggle with an incompatible infrastructure, low access to services and products (both in terms of availability and price), and a lack of collective sources of meaning.

As noted above, the context of the transition adds its specific ambivalences and tensions to society. Soviet norms and value systems, still alive at least at the level of memory, clash and compete with (late) modern symbols and practices characteristic of the Westernized consumer society, in which consumerism as one of the building blocks of self-expression is exercised in the context of abundance, quick obsolescence of goods complemented by the ever-growing normative rhetoric of 'down-shifting' (i.e. consuming less) and eco-friendly consumption. In this context, we cannot forget the inherent ambivalence and tension within Western late modern consumer society itself.

As Campbell has theorized in his seminal study (1987), the hedonistic or romantic ethic has become the main engine of contemporary consumerism by making the pursuit of pleasure through goods of primary importance. This, in turn, is in continuing conflict with the puritan ethic of frugality and restraint and the utilitarian ethic of rational satisfaction of needs, forcing consumers to constantly face moral dilemmas in their everyday consumption decisions. But what does the new ethic of sustainable consumption consist of? We may assume that it is a complex mix of the puritan ethic, based on the idea of restraint and thrift, which considers all types of excess and waste reprehensible (as epitomized in the 'consume less' slogan). However, this time it is not from the viewpoint of individual morality but for the sake of the planet. On the other hand, there is an element of the romantic ethic in the discourse of sustainable consumption, which seeks pleasure in the idea of 'green goods' being pure, wholesome and benevolent in their potential for benefiting the planet and human beings, which is particularly prominently expressed in the growing popularity of goods, ranging from organic local foodstuffs to eco-labeled household cleaning products and clothing. Our objective is to inquire as to how these different orientations to consumerism and sustainability exist side by side in the attitudes and practices of Estonian consumers who live in a rapidly developing consumer society, in which the memory of the Soviet time is still vivid.

## Age and Ethnicity in the Context of Consumption

As mentioned above, our particular interest in the context of consumerism and sustainability lies in age and ethnicity, i.e. how and why consumption patterns of different age and ethnic groups stand apart.

Research on consumption in relation to children and young people is a fast developing area [for recent studies see for example, Ekström and Tufte (2007)], and it is not possible in this essay to give a thorough overview of this. A large number of studies on youth consumer culture reveal youngsters as particularly receptive to the (potentially harmful) impact of transnational consumer and media culture. As Langer has put it: 'Global commercial culture, whether accessed through the media or encountered as part of the landscape of consumer capitalism, is an important source of symbolic material for children as they put together their projects of self' (2005, p. 264). Thus, there is reason to assume that the youngest age groups in Estonia, like their peers elsewhere, are the most consumerist- and brand-prone in their orientations.

Also, different Estonian analyses of pro-environmental behavior from 1983 onwards (Kaasik et al. 1996; Kiisel 2002; Lauristin 1987; Raudsepp 2001a, 2001b, 2003; Sööt 2004) have shown that younger age groups score lowest in pro-environmental behavior measures and nature contacts. Environmental practices tend to increase with advancing age.

Ethnicity is another variable that we find intriguing in the given context. Although approximately one-third of the Estonian population is Russian-speaking, consumption patterns by Estonian Russians are a poorly researched area. In-depth studies on the development of consumer culture (see Keller 2004; Kõresaar 2003; Rahu 2004; Rausing 1998) have focused solely on ethnic Estonians.

It is probable, though, that ethnic Estonian and Estonian Russian consumers are faced with a different set of influences in their everyday lives as consumers. Ethnic Estonians experience complicated interrelationships between home culture and transnational consumer and media culture, while in the case of Estonian Russians, a third aspect (Russian home and diaspora culture), combined with their perceived minority status, is added to the configuration of cultural impacts (cf. Askegaard et al. 2005; Campbell 2005). Another important nuance is the different experience of transition in Estonia of ethnic Estonians and Estonian Russians, including varying perceptions of cultural disruption (cf. Vihalemm & Kalmus 2008). However, Hamlett et al. point out that 'Any evaluation of the influence of ethnic identity over consumption must be framed within a wider understanding of the operation of other categories of social identity' (2007, p. 110).

Several earlier analyses have shown that Estonian Russians estimate their sustainable consumption habits, and especially their readiness to behave in a pro-environmental manner, relatively higher than ethnic Estonians do, with the exception of overall waste and recycling behavior (Kaasik et al. 1996; Kiisel 2002; Raudsepp 2003).

## Data and Method

### Data

Our analysis is based on data from the representative population survey *Me. The World. The Media*, carried out in Estonia in November 2005. The survey covered the Estonian population aged 15–74, with a total sample size of 1,475. A proportional model of the general population (by areas and urban/rural division) and multi-step probability random sampling was used. In addition, a quota was used to include a proportional number of ethnic Estonians and Estonian Russians in the sample. A self-administered questionnaire, together with a follow-up interview, was used.

*Measures*

The questionnaire included a number of indicators of different consumption practices and preferences, indicators of the awareness and practices of sustainable consumption, oppositional assertions about the importance of brands, assertion pairs representing popular versions of the 'endangered *versus* empowered child' debate in consumer and media studies (for details, see Keller & Kalmus forthcoming), value statements about the environment developed by Inglehart (1997), Rokeach's (1973) value indicators, etc.

On the basis of single variables we formed several indices. Two indices form the main axes of our analysis: consumerism and sustainable consumption. The index of consumerism measures a more 'symbolic' aspect of consumption, i.e. consumption practices and preferences that are more expressive and revealing of people's identity building and lifestyles.[2] The index of sustainable consumption is comprised of the sub-index of the use of sustainable solutions[3] and five indicators of the awareness and practices of sustainable consumption, presented in Table 3 (an extremely positive answer, for example, 'always', added two points to the index; a positive answer, such as 'sometimes', added one point). In addition, we used the index of valuation of brands[4] and the index of protectionism of children against advertising and consumption.[5]

*Analysis*

Previous analyses of the same survey data have shown that generational and ethnic dimensions have a considerable explanatory force in interpreting the cultural aspect of individuals' adaptation to transition in Estonia (Kalmus & Vihalemm 2008; Vihalemm & Kalmus 2008, 2009). Previous analyses also found that, in general, consumerism was very well predicted by age (Keller & Kalmus 2004, forthcoming). We assume that various age groups and ethnic Estonians and Estonian Russians differ in a number of ways when we look at their attitudes and practices related to consumption and environment. In the first section of results we compare the mean values of the indices of consumerism, and the valuation of brands and sustainable consumption between age groups, and between ethnic Estonians and Estonian Russians.

We proceed from the assumption that orientations to material well being and self-realization as a consumer cannot be unequivocally opposed to sustainable or 'anti-consumerist' orientations. These seemingly conflicting sets of attitudes and practices may go hand in hand and form complicated interlacing patterns. To analyze these patterns in detail, we carried out a K-means cluster analysis based on shortened indices of consumerism and sustainable consumption.[6] In proceeding from the two main axes, with the aim of creating an easily interpretable typology, we set the number of clusters at four. Thus, we constructed four consumer types, partly inductively, based on the empirical analysis of the data, and partly relying on the theoretical assumption regarding possible co-variation patterns between consumerist and sustainable attitudes and practices.

The second section of results presents the typology of consumers, consequent from the cluster analysis, and characterizes the types regarding their awareness and particular practices of sustainable consumption, relationship with nature, attitudes towards brands, consumer culture and children, and value orientations, and describes the types socio-demographically (by analyzing relationships with age, gender, education, income, social status, type of residence and ethnicity).

# Results

## Consumption in different age groups

Table 1 reveals that respondents' age differentiates significantly between all main dimensions of consumption analyzed in this study. The youngest consumers (aged 15–19) valued expressive dimensions of consumption most. The relation between consumerism and age was strictly linear: more expressive consumption preferences and practices became less prevalent as age increased: in the oldest age group, the index of consumerism was more than twice as low as it was amongst teenagers. It is noteworthy that, in a similar survey carried out at the end of 2002, only 10% of the youngest age group reported 'very high' consumerism (see Keller & Kalmus 2004), whereas in this study the same indicator was 23%. Thus, consumerism is growing most rapidly among teenagers, along with the general rise of the living standard in Estonia.

Valuation of brands followed almost the same pattern of distribution in age groups as consumerism. Respondents in their twenties stood out, together with teenagers, as the most brand-oriented consumers.

Sustainable consumption was highest among 45–64 year-olds, and dropped significantly in the group which had reached retirement age (65–74 year-olds). Teenagers showed the lowest levels of sustainable consumption. These results correspond to the findings of a survey of pro-environmental behavior from 1994 (Kaasik et al. 1996) and a study of consumption of environmental information from 1983 (Lauristin 1987).

Among the oldest people, the lower index value seems to be conditioned by two factors. On the one hand, this age group showed the lowest level of environmental awareness (for example, 22% claimed not to know eco-labels and 28% could not judge the environment-friendliness of packaging). On the other hand, they lacked material resources (40% were not able to pay more for environmentally sustainable products or services). Teenagers tended not to acknowledge either a lack of awareness

**TABLE 1** Consumerism, valuation of brands and sustainable consumption by age (means)

| Indices | 15–19 | 20–29 | 30–44 | 45–54 | 55–64 | 65–74 | F | Sig. |
|---|---|---|---|---|---|---|---|---|
| N | 151 | 273 | 393 | 263 | 209 | 186 | | |
| Consumerism (max 11) | 3.20 | 2.90 | 2.69 | 1.96 | 1.86 | 1.39 | 36.2 | 0.000 |
| Valuation of brands (max 4) | 0.43 | 0.45 | 0.33 | 0.22 | 0.30 | 0.18 | 5.4 | 0.000 |
| Sustainable consumption (max 19) | 5.15 | 6.19 | 6.27 | 6.76 | 6.80 | 5.75 | 8.5 | 0.000 |

or a lack of resources (for example, 74% were ready to pay more for sustainable products or services); rather, they did not attempt to hide their careless attitude (for example, 47% declared that they never paid attention to eco-labels when shopping and 38% never tried to select products with eco-friendly packaging).

*Consumption in different ethnic groups*

Table 2 indicates that consumerist orientation was, in general, significantly stronger among Estonian Russians compared with ethnic Estonians. The most remarkable difference appeared in the group of 20–29 year-olds: young Estonian Russians were significantly more consumerist than their Estonian peers (the index means being 3.20 and 2.76, respectively). Teenagers of the ethnic majority and the minority, however, did not differ from each other in this respect.

The index of brand valuation differed between the two ethnic groups in the opposite direction: ethnic Estonians were significantly more brand-oriented than Estonian Russians, whereas the sharpest distinction appeared between teenagers of the two ethnic groups (the index means were 0.50 among Estonians and 0.22 among Estonian Russians). This difference is largely due to the assertion pair 'The brands someone consumes tell a lot about the person' *versus* 'One cannot judge people based on the brands they consume': Estonian Russians, including teenagers, were more inclined to refrain from judging people based on signs of consumer culture.

No significant differences in the overall index of sustainable consumption between ethnic Estonians and Estonian Russians, either in general or in particular age groups, existed; distinctions, however, appeared in all particular attitudes and practices. Estonian Russians demonstrated, on the one hand, higher normativity on the macro level: for instance, 18% of Russians (compared to 6% of Estonians) considered themselves to be highly aware of sustainable consumption, and 12% of Russians (compared to 5% of Estonians) claimed that they always paid attention to eco-labels. On the other hand, a larger percentage of Estonian Russians (compared to ethnic Estonians) admitted to a lack of particular knowledge: 23% of Russians (11% of Estonians) were not able to judge the environment-friendliness of packaging, and 13% of Russians (8% of Estonians) claimed not to know eco-labels. In earlier studies, Estonian Russians also reported relatively less personal control (knowledge of what to do and belief in its outcome) over everyday environmental practices (43% compared to 65% of Estonians: Raudsepp 2003).

**TABLE 2** Consumerism, valuation of brands and sustainable consumption by ethnic groups (means)

| Indices | All | Estonians | Estonian Russians | $t$ | Sig. |
|---|---|---|---|---|---|
| N | 1475 | 1033 | 442 | | |
| Consumerism (max 11) | 2.37 | 2.29 | 2.54 | −2.5 | 0.012 |
| Valuation of brands (max 4) | 0.32 | 0.34 | 0.26 | 2.2 | 0.029 |
| Sustainable consumption (max 19) | 6.24 | 6.25 | 6.22 | 0.2 | 0.868 |

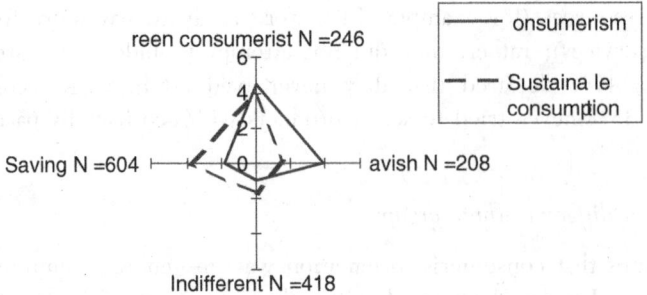

**FIGURE 1** Levels of consumerism and sustainable consumption (index means) in consumer types

Ethnic Estonians demonstrated a higher level of sustainable practices: they were more active in recycling and tended to use more technology-based sustainable solutions in housekeeping. An earlier study by Raudsepp (2003), however, shows that the differences between Estonians and Estonian Russians in tradition-based saving practices (for example, repairing old and broken items and buying food products from acquaintances in the countryside) are not that significant.

## Typology of consumers

A statistically significant positive correlation between the indices of consumerism and sustainable consumption ($r = 0.13$; $p < 0.000$) suggests that these two are not mutually exclusive or opposing phenomena. A typological analysis, however, shows a more complicated relationship between these dimensions of consumption. Figure 1 shows four consumer types that resulted from cluster analysis. The largest percentage of respondents (41%) belonged to the cluster which is characterized by a high level of sustainable consumption and below average consumerism. We labeled this cluster the 'Saving' type. The second biggest cluster (28% of respondents) displayed low levels of both consumerism and sustainable consumption. This cluster is labeled as the 'Indifferent' type (indifferent towards consumption and the environment). A significant percentage of respondents (17%) belonged to the type, which scored high on both dimensions of consumption. They bear the name 'Green Consumerists'. The smallest share of people (14%) showed a high level of consumerism and a low level of sustainable consumption. We labeled this cluster the 'Lavish' type.

The following characterization of consumer types is based on a number of indicators related to environment and consumption, and socio-demographic variables (see Tables 3 and 4, respectively).

## The Saving type

Respondents in this cluster stood out due to their very high extent of sustainable everyday practices: they were most active in recycling and in using sustainable solutions in housekeeping (see Table 3). Also, they tended to display a relatively high level of environmental awareness and related consumption practices. Respondents of this type had a rather active relationship with nature: nearly 60% went hiking or out

**TABLE 3** Characterization of consumer types (% in the type)

| | Total N | Saving type | Indifferent type | Green consumerist type | Lavish type |
|---|---|---|---|---|---|
| N | 1475 | 604 | 418 | 246 | 208 |
| % in the population | 100 | 40.9 | 28.3 | 16.6 | 14.1 |
| *Indicators of the awareness and practices of sustainable consumption* | | | | | |
| Considers oneself aware of sustainable consumption (highly or rather)** | 137 | 86.4 | 44.7 | 87.8 | 47.6 |
| Pays attention to eco-labels when shopping (always or sometimes)** | 859 | 78.2 | 31.1 | 81.8 | 34.2 |
| Tries to select products with environmentally-friendly packaging (always or sometimes)** | 868 | 78.0 | 30.4 | 86.7 | 36.0 |
| Is ready to pay more for an environmentally sustainable product or service (much or a bit)** | 943 | 77.9 | 42.3 | 84.9 | 52.4 |
| Separates recyclable rubbish at home (always or at convenience)** | 1111 | 90.1 | 63.8 | 88.1 | 52.2 |
| Index of use of sustainable solutions (max 9, mean values)** | 1475 | 3.38 | 1.48 | 3.37 | 1.35 |
| *Indicators of relationship with nature* | | | | | |
| Has participated in green activists' bicycle trips, cleaning away rubbish, etc.** | 291 | 21.3 | 12.3 | 31.0 | 19.2 |
| Goes hiking, to the nature (often or sometimes)** | 821 | 59.4 | 43.2 | 74.4 | 53.9 |
| *Consumption-related indices (mean values)* | | | | | |
| Valuation of brands (max 4)** | 1475 | 0.30 | 0.21 | 0.43 | 0.45 |
| Protectionism of children against advertising and consumption (max 6)** | 1475 | 2.45 | 2.01 | 2.43 | 2.23 |
| *Value statements about the environment* | | | | | |
| Agrees to an increase in taxes, if the extra money is used to prevent environmental pollution** | 736 | 59.8 | 37.9 | 62.9 | 38.8 |
| Does not agree that if we want economic development, we can't pay too much attention to environmental protection** | 1109 | 79.9 | 72.0 | 86.5 | 72.9 |
| *Selected Rokeach values (max 5, means)* | | | | | |
| Clean environment** | 1475 | 4.75 | 4.61 | 4.77 | 4.51 |
| World of beauty** | 1475 | 4.36 | 4.22 | 4.37 | 4.21 |
| Wealth* | 1475 | 3.90 | 4.01 | 4.02 | 4.06 |
| Comfortable life** | 1475 | 3.98 | 4.04 | 4.15 | 4.20 |

*Notes*: *Difference between the groups is statistically significant at $p<0.05$. **Difference between the groups is statistically significant at $p<0.01$.

**TABLE 4** Distribution of socio-demographic groups in consumer types

|  | Total N | Saving type | Indifferent type | Green consumerist type | Lavish type |
|---|---|---|---|---|---|
| N | 1475 | 604 | 418 | 246 | 208 |
| % of the population | 100 | 40.9 | 28.3 | 16.6 | 14.1 |
| *Age*** | | | | | |
| 15–19 | 151 | 20.5 | 27.2 | 16.6 | 35.8 |
| 20–29 | 272 | 35.3 | 21.3 | 23.9 | 19.5 |
| 30–44 | 393 | 37.7 | 23.9 | 22.4 | 16.0 |
| 45–54 | 264 | 51.5 | 27.3 | 12.9 | 8.3 |
| 55–64 | 209 | 52.2 | 32.1 | 12.4 | 3.3 |
| 65–74 | 186 | 45.2 | 46.2 | 3.8 | 4.8 |
| Mean value | 41.95 | 45.16 | 45.72 | 36.45 | 31.56 |
| *Gender*** | | | | | |
| Male | 687 | 43.4 | 29.6 | 12.5 | 14.4 |
| Female | 788 | 38.8 | 27.3 | 20.2 | 13.7 |
| *Education*** | | | | | |
| Primary | 281 | 35.6 | 41.6 | 7.5 | 15.3 |
| Secondary | 817 | 43.8 | 27.1 | 15.1 | 14.1 |
| Higher | 339 | 39.5 | 17.7 | 28.9 | 13.9 |
| *Income*** | | | | | |
| Low | 502 | 42.6 | 33.9 | 11.0 | 12.5 |
| Average | 462 | 42.2 | 28.6 | 16.0 | 13.2 |
| High | 455 | 38.5 | 20.4 | 24.8 | 16.3 |
| *Status*** | | | | | |
| Lower | 163 | 37.4 | 45.4 | 8.0 | 9.2 |
| Lower-middle | 271 | 40.2 | 36.9 | 10.0 | 12.9 |
| Middle | 498 | 43.4 | 28.7 | 14.7 | 13.3 |
| Upper-middle | 301 | 43.5 | 18.3 | 22.3 | 15.9 |
| Upper | 185 | 43.2 | 9.7 | 35.1 | 11.9 |
| *Type of residence** | | | | | |
| Capital city | 446 | 41.3 | 24.9 | 20.0 | 13.9 |
| Big city | 287 | 39.7 | 28.6 | 14.3 | 17.4 |
| Small city | 301 | 45.5 | 25.2 | 17.6 | 11.6 |
| Countryside | 438 | 38.4 | 33.8 | 14.2 | 13.7 |
| *Ethnic groups* | | | | | |
| Ethnic Estonians | 1033 | 41.6 | 28.6 | 16.5 | 13.2 |
| Estonian Russians | 442 | 39.4 | 27.6 | 17.0 | 16.1 |

*Notes*: *Difference between the groups is statistically significant at $p<0.05$. **Difference between the groups is statistically significant at $p<0.01$.

into nature at least occasionally and a fifth had participated in events organized by green activists.

These respondents were not fascinated with consumer culture: their valuation of brands was slightly below the average and they were most protective of children against advertising and consumption. Their personal value orientations were highly post-materialist: they tended to value a clean environment and a world of beauty very highly, and showed the lowest valuation of wealth and a comfortable life. When it came to macro-level value decisions regarding tax-raising and a sustainable economy for the sake of environmental protection, respondents of the Saving type were slightly less post-materialistic compared with Green Consumerists.

Respondents of the Saving type were more often middle-aged or elderly people (more than half of 45–64 year-olds belonged to this type – see Table 4). Males, significantly more often than females, belonged to this type. The Saving type was characterized by the prevalence of people with a secondary education and low or average incomes. When it came to self-estimated status in the social hierarchy, the middle, upper-middle and upper strata were equally strongly represented in this cluster. The Saving type was most common among residents of small cities. No statistically significant relationship between consumer types and ethnic groups existed.

In general, the Saving type embodied ideal-typical features of the social portrait of the petty bourgeoisie and the values of the Protestant ethic in their late modern form, specifically molded in transition culture, representing thrift, wariness, mettle, moderation and socially desirable conduct.

## The Indifferent type

Respondents in this cluster showed a significantly lower engagement in sustainable everyday practices than those of the Saving type and Green Consumerists, yet they were slightly more active in recycling and in using sustainable solutions than the Lavish type respondents (see Table 3). Respondents of the Indifferent type displayed the lowest level of environmental awareness and related consumption practices. Also, they had by far the most passive relationship with nature: only 43% went hiking or out into nature at least occasionally and 12% had participated in green activist events.

This type of respondent seemed to have the weakest connection with consumer culture: they scored lowest on the indices of valuation of brands and protectionism of children against advertising and consumption (largely because they tended to answer 'Difficult to say' to the index questions). Their personal value orientations were relatively materialistic: they gave less importance, compared with Green Consumerists and the Saving type, to a clean environment and the world of beauty, and tended to value wealth highly (probably as a scarcity value). Respondents of the Indifferent type were most materialistic when it came to the macro-level issues of tax raising for the sake of environmental protection and economic development at a cost to the environment.

Respondents of the Indifferent type were most often male, elderly people (46% of 64–74 year-olds belonged to this type; the average age was highest in this type – see Table 4). This cluster was characterized by the dominance of people with a primary education and low incomes. They were most likely to estimate their social status as lower or lower middle. The Indifferent type was most common among people residing in the countryside.

In general, this type represents a lagging behind or withdrawal from new cultural flows of consumerism and environmentalism, and encapsulation in a certain inveterate lifestyle – partly due to lack of resources, and partly because of attitudes of indifference and carelessness.

## The Green Consumerist type

Respondents in this cluster stood out as having the highest level of environmental awareness and related consumption practices (see Table 3). Their extent of engagement in sustainable everyday practices was almost as high as in the case of the Saving type. Moreover, Green Consumerists had the most active relationship with nature: three quarters went hiking or out into nature at least occasionally and almost a third had participated in green activist events.

This type of respondent tended to have a clear opinion about consumer culture: they considered brands relatively important, while being at the same time highly protective of children against advertising and consumption. Their macro-level value decisions regarding tax-raising and a sustainable economy for the sake of environmental protection were most post-materialist; also, they tended to value a clean environment and the world of beauty most highly. At the same time, they considered wealth and a comfortable life relatively important – probably not as scarcity values, but as a means for, and a part of, a consumerist and hedonistic lifestyle.

Green Consumerists were most often younger people (aged 20–44) and predominantly female (see Table 4). This type was characterized by the prevalence of people with a higher education and high incomes. When it came to self-estimated status in the social hierarchy, the upper and upper-middle strata were highly over-represented in this cluster. Green Consumerists were more likely residents of the capital and small cities.

This type can be characterized as one very well adapted to new cultural flows in the transitional society. Green Consumerists were highly reflective and conscious of the potential hazards and negative impact, both for the environment and children, imposed by the emerging consumer society. At the same time, they appropriated commercially produced and branded goods and services as well as related values into their personal life-worlds.

## The Lavish type

Respondents in this type stood out for having the most modest engagement in sustainable everyday practices (see Table 3). Also, they displayed a relatively low level of environmental awareness and related consumption practices. Respondents of the Lavish type had a somewhat less active relationship with nature; they were, however, more active than the Indifferent type was.

This type of respondent scored highest on the index of valuation of brands. They were less protective of children against advertising and consumption than Green Consumerists and the Saving type were. This can partly be explained by the high proportion of under-age respondents in the cluster: probably they had no wish to admit to their own vulnerability and manipulability. The personal value orientations of respondents of this type were the most materialistic: they gave least importance to a clean environment and the world of beauty, and valued most highly wealth and a comfortable life. Also, respondents of the Lavish type were highly materialistic when it came to the macro-level issues of tax raising for the sake of environmental protection and economic development at a cost to the environment.

Respondents of the Lavish type were most often teenagers: the largest number of 15–19 year olds (36%) belonged to this type (see Table 4). Also, young people aged 20–29 were highly represented and the average age was lowest in this cluster.

Gender distribution was most even in this type compared with the others. The Lavish type was characterized by the slight predominance of people with a primary education but high incomes per family member, which can be explained by the large proportion of high school students in the cluster. Respondents of this type were most likely to estimate their social status as upper-middle and to reside in big cities. A difference between ethnic groups was notable only in this consumer type: slightly more Estonian Russians belonged to the Lavish type.

## Conclusions and Discussion

Our findings confirmed the assumption that the youngest age groups (aged 15–29) would be most consumerist and brand-oriented, offering a sharp contrast to the generations of their grandparents, whose most active 'consumer years' fell during the Soviet period and for whom Western consumerism is not the dominant building block of their lifestyle.

The two youngest age groups were born in 1976–1990; thus, their formative years, i.e. adolescence and early adulthood, coincide mostly or entirely with the period of transition. They can be called the generation of the 'children of freedom', or the 'post-revolutionary generation' (cf. Marada 2004). According to Sztompka (2004), this generation has been basically insulated from the cultural impact of the communist system. Instead they have had, in many ways, a more open and liberal society to grow up in. Obviously, they have been the most receptive to new cultural flows of self-expressive consumerism and the sign system of commercially produced and branded goods and services (Langer 2005).

As the Czech sociologist Marada (2004) argues, the post-revolutionary generation has also developed a more competitive and less moralistic relationship with the social world. This may explain, on the one hand, the importance of brands as status symbols for these young people and, on the other hand, the more openly careless attitude towards sustainable consumption among a large part of this age group. Also, as Vihalemm and Kalmus (2008) have shown, younger people are more exposed to transnational self-identification and orientation to imagined or virtual communities, largely based on globalizing consumer and media culture, which tends to go hand in hand with certain emancipation from the concerns of one's immediate social and physical environment. This emancipation can also be explained by the degeneration of a nature-related lifestyle and contacts during the transition (see Kaasik et al. 1996). Raudsepp's (2001a) analysis has shown that younger people report relatively few nature contacts from childhood. These facts correspond to Beck's concept of a 'sudden plunge into modernity' and a dissolution of traditional meaning references due to that plunge. However, although the 'children of freedom' are a substantially different generation from that of their parents since they do not have many active memories of the Soviet time, the attitudes towards consumption and sustainable practices, in particular, are also related to life course. We may assume that when these youngsters establish families of their own, have children and grow older, their orientations may become more environmentally conscious, as the tendency to report more pro-environmental concerns and practices with advancing age has been predominant in previous studies, from 1983 onwards (for example, Kaasik et al. 1996; Lauristin 1987).

Our results indicated that a consumerist orientation was, in general, significantly stronger among Estonian Russians compared with ethnic Estonians. The latter were, at the same time, significantly more brand-oriented than Estonian Russians. This can be explained by the different set of influences experienced by the two ethnic groups in the transformational society. Among these, the strong feeling of social exclusion by Estonian Russians, extensively brought to light in studies conducted after the disruptive 'April Events' in 2007 (see Vihalemm & Kalmus 2009), has to be taken into account. We may assume that a market-based consumer culture, which in its Western definition is, at least theoretically, universal, impersonal and open to all (Slater 1997), is the most neutral, non-discriminating and accessible area where Estonian Russians' feeling of exclusion is alleviated. In a shopping mall, everybody is treated equally and for window-shopping no money is required (see also Keller 2005).

Studies based on the same survey data (*Me. The World. The Media* 2005) indicated that the thought pattern called 'Sub-Cultural Identity and Desire for Capital', which probably emerged from the opportunities and pleasures of identity construction offered by consumer culture and valuation of the means necessary to afford it, was more widespread among the Russian minority (Vihalemm & Kalmus 2009). In the case of the youngest age group (15–19 year-olds), the difference in consumerism seems to be leveling out due to the increasing influence of the transnational consumer and media culture experienced by youngsters of both ethnic groups. This leads us to hypothesize the birth of a new consumer, for whom the symbolic resources for everyday identity creation and meaning making are, to a large extent, commercially produced on a global scale.

At the same time, Estonian Russians were significantly more subjected to the thought pattern which attaches importance to solidarity with community members and spiritual harmony, and de-emphasizes high social position (Vihalemm & Kalmus 2009). This mental structure probably represents the mixed legacy of the Soviet ideology and the ethic of Russian Orthodoxy, both characterized by ideals of community, unanimity and rejection of economic competition (cf. Chaplin 2004). This deep-rooted ethical maxim helps to explain why Estonian Russians, including teenagers, were more inclined to refuse to judge people based on the brands they consume, which, however says little about their actual brand consumption.

No significant differences in the overall level of sustainable consumption between ethnic Estonians and Estonian Russians was shown. The latter, however, declared a higher macro-level normativity, while showing a greater lack of particular knowledge of sustainable consumption and a lower level of engagement in eco-friendly everyday practices, especially recycling behavior. A recent study from 2007 (Kuldna & Kaldaru 2007) shows that this tendency has not disappeared in the recent years of the active introduction of instrumentalized environmentalism. The reasons for lower engagement in eco-friendly consumption and recycling practices among Estonian Russians can be traced to a lower level of knowledge of the environmental impacts of different practices, the lower impact of public information sources on environmental knowledge, and less personal control over environmental behavior. Ethnic Estonians have more active and pragmatic relations with nature than Russians, although there are no clearly discernible major differences between the two ethnic groups in terms of recreational nature-habits (Enterprise Estonia Tourism Development Center 2007; Raudsepp 2005). Substantially more Russians than Estonians report nature as central to their life-world and define themselves as nature-lovers; they also report more abstract and spiritual relations with nature than Estonians (Raudsepp 2005). This, along with different realms of information and media consumption, may explain Estonian Russians' greater self-reported readiness for pro-environmental behavior. However, their actual knowledge and behavior may sometimes conflict with their positive attitudes.

The findings of our typological analysis of Estonian consumers lend support to Sztompka's (2004) thesis of the ambivalence of the cultural context of transition and the parallel existence of old and new 'cultural templates'. The distribution of various post-materialist attitudes and practices, and different age groups in consumer types suggest that no unambiguously 'old' types exist. The higher average age of respondents in the Indifferent type and the Saving type, however, hints that the role of the Soviet heritage is probably greater in the formation of the characteristics of these types, including their lower levels of consumerism and valuation of brands. It is also interesting that in Estonian, SC is translated as *säästev tarbimine*, which literally means 'saving consumption'. Thus, sustainability in this context acquires an additional connotation of thrift, which stems from the puritan ethic of restraint combined with the rational–utilitarian orientation to efficiency and the minimization of waste. Thus we may assume that the Saving type embodies less of the late modern 'green ethic' of individual environmentalism for the planet's sake, and more of an ethic of thrift, intermixed with a certain traditional holistic attitude to nature, which is valued for its beauty, spirituality and totality.

In the case of the Indifferent type, the high proportion of country people is noteworthy. This may suggest a certain stratification of the Estonian society on the axis of city–country, as well as indicating that for a large number of country people the relationship with the environment is more taken for granted, habitual and pragmatic, and not worthy of special concern in relation to their consumption practices. Also, in the countryside a certain set of attitudes that we may call '*kolkhoz*-mentality' still prevails. It is a rudiment of the Soviet era, when relationships with the natural environment were exclusively instrumental in the collective farms, where nationalization of land and private property had contributed to dissolving respect for common responsibility. In addition, we may assume that consumerist lifestyle construction, including brand consumption, as well as the normative framework of SD, are perceived as irrelevant, as 'not for us', by a large number of people living in the country. Also, at least in some cases, material deprivation plays a role in making consumerist orientations inaccessible.

Two other types, the Lavish type and Green Consumerists, belong rather clearly to 'new' cultural templates, representing two different faces of the emerging consumer culture in transformational Estonia. Both of these types are characterized by a high level of appropriation of commercially produced and branded goods and services, as well as the related values in their life-world, and by a lower average age compared with the Saving type and the Indifferent type. Green Consumerists have developed a critical awareness of problems and hazards inherent in consumer society and are trying to adjust their lifestyle and everyday practices to come to terms with the late modern ethic of sustainability, in which we may imagine a considerable number of everyday tensions and dilemmas, as well as a high level of reflexivity stemming from this. Here we may assume the rise of the new green romantic ethic in which consumer satisfaction is derived from the perceived purity, locality and 'naturalness' of goods. They are enjoyed for individual health and pleasure, as well as for the sake of benefiting the planet and future generations. Soper (2007) has referred to this as 'alternative hedonism'. These people are, however, also active consumers who willingly purchase non-green goods and for whom self-expression and lifestyle are, to a large extent, linked with consumption of goods and services.

Their active relationship with nature resonates with the idea that the growing distance between society and nature, evident in the increasing volume of consumption, may at the same time reconnect people with nature through the re-invention of a natural lifestyle, often in the framework of commodification and campaigning, or at least through a set of behaviors and attitudes that are believed to be environment-friendly ('the best I can do'). It can be postulated that 'old' nature relations, which declined during the transition period, have not been simply reincarnated, but also reinvented and modified in the context of commodification and consumption (see EETDC 2007). This explains the close nature relations among high consumerists, such as the respondents of the Green Consumerist type. We can also say that the perception of the nature–society divide peculiar to the individuals of late modernity has not fully 'invaded' Estonia yet, since high consumerism has not displaced uncommodified nature-related habits, that is, traditional lifestyle interwoven with SC practices.

Respondents of the Lavish type, almost equal in number to Green Consumerists and even younger on average, have neither developed discursive consciousness of the problems of over-consumption nor internalized sustainable practices. Young consumers of this type have, in principle, three possible ways of socialization in their future: they may enhance their awareness of environmental issues and join Green Consumerists; they may develop into a type of their own, which would be more prominently represented in older age groups; or, most improbably, they may lose their fascination with consumerism and merge into the Indifferent type.

A more sustainable path of development is clearly not a value-neutral academic concept, but a moral and normative framework, which seems to be at least officially and publicly desirable on the global level. Thus, the question remains as to how (and by whom) today's youngest consumers can be socialized and influenced in the direction of sustainability. As things stand, sustainability is of low importance to a remarkably large number of this group, who seem to be overpowered by the lure of the attractive commercial symbolism of global popular and consumer culture. Will they become Green Consumerists on their own as they grow older and more experienced, or do we need more conscious and coordinated action to promote what is termed 'consumer literacy'?

## Acknowledgements

The preparation of this essay was supported by grant No. 6968, financed by the Estonian Science Foundation, and grant No. SF0180017s07, financed by the Estonian Governmental Scientific Research Support Scheme.

## Notes

1. The Index of Actual Individual Consumption, provided by Eurostat, is comprised of household final consumption expenditure, as well as consumption of individual services (for example, health and education).
2. The index of consumerism summarized positive answers to questions on 11 consumption practices and preferences. Each positive answer added one point to the index, with the scale ranging from zero to 11: having clothes tailor-made, preference for certain clothing brands, buying clothing abroad, considering fit of clothing more important than price, considering brand of clothing more important than price, following a specific style of home decoration, having a personal hairdresser, having a personal cosmetician, having a personal masseur, regular gym-going and doing aerobics.
3. The sub-index of use of sustainable solutions summarized positive answers to nine questions on using sustainable solutions in housekeeping. Each positive answer added one point to the index, with the scale ranging from zero to nine: sustainable car fuels, energy-saving household machines, energy-saving light bulbs, recycled paper, 'Green Energy' option in electricity consumption, composter, sustainable household chemistry (for example, non-synthetic or phosphate-free washing powder), water-saving mixers (with interrupters) or something else.
4. The index of valuation of brands summarized a respondent's agreement with two assertions: 'The brands someone consumes tell a lot about the person' and 'It is important to me what impression the brands I consume make' (the answer 'I totally agree' added two points to the index; 'I rather agree' added one point; the scale ranges from zero to four).
5. The index of protectionism of children against advertising and consumption summarized a respondent's agreement with three assertions: 'Children are defenseless in the face of advertising and it is easy to manipulate them'; 'Advertising targeted at children is harmful; it increases excessive consumerism'; and 'Children should be kept away from all kinds of advertising and shopping malls, because consumer society corrupts children' ('I totally agree' added two points to the index; 'I rather agree' added one point; the index scale ranges from zero to six).
6. In following normal distribution, the original indices of consumerism and sustainable consumption were reduced to short and comparable scales ranging from '0 – missing' to '5 – very high', in the case of consumerism, and from '1 – very low' to '5 – very high', in case of sustainable consumption.

## References

Alexander, J. C., Eyerman, R., Giesen, B., Smelser, N. J. & Sztompka, P. (eds) (2004) *Cultural Trauma and Collective Identity* (Berkeley, CA, University of California Press).

Askegaard, S., Arnould, J. & Kjeldgaard, D. (2005) 'Postassimilationist Ethnic Consumer Research: Qualifications and Extensions', *Journal of Consumer Research*, 32, 2.

Bauman, Z. (1992) *Intimations of Postmodernity* (London, Routledge).

Beck, U. (1995) *Ecological Politics in an Age of Risk*, translated by A. Weisz (Cambridge, Polity Press).

Beck, U. & Beck-Gernsheim, E. (2002) *Individualization: Institutionalized Individualism and Its Social and Political Consequences* (London, Sage).

Campbell, C. (1987) *The Romantic Ethic and the Spirit of Modern Consumerism* (Oxford, Blackwell).

Campbell, H. (2005) 'Chicano Lite: Mexican–American Consumer Culture on the Border', *Journal of Consumer Culture*, 5, 2.

Chaplin, V. (2004) 'Orthodoxy and the Societal Ideal', in Marsh, C. (ed.) (2004).

Eder, K. (1996) 'The Institutionalization of Environmentalism: Ecological Discourse and the Second Transformation of the Public Sphere', in Lash, S., Szerszynski, B. & Wynne, B. (eds) (1996).

Ekström, K. & Tufte, B. (eds) (2007) *Children, Media and Consumption: On the Front Edge* (Göteborg, The International Clearinghouse on Children, Youth and Media, Nordicom, Göteborg University).

Enterprise Estonia Tourism Development Center (EETDC) (2007) *Aktiivsed harrastused Eesti-sisestel reisidel: elanikkonna küsitluse tulemused* [*Habits of In-Country Traveling: Report of Public Survey*] (Tallinn, Enterprise Estonia Tourism Development Center).

Feher, F., Heller, A. & Markus, G. (1984) *Dictatorship over Needs: An Analysis of Soviet Societies* (Oxford, Blackwell).

Hamlett, J., Bailey, A. R., Alexander, A. & Shaw, G. (2007) 'Ethnicity and Consumption: South Asian Food Shopping Patterns in Britain, 1947–75', *Journal of Consumer Culture*, 8, 1.

Inglehart, R. (1997) *Modernization and Postmodernization: Cultural, Economic, and Political Change in 43 Societies* (Princeton, Princeton University Press).

Kaasik, T., Peterson, K. & Kaldaru, H. (1996) *Inimene ja keskkond: muutused Eesti keskkonnateadvuses, 1983–1994, võrdlusjooni maailmaga* [*Human and Environment: Changes in Estonian Public Environmental Awareness, 1983–1994: Global Comparison*] (Tallinn, Stockholm Environment Institute).

Kalmus, V., Lauristin, M. & Pruulmann-Vengerfeldt, P. (eds) (2004) *Eesti elavik 21. sajandi algul: ülevaade uurimuse Mina. Maailm. Meedia tulemustest* [*Estonian Life-World at the Beginning of the 21st Century: Overview of the Findings of the Survey Me. The World. The Media*] (Tartu, Tartu University Press).

Kalmus, V. & Vihalemm, T. (2006) 'Distinct Mental Structures in Transitional Culture: An Empirical Analysis of Values and Identities in Estonia', *Journal of Baltic Studies*, 36, 1.

Kalmus, V. & Vihalemm, T. (2008) 'Patterns of Continuity and Disruption: The Specificity of Young People's Mental Structures in Three Transitional Societies', *Young*, 16, 3.

Keller, M. (2004) *Representations of Consumer Culture in Post-Soviet Estonia: Transformations and Tensions* (Tartu, Tartu University Press).

Keller, M. (2005) 'Needs, Desires and the Experience of Scarcity: Representations of Recreational Shopping in Post-Soviet Estonia', *Journal of Consumer Culture*, 5, 1.

Keller, M. & Kalmus, V. (2004) 'Konsumerismist tarbimisliku ükskõiksuseni: tarbimisorientatsioonid tänases Eestis' ['From Consumerism to Indifference towards Consumption: Consumer Orientations in Today's Estonia'], in Kalmus, V., Lauristin, M. & Pruulmann-Vengerfeldt, P. (eds) (2004).

Keller, M. & Kalmus, V. (forthcoming) 'Between Consumerism and Protectionism: Attitudes towards Children, Consumption and the Media in Estonia', *Childhood: A Journal of Global Child Research*.

Keller, M. & Vihalemm, T. (2005) 'Coping with Consumer Culture: Elderly Urban Consumers in Post-Soviet Estonia', *Trames*, 9, 1.

Kennedy, M. D. (2002) *Cultural Formations of Post-Communism: Emancipation, Transition, Nation, and War* (Minneapolis & London, University of Minnesota Press).

Kiisel, M. (2002) *Olmejäätmete käitlemine Tartu elanike seas* [*Recycling of Domestic Waste among Inhabitants of Tartu*], unpublished report (Tartu, University of Tartu).

Kiisel, M. (2005) *Keskkonnateadvuse kujunemine Eestis 1980ndatest 2005ni* [*Formation of Environmental Consciousness in Estonia from the 1980s to 2005*], unpublished MA thesis (Tartu, University of Tartu).

Kõresaar, E. (2003) 'Hea elu normatiivsus. Nõukogudeaegse defitsiidikogemuse kujutamine elulugudes' ['Normativity of Good Life: Depiction of the Soviet Shortage of Goods in Life Stories'], in Kõresaar, E. & Anepaio, T. (eds) (2003).

Kõresaar, E. & Anepaio, T. (eds) (2003) *Mälu kui kultuuritegur: etnoloogilisi perspektiive* [*Ethnological Perspectives on Memory*] (Tartu, Tartu University Press).

Kuldna, P. & Kaldaru, H. (2007) *Inimene ja keskkond: muutused elanike keskkonnateadvuses 1994–2007* [*Human and Environment: Changes in Estonian Public Environmental Awareness 1994–2007*] (Tallinn, Stockholm Environment Institute).

Langer, B. (2005) 'Research Note: Consuming Anomie: Children and Global Commercial Culture', *Childhood*, 12, 2.

Lash, S., Szerszynski, B. & Wynne, B. (eds) (1996) *Risk, Environment and Modernity: Towards a New Ecology* (London, Sage).

Lauristin, M. (1987) 'Empiricheskaya tipologija ekologicheskovo soznanija', in Lauristin, M. & Firsov, B. (eds) (1987).

Lauristin, M. (2004) 'Eesti ühiskonna kihistumine' ['Stratification of the Estonian Society'], in Kalmus, V., Lauristin, M. & Pruulmann-Vengerfeldt, P. (eds) (2004).

Lauristin, M. & Firsov, B. (eds) (1987) *Massovaja kommunikatsija i ohrana sredy* [*Mass Communication and Environmental Protection*] (Tallinn, Eesti Raamat).

Lauristin, M. & Vihalemm, P. (2009) 'External and Internal Dimensions in Estonian Political Agenda during Different Periods of Transformation', *Journal of Baltic Studies*, 40, 1.

Marada, R. (2004) 'Social Construction of Youth and Formation of Generational Awareness after Socialism', in Mareš, P., et al. (eds) (2004) *Society, Reproduction and Contemporary Challenges* (Brno, Barrister & Principal).

Marsh, C. (ed.) (2004) *Burden or Blessing? Russian Orthodoxy and the Construction of Civil Society and Democracy* (Boston, Institute on Culture, Religion and World Affairs, Boston University).

Miller, D. (1987) *Material Culture and Mass Consumption* (Oxford, Blackwell).

Miller, D. (ed.) (1998) *Material Cultures: Why Some Things Matter* (London, UCL Press).

Oja, A. (ed.) (2003) *Keskkonnaeetikast säästva ühiskonna eetikani: inimese ja looduse vaheline tasakaal kui jätkusuutlikkuse aluspõhimõte* [*From Ethics of Environment to Ethics of Sustainable Society: The Balance between Human and Nature as the Principle of Sustainability*] (Tallinn, Stockholm Environment Institute).

Outhwaite, W. & Ray, L. (2004) *Social Theory and Postcommunism* (Oxford, Blackwell).

Rahu, K. (2004) *Šoppamise sooline representatsioon* [*Gendered Representation of Shopping*], unpublished MA thesis (Tartu, Department of Journalism and Communication, University of Tartu).

Raudsepp, M. (2001a) 'Environmental Belief Systems: Empirical Structure and a Typology', *Trames*, 5, 3.

Raudsepp, M. (2001b) 'Values and Environmentalism', *Trames*, 5, 3.

Raudsepp, M. (2003) 'Kui keskkonnasõbralikud on eestlased?' ['How Friendly are Estonians to Nature?'] in Oja, A. (ed.) (2003).

Raudsepp, M. (2005) 'Eesti elanike suhe loodusesse ja subjektiivne heaolu' ['Nature-Relations of Estonian Inhabitants and Subjective Well-Being']', *Estonian Social Science Online*, 3.

Rausing, S. (1998) 'Signs of the New Nation: Gift Exchange, Consumption and Aid on a Former Collective Farm in Northwest Estonia', in Miller, D. (ed.) (1998).

Rokeach, M. (1973) *The Nature of Human Values* (New York, Free Press).

Slater, D. (1997) *Consumer Culture and Modernity* (London, Routledge).

Sööt, M. (2004) *Keskkonnasäästliku tarbimise võimalikkusest* [*On Possibility of Sustainable Consumption*], unpublished survey (Tartu, University of Tartu).

Soper, K. (2007) 'Re-thinking the "Good Life": The Citizenship Dimension of the Consumer Disaffection with Consumerism', *Journal of Consumer Culture*, 7, 2.

Svennebye, L. (2008) 'GDP per Capita, Consumption per Capita and Comparative Price Levels in Europe', in *Statistics in Focus. Economy and Finance. Eurostat 3/2008*, available at: epp.eurostat.ec.europa.eu/portal/page?_pageid=1073,46587259&_dad=portal&_schema=PORTAL&p_product_code=KS-SF-08-003, accessed 31 March 2008.

Sztompka, P. (2004) 'The Trauma of Social Change: A Case of Postcommunist Societies', in Alexander, J. C., Eyerman, R., Giesen, B., Smelser, N. J. & Sztompka, P. (eds) (2004).

Vihalemm, T. & Kalmus, V. (2008) 'Mental Structures in Transition Culture: Differentiating Patterns of Identities and Values in Estonia', *East European Politics and Societies*, 22, 4, pp. 901–27.

Vihalemm, T. & Kalmus, V. (2009) 'Cultural Differentiation of the Russian Minority: Mental Structures in Estonia and Latvia', *Journal of Baltic Studies*, 40, 1.

Vogt, H. (2005) *Between Utopia and Disillusionment: A Narrative of the Political Transformation in Eastern Europe* (New York, Berghahn Books).

WSSD (2002) *World Summit on Sustainable Development: Plan of Implementation* (Johannesburg, United Nations Division for Sustainable Development), available at: http://www.un.org/esa/sustdev/documents/docs_key_conferences.htm, accessed 20 March 2008.

# THE PATTERNS OF CULTURAL ATTITUDES AND PREFERENCES IN ESTONIA

## Maarja Lõhmus, Marju Lauristin and Eneli Siirman

### Introduction: Changing Normative Meaning of Culture in a Post-communist Society

The meaning of cultural consumption is greatly influenced by the connotations that the word 'culture' has in a particular society. On the one hand, consumption of 'culture' is framed by the social settings that define *normative aspects of cultural preferences*. 'People act in part upon the basis of myths, dogmas, ideologies and "half baked" theories' (Denzau & North 1994, p. 3), and this is also relevant for cultural consumption, especially if we consider how cultural consumption is affected by the notion of 'high' *vs.* 'low' culture. On the other hand, the way people participate in cultural activities is always embedded in individual needs, and depends on personal reflectivity and creativity, which compound internal and non-normative aspects of cultural preferences. In a sociological interpretation of cultural consumption, it is important to understand how these two aspects are inter-related, and how the predefined system of social values is transformed and reflected in individual cultural preferences.

The empirical sociological research of cultural consumption has often been focused on social patterns of individual choices ('taste'), or has dealt with the practices of cultural consumption related to certain social statuses and lifestyles (Chan & Goldthorpe 2007; Rausell & Carrasco 1998).

The normative approach to people's cultural behavior, which has long dominated empirical studies of cultural preferences, has been based on a clear distinction between 'high' culture and 'low' or 'mass' culture. The quality of participation in culture has been, first and foremost, valued as the ability to participate in high culture, i.e. to enjoy aesthetically demanding pieces of art. Low culture has meant a preference for products of mass culture, adapted to more simple tastes and pop culture. One of the representatives of such a normative approach, Herbert J. Gans (1999, pp. 100–20), has differentiated Americans' cultural preferences and choices as a hierarchy of tastes.[1]

This kind of normative approach was also clearly applicable for the research of cultural consumption in Soviet society, where a very strict hierarchy of 'good' and 'poor' taste was introduced through education and the ideological system. The 'good taste' taught in schools was defined as a preference for the 'classical' forms of high culture, while 'bad taste' was exemplified by 'Western' popular culture.

The existence of strong normative beliefs about the meaning of culture in Soviet society was confirmed in sociological studies conducted in Estonia during the 1970s and 1980s. The results of surveys proved the importance of 'high' culture[2] as a value for the vast majority of the Estonian population (Hion *et al.* 1988; Järve 1985; Kask & Vellerand 1980; Narusk 1995; Rannik 1985). According to the Estonian national survey from 1984, conducted by Estonian Radio (*Eesti Raadio*), the satisfaction of cultural needs was considered 'very important' by 65%, and 'rather important' by 27% of the respondents, and only 8% of the respondents said that culture was not important or was irrelevant for them. The notion of 'culture' in Soviet ideology had the connotation of a 'high spiritual value', 'classical tradition' and a 'well educated personality', whereas 'entertainment' was considered to characterize 'lower', 'less educated' and 'Western' cultural attitudes. Therefore, in the same survey, 'entertainment' was valued less than 'culture': it was 'very important' for 41%, 'rather important' for 36% and 'not important' for 22% of the respondents (Saar *et al.* 1985). Cultural activities, such as reading books and journals, and visiting theaters, concerts and art exhibitions, were positively correlated with the higher self-esteem and better social and economic position of individuals. For example, according to the typology of lifestyles developed on the basis of the data collected in 1978–1983, the group characterized by a high level of involvement in various cultural activities included 30–35% of Estonians. This group of the culturally most active people also had a higher social position and was more satisfied with their lives (Hion *et al.* 1988, p. 118).

The high value of culture and widespread interest in 'serious' cultural forms (theater, poetry, classical and Soviet novels, classical and Soviet music, art exhibitions, quality films, etc.) in Soviet society could be explained mainly by ideological reasons: first, the whole area of 'culture' was officially recognized as an important 'ideological' field and means for socialization; second, access by the 'ordinary people' to 'high culture' was claimed to be one of the major achievements of socialism ('Art belongs to the people!' was an official slogan of the Bolsheviks). But this highly ideological valorization of cultural activities also had its positive effects for people: cultural consumption under the conditions of Soviet 'deficit economy' was the only field where people had a comparatively rich variety of personal choices; also, and not least, despite the efforts of censorship to control the dissemination of ideas, metaphorical artistic forms were often used to send 'hidden messages' containing forbidden ideas, offering an opportunity to express in public critical views and alternative experiences excluded from explicit political discussion. Namely for that reason, poetry and theater, in particular, became enormously popular in Estonia in the 1960s and 1970s. Less opportunities for effective ideological control over the complicated forms of the 'fine arts' (compared to the political field and the media) made self-expression in the cultural field a substitute for the non-existent political public sphere (Lõhmus 2002; Vihalemm & Lauristin 1997). The mission of cultural resistance and preservation of national identity contributed to the 'seriousness' of cultural beliefs. On the other hand, artistic forms provided rich opportunities for language games, which also contributed to the popularity of culture, especially to the genres containing irony and humor:

> In the case of the totalitarian regime, normative symbols, as well as textual symbols and especially ambivalent humour, have more interpretations than in a democratic open system, for the reason that having been closed and silent has provided an especially dense area of possibilities for different meanings. (Lõhmus 2004, p. 264)

During the 'Singing Revolution' at the end of the 1980s and beginning of the 1990s, freedom of political expression in Estonia was fully restored, and the need for politically ambivalent entertainment decreased (Lõhmus 2002, pp. 78–9). In the course of economic liberalization, both the production and consumption of culture were more and more commercialized. The normative meaning of culture and the high prestige of cultural activities started to dissolve under the pressure of rising consumerism. The 'spiritual value' of culture was, for many people, replaced by an understanding of culture as a commodity. The value of arts was merchandized. The functions of culture were reconsidered: the 'spiritual', aesthetic and ethical values ascribed to cultural consumption by a majority of respondents in surveys from the 1970s and 1980s were replaced by 'commodity values', which included practical knowledge, social recognition, prestige, and the needs of individuals to adjust to the new environment of a consumer society and to form their group identity. In the present essay, we try to describe this new situation, using data on cultural preferences and activities from surveys we conducted in 2002 and 2005.

## Culture as a Field: Variety of Preferences

An alternative view of the normative model of cultural consumption was developed by Pierre Bourdieu's theory of the 'cultural field'. His approach interprets culture as a domain which does not have a unidimensional hierarchical nature, but where participants relate to one another through mutual *symbolic differentiation* in the multidimensional space of preferences (Bourdieu 1984, 1992). The concept of *cultural field* makes it possible to use the empirical patterns of cultural consumption as an indication of the differences in 'cultural capital' which define the mutual positions of the social actors in this field:

> There are thus as many fields of preferences as there are fields of stylistic possibilities. Each of these worlds – drinks (mineral waters, wines and aperitifs)

or automobiles, newspapers or holiday resorts, design or furnishing of house or garden, not to mention political programmes – provides the small number of distinctive features which, functioning as a system of differences, differential deviations, allow the most fundamental social differences to be expressed almost as completely as through the most complex and refined expressive systems available in the legitimate arts, and it can be seen that the total field of these fields offers well-nigh inexhaustible possibilities for the pursuit of distinction. (Bourdieu 1992, p. 226)

Bourdieu had stressed social and economic differences in a class society as the main factor behind cultural differences (Bourdieu 1992, p. 228). More recently, Finnish sociologist Taru Virtanen, seeking a deeper understanding of differences in cultural consumption, has raised the question of the universality of taste in contemporary Europe. The most important cultural indicator that Virtanen points to is the amount of *time* that individuals need to spend in order to enjoy the various forms of culture. In other words, some cultural domains require a greater devotion of time than others. This finding points to the lessening role of economic and material constraints *vis-à-vis* personal choices in using one's own time as a resource. As a result of her analysis, Virtanen has stressed the variety of pattern, characterizing cultural consumption in Europe. She finds that '[E]ach country has its own cultures of taste' (Virtanen 2007, p. 241). Looking at cultural activities through the analytical lens of time relates the notion of cultural preferences and taste with lifestyle research, where culture is just one of the choices made by an individual who decides upon the uses of his or her own leisure time. When present in the lifestyles of people in communist societies, culture was one of the few spheres where a variety of choices was possible and legitimate, and therefore cultural consumption dominated other fields. In the new context of the free market this situation has changed for the majority of people, who now prefer 'materialist' values over 'spiritual' ones. Even if the high value of culture remained unchanged as a normative belief, the reality of consumer culture is different (see Kalmus *et al.* 2009).

In our study,[3] we do not focus on tastes in their normative meaning ('good' *vs.* 'bad', 'high' *vs.* 'low'), but rather as closer to the 'field' approach. In our survey, we have tried to disclose the value of cultural activities from the viewpoint of personal needs and preferences, indicated by people themselves. Cultural preferences include a person's idea of the standards and principles he or she believes that they are following and his or her self-evaluation as an actor participating in the cultural field. In this sense, cultural preferences could also be considered to be 'ideological beliefs', in the meaning developed by van Dijk (1998).

Rausell and Carrasco (1998) focused on cultural consumption as a symbolic act within defined categories. They found differences between *real* and *ideal* time spent in leisure activities. They asked the following questions: why do people not act according to their ideal preferences? And what kind of constraints do not allow people to behave according to their ideal options? These questions remind us of the need to analyze changes in cultural orientations not only on the level of normative beliefs, but also taking into account the changing availability of time or economic resources. In our empirical study we have differentiated 'cultural activities' from 'cultural beliefs' and 'cultural resources'. *Cultural beliefs* is defined as the possession of certain normative principles which inform personal relationships with culture. We assume that those normative principles are represented in the personal assessments of the value of culture, and in definitions of needs, expectations and preferences in the process of cultural consumption. We have studied *cultural activities* as a part of personal lifestyle (engagement in 'cultural hobbies' such as singing in a choir, recording music, making movies, participating in performances and collecting cultural artifacts) or as cultural consumption habits, interests and tastes: regularity of participation, preferences for certain kinds of cultural products (books, films, music etc.). *Cultural resources* are measured through level of education, possession of cultural artifacts (for example, the number of books in a home library) and the possession of sufficient means for access to cultural events and activities (Lõhmus *et al.* 2004). In the present essay we present an empirical typology of cultural orientations. This typology reflects empirical patterns of cultural activities combined with certain beliefs about the personal meaning of culture. These patterns of cultural activities involve access to cultural resources, which are connected with the demographic and social backgrounds of respondents. We try to distinguish between different types of 'cultural consumption' in today's Estonian society, and assess what the relative importance of these types or patterns of cultural orientations is. Our main interest is in discovering how changes in society, *inter alia* marketization of the cultural domain, have affected both the normative beliefs that people hold about the role of culture in their lives and their real cultural activities.

## Methodology and Data

For the data collection in the 2005 national survey *Me, My World and the Media* (*Mina. Maailm. Meedia*), mainly referred to in this essay, we used a questionnaire comprised of two parts: a self-assessment form and an interview form. In the self-assessment part, along with a range of questions about other areas (altogether 800 items), respondents were asked to assess the general importance of culture in their lives, the role of cultural activities in their lifestyles, the regularity of their contacts with cultural events, their usage of cultural media, their book preferences, their values, and their social and economic status (education, social position, income, sufficiency of means for consumption of different products and services, etc.). In order to study cultural beliefs, we invited respondents to express their agreement/disagreement with 25 statements defining personal expectations and values in relation to culture. The statements were constructed along five dimensions: (1) cognitive value of culture as a source of knowledge; (2) aesthetic value of culture as a source of spiritual experience, beauty and harmony; (3) value of culture for self-expression and social recognition; (4) value of culture as a source of emotional satisfaction and relaxation; and (5) ethnocentric *vs.* cosmopolitan character of cultural preferences. Respondents were asked to sort these statements according to a five-point scale of personal relevance: from very important and relevant statements to absolutely irrelevant ones. Missing answers were taken to have zero value in the analysis, meaning that these statements were absolutely unimportant to the respondent.

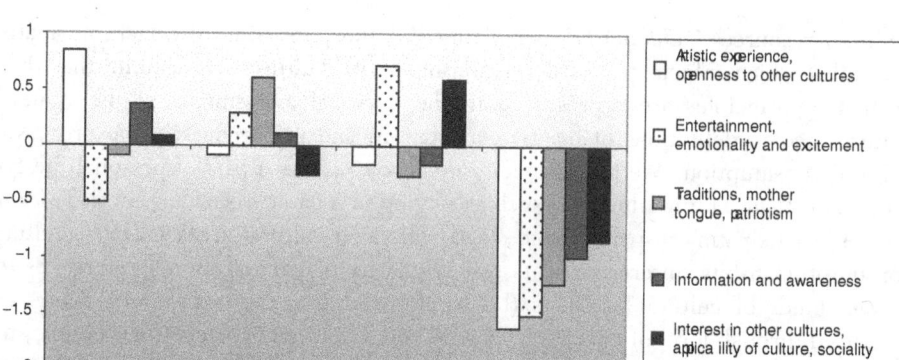

**FIGURE 1** Profiles of cultural beliefs in clusters of cultural orientations (average factor scores of cultural beliefs by each cluster).

*Factor analysis of cultural beliefs – aesthetic* vs. *consumerist, ethnic* vs. *cosmopolitan, rational* vs. *emotional dimensions*

The patterns of cultural beliefs were described using a factor analysis (principal axis method, Varimax rotation) of the ratings of the 25 above described statements. The five-factor solution of the 25 statements revealed general patterns which confirmed the relevance of the initial classification of the cultural beliefs in our study: as alternative factors, the combination of the 'normative' aesthetic and cognitive cultural orientation on the one side (*the first factor*), and consumerist–hedonistic orientation on the other side (*the second factor*) emerged. *The third and fourth factors* revealed a polarization between conservative ethnocentric orientation and cosmopolitan orientation in cultural relationships. *The fifth factor* mainly pointed to a rational and non-engaged attitude concerning arts as the source of social recognition. Those categories were used in a further analysis in order to create a typology of cultural orientations (by using the k-means method of cluster analysis based on factor scores). Factor-based components of the clusters can be seen in Figure 1 and in the Appendices.

*Factor analysis of cultural activities – the five dimensions of lifestyles (socializing with friends, self-realization in work and studies, family and home oriented, involvement in technical hobbies, creative activities)*

In our survey, we asked respondents to evaluate the regularity of their engagement in various cultural activities, listing 38 activities for evaluation. We present briefly the five-factor solution of these 38 indicators (principal axes method, Varimax rotation). The results of this analysis are reflected in Figure 3. *The first factor* represents a leisure-centered socializing lifestyle. It includes a variety of social entertainments that particularly characterize youth culture: enjoying good company, visiting clubs and discos; sitting with friends in restaurants, pubs and cafés; watching films (videos, DVDs and downloads); engagement in computer-related hobbies (games, chat-rooms,

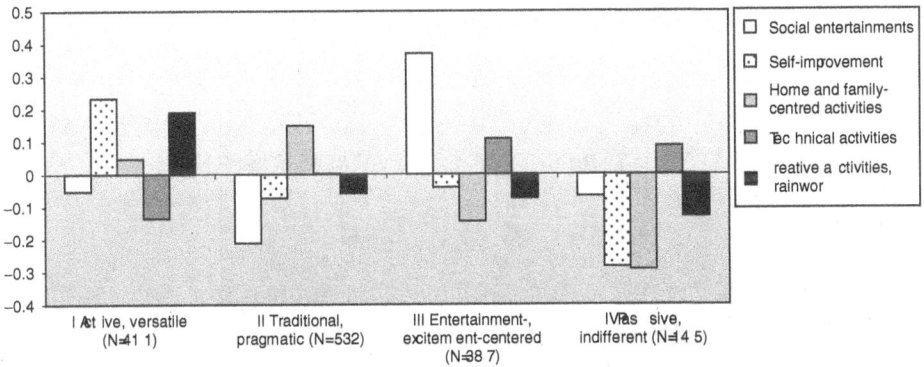

**FIGURE 2** Profiles of cultural activities related to the type of cultural orientations (average factor scores of cultural activities by clusters of cultural orientation).

computer music etc.); music, dancing, sports and physical exercise; audiovisual hobbies such as photography, film-making, and recording videos or music; grooming (massage, beauty salons, solarium etc.); visits to friends and relatives; and gambling (casinos and slot-machines). *The second factor* is characterized by activities targeted to self-realization and self-improvement: participation in seminars, conferences, courses, meetings and debates; reading professional and hobby-related literature; enjoying theater, arts, concerts of classical music, jazz, folk and rock music; and traveling and hiking. *The third factor* is comprised of home and family-centered activities: housekeeping and decorating; taking care of family members and relatives; gardening; cooking; dealing with children; handicrafts; solving crossword puzzles; activities with pets; and visits to church. *The fourth factor* represents technical activities: leisure time activities involving cars, boats and motorbikes; and engagement in the rebuilding and renovation of one's home. *The fifth factor* involves the importance of creative and intellectual activities: reading fiction, visiting a library, drawing, painting and making applied arts; collecting various objects; and solving crosswords.

*Factor analysis of book preferences: distinction between main orientations in readers' interests*

As an indication of cultural preferences, we used questionnaire data on the choices made among 30 types of books (see Appendix 2). These data were also aggregated using a factor analysis. The five-factor solution of book preferences revealed the following tendencies in cultural preferences (see Figure 2): *the first 'home and garden' factor* revealed combined interest in home and family-centered 'how-to' literature (cooking, health, interior design and interpersonal relations) with light reading (romance, mystery, spiritual matters and horoscopes) and children's books. *The second 'curiosity' factor* is dominated by an interest in history and nature (travel, nature, history and biography), combined with various reference books. *The third 'intellectual' factor* represents a 'high-brow' interest in philosophy and the arts, together with professional literature and politics. *The fourth 'fiction' factor* is comprised of an interest in fiction: translations of modern fiction, classics of world literature, modern Estonian

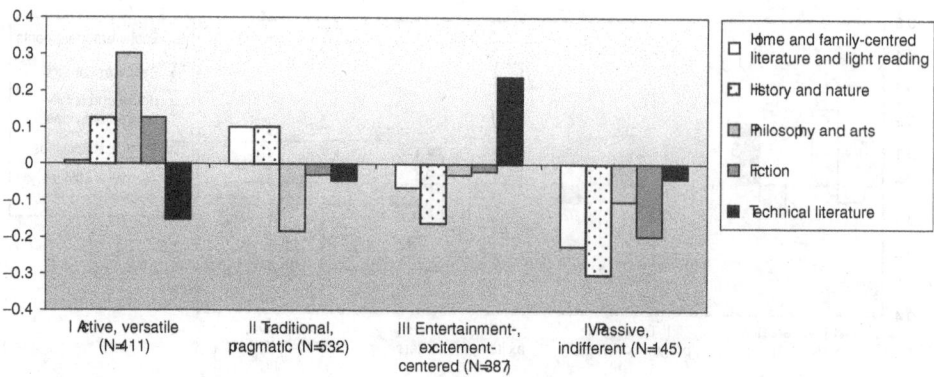

**FIGURE 3** Profiles of book preferences in different types of cultural orientation (average factor scores of book preferences by the clusters of cultural orientations).

literature and Estonian literary classics, crime and suspense. *The fifth 'practical' factor* consists of an interest in technical literature and the economy: economics, management, marketing, cars and computers, building and renovation, and sports.

*Formation of the generalized typology of cultural orientations*

As the next step of the analysis, the above-mentioned results of factor analysis were used for a multidimensional classification (cluster analysis) of respondents, in order to create a typology of cultural orientations. For this purpose, the individual scores of the factors of cultural orientations, lifestyles and book preferences were computed, and on this ground, all respondents were described as belonging to one of the revealed four patterns (clusters) of cultural beliefs (see Figures 2 and 3). These empirical clusters were characterized as 'the types of cultural orientations' from the one side by the distinctive profile of 'cultural factors', and on the other side, by the social and ethnic composition behind each cluster.

## Typology of Cultural Orientations

As described above, the basis of the cultural typology is formed by a cluster analysis of respondents, using the factor scores of cultural beliefs, lifestyle and book preferences as personal variables. The analysis of the main dimensions, which have differentiated cultural orientations of respondents belonging to the same cluster, revealed two basic characteristics behind the variety of patterns. The first is high versus low general interest in culture. The second is the level of divergence in interests and preferences. On these grounds, the four types of cultural orientations could be described as follows. The first cluster includes people characterized by active and versatile involvement in cultural activities (28%). The second cluster united people whose relatively active relations with the cultural domain were predominantly restricted to traditional cultural activities and to pragmatic beliefs (36%). The third, also relatively active cluster is characterized by excitement-centered cultural orientation, preferring entertainment to the 'serious' forms of cultural activities (26%). The fourth cluster indicates the low importance of culture, and passive and indifferent attitudes concerning any cultural activities (10%). Figure 1 shows a profile of cultural beliefs (average factor scores by cluster) characterizing each cluster (see also Appendix 1 describing the composition of the factors of cultural orientations depicted in this figure). Figure 2 illustrates the role of certain cultural activities in the profile of each of the clusters. Adding even more details, the tendencies in book preferences related to the cluster membership are visible in Figure 3. The ethnic and social background of cluster membership is represented in Appendix 1.

Looking at the results presented above, we can describe the following four empirical types of cultural orientations that represent the different attitudes and preferences of Estonians concerning participation in the cultural field.

## 1. Active and versatile type of cultural orientation (28%)

This type of cultural orientation was shared by 28% of respondents. People belonging to this type express predominantly aesthetic and cognitive attitudes towards culture and the arts. Participation in culture is interpreted as a deep personal experience, providing spiritual self-expression and openness of mind. The basic factor of cultural beliefs behind this type ('Artistic experience, openness to other cultures') is characterized by statements such as 'Good works of art make us better understand life and people', 'Art allows us to perceive the divine essence of man and the harmony of the world', 'I like art that knows no boundaries and lets me feel a part of world culture', 'Art expresses my deeply personal internal being', 'Total freedom of the creative personality is the most important characteristic of art', 'I like to discover and experience other cultures', 'Books, theater, music and art play an essential role in the development of personality', 'I recognize and can appreciate works of high artistic value'. The characteristics of this rich cultural orientation are not only related to personal involvement and self-expression, but also include reflectivity and intellectual interest in the arts: scores in Factor 4 of cultural beliefs ('Information and awareness') are also high for this cluster. This factor includes agreement with the statements 'I regularly follow radio and TV broadcasts, articles, and criticism and reviews concerning culture', and 'I try to follow all new and important phenomena in modern culture'. In the cultural activities and book preferences of this cultural type, active interest in reading and diversity of book choices predominate. Illuminating is the higher than average interest in philosophy, art and fiction. The involvement in creative activities in this cluster is also higher than average (42% are engaged in various active forms of cultural participation, compared to the overall average of 33%). A participatory and active attitude characterizes not only relations with culture but also the overall life of this type of person. They also express a higher than average level of social trust, and are used to more active participation in other spheres of social life.

Looking at the social background of this distinctive type of high cultural and artistic involvement (see Appendix 2), it is surprising to discover that status characteristics, such as material wealth and social class, are not very different from the average distribution. Also, age seems not to have a big impact on this quality of cultural orientation. The most predictable social distinction producing this kind of 'high culture' orientation is related to higher education. However, differences are also remarkable in terms of the gender and ethnicity profile of this cluster: we can see here a quite clear tendency in favor of 'weaker' groups, i.e. women and representatives of the Russian-speaking population. Compared to the above-mentioned similar active type of cultural participation revealed in our studies during the Soviet time, where it was related to higher social status and better adjustment in society, in the new conditions of the market society, this type of cultural orientation preserves the compensatory character of cultural consumption, but its social background has shifted towards the less adjusted, socially marginalized groups of society.

## 2. Active traditional, pragmatic type of cultural orientations

The largest share of the respondents (36%) falls into this cluster. Cultural beliefs of this type are embedded in traditions. Culture (presumably in the mother tongue) is considered to be a medium of national values and a source of identity and ethics: 'For me, culture is primarily my mother tongue, traditions, and common cultural values that make us members of our ethnos', 'Culture teaches people to live more ethically, in a more proper way', 'Cultural activities give me the chance to spend time with other people and feel that something unites us', 'I feel that folk culture and national heritage are especially close to me'. Attitudes towards the arts are less critical, less selective and more centered on emotions than that of the first type.

Membership in this cluster of cultural beliefs coincides with a family-centered lifestyle, active media consumption and a lively interest in political life. In accordance with the lifestyle, preferences are mostly for practical and home-centered books.

The social background of this cultural type is characterized by the dominance of Estonian ethnicity, and by a small shift towards older age groups and more rural than urban residence. Women are also slightly predominant in this type. The widespread character of this traditional identity-centered attitude reveals that stability and conservatism still prevail in the cultural attitudes of Estonians.

## 3. Less active entertainment- and excitement-centered cultural orientations (26%)

This type of cultural orientation is characterized by low reflectivity and strong emotional involvement, and a preference for cultural forms providing excitement and entertainment. At the same time, this entertainment-centered attitude also embraces a higher than average interest in technical matters. Among factors of cultural beliefs, the most dominant is Factor 2, 'Entertainment, emotionality, excitement' (Figure 1). The typical beliefs are expressed in agreement with statements such as 'I have no specific preferences in culture and art', 'What I like depends on my mood and the company I am with', 'I like to experience concerts, plays, books and films, not to argue about them', 'A good book, film or theater performance has to be exciting and to offer spicy experiences', 'All lectures on culture are too serious; actually, culture is still entertainment', 'Most of all, I enjoy the elevated mood of public activities and the lively atmosphere of cultural events', 'My life would be poor and dull without films, books and music'. The other outstanding quality of this type of cultural orientation is the combination of status-symbolism and cultural 'cosmopolitanism' (high scores on Factor 5 'Interest in other cultures, applicability of culture, sociability') characterized by statements such as 'My friends appreciate my taste and respect my opinions on works of art', 'Generally, I am more interested in translations than in books by Estonian authors', 'I like to watch films in original languages (or with subtitles), instead of dubbing or voice translation', 'Artistic works can provide witty ideas that can be used in one's own work'.

Excitement, status-symbolism and cosmopolitan cultural attitudes are connected with activities related to technical and business matters. The general interest in books is modest, and the choice is dominated by books of practical and cognitive content, providing information about technology, science, management and the economy (see Figure 3). Comparing the social background of this cluster with the previous two, we have to stress, above all, the younger age of people sharing this entertainment-focused and instrumental cultural orientation. Men are dominant in this cluster. Some bias towards ethnic Estonians and the higher-middle class should also be noted.

*4. Passive and indifferent attitude toward culture (10%)*

This type of cultural orientation is characterized by a general lack of interest in culture. The cluster is made up of respondents who left all or the majority of the 25 statements about the significance of culture unanswered. These respondents can be divided into two groups: half of them declared that culture was for them absolutely unimportant, and consequently skipped altogether the part of the questionnaire containing questions about cultural attitudes. The other half of this group of respondents gave negative answers to the vast majority, if not to all, questions concerning their cultural beliefs and preferences. Nevertheless, some of them answered the questions about book preferences. Typically having a limited interest in books in general, they were interested in books on technical and practical subjects. Interest in fiction was low and included only 'light reading' that enabled them to escape the realities of everyday life. This type is characterized by little mobility, a lack of openness and low trust in institutions.

The social profile of this group (see Appendix 2) is biased towards men with lower status and education, living in the capital city. Russian-speaking respondents were slightly dominant. Regardless of the particularly poor cultural capital of this group, it was not significantly different from the other types in terms of income and age.

## Financial Constraints Limiting Cultural Consumption

After examination of the subjective side of cultural participation, let us ask: how are the attitudes and preferences in cultural participation related to the material resources available to people? Is there a simple factor of economic inequality behind the more active or passive cultural participation? As we have seen in the overview of cultural orientations, differences in personal incomes did not clearly explain the differences in cultural orientations. But when we look not at incomes, but at subjective assessments of material opportunities, a different picture appears (see Figure 4). In the table, the average scores of the three indices characterizing 'material well-being' in each cluster of cultural orientations are presented. These indices are based on summaries of

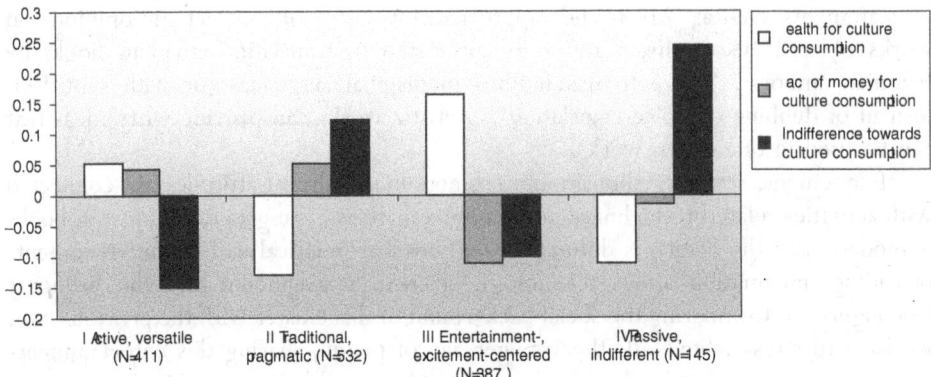

**FIGURE 4** Sufficiency of means for cultural consumption in clusters of cultural preferences (the averages of summarized index for each cluster of cultural participation).

answers to the questions about sufficiency or lack of money for consumption of different goods and services or expressed absence of need in particular goods or services.[4]

The largest differences between the cultural orientations regarding material opportunities (see Figure 4) can be noticed in the case of the wealth index (summarizing the number of answers reflecting sufficiency of means for the desired goods and services) and the indifference index (summarizing the number of answers 'I do not need that at all').

We discovered that an insufficiency of finances was sharply felt by people belonging to the first type of cultural orientations: they have the most diverse and demanding cultural expectations, are selective and appreciate high quality performance. At the same time, the level of income (see Appendix 2) in this group is not different from the general population. This means that cultural activities are an important item of their personal budget, and financial constraints in this area are sensed with a greater intensity. The second type, people with a traditional cultural orientation, suffer at times from financial constraints, but they are also more indifferent towards culture. However, people with a high interest in entertainment do not feel that financial constraints restrict their access to (popular) culture. Finally, indifference to culture was widespread among people who also expressed indifference and a lack of interest concerning a number of other needs and opportunities. The level of income in this group is similar to the average distribution among all respondents.

We can conclude that sufficiency of financial resources in itself seems to have little impact on cultural orientations. Economic constraints reveal themselves not in terms of income, but rather as a lack of money for some specific cultural needs. In previous studies we witnessed similar results (see Lõhmus et al. 2006). In all categories of income, we found people who are indifferent to culture and people who are able to fulfill their cultural needs. People whose extensive cultural needs could not be satisfied because of a lack of money could be found as often among the well off as among the poor. But the most important conclusion from a comparison of financial opportunities and cultural attitudes is that sufficiency of means in itself is not able to create a richer spectrum of cultural consumption, but rather makes it possible to enjoy more entertainment and more exciting leisure forms.

## Discussion and Conclusions

The presented empirical typology of cultural orientations reveals that, in general, Estonia continues to be a country where the vast majority of people actively participate in cultural activities. Only 10% of respondents in our research could be classified as 'culturally indifferent and passive'. The normative beliefs of middle-aged and older people are still strongly influenced by education and socialization given during the Soviet time when the notion of 'culture' had strong spiritual and ethnic connotations. When looking back at the picture of cultural attitudes in the Soviet time, it seems that the normative beliefs attaching high importance to 'classical culture' and engagement in spiritual values are alive among the Estonian population. Notable is a high evaluation of spiritual values among minority groups with higher education but lower social status, who feel deprived of their previous position in society. Comparing the ethnic background of cultural orientations, we discovered a trend which revealed itself also in the analysis of value orientations (see Vihalemm & Kalmus 2009): among the Russian speaking minority identification with the artistic (versatile) cultural orientation is stronger, compared to the more pragmatic and hedonistic orientation of ethnic Estonians. However, the dramatic changes in society during the last two decades had contributed to the dissolution of the old cultural hierarchies.

Comparing the presented empirical typology of Estonian cultural orientations with the classical model of the 'hierarchy of tastes' (Gans 1999), or with the class-related structure of the cultural field presented by Bourdieu (1984), we could not identify any clear structural compatibility between 'high' and 'low' tastes, and lower or higher socio-economical position in society. Our results tell us that the most active and versatile relationship with culture occurs among people who belong to the 'middle layer', and even among socially disadvantaged minority groups, rather than to the 'high layer' of society. At the same time, the forms of 'lower' entertainment culture are popular among younger age groups having comparatively higher social and economic positions in Estonian society. Due to the usage of quite expensive electronic equipment, involvement in the popular entertainment culture, which often had been associated with the lower layers of social structure, even has a relatively elitist character in Estonia.

We can conclude that, in the situation of post-communist transformation, the patterns of cultural participation do not correspond to any one-dimensional hierarchy of cultural preferences, and differentiating between 'high' and 'low' forms of culture is not fruitful from a sociological viewpoint. The patchy picture of cultural orientations in post-communist Estonia resembles the 'post-modern' cultural condition. Nevertheless, the Estonian cultural field had preserved some pre-modern features: the visible presence of conservative and traditional cultural attitudes, related to the quite clear-cut division between 'male' and 'female' patterns of cultural preferences and a strong connection between cultural attitudes and ethnic identity.

The most significant change in cultural attitudes is the rising position of entertainment. From the status of culturally 'bad' (in the 1980s), it has progressed towards the status of culturally 'good' (starting in the second half of the 1990s). Compared with the 1980s, consumption-oriented cultural patterns have become more prominent – this is a new type of relatively passive, leisure-focused and non-critical cultural orientation, whose representatives, however, are able to spend more money and time on their cultural practices and hobbies. Products of the entertainment industry, consumed by young people with smaller incomes and uncompleted education in 2002, in 2005 became a pastime for a more middle-aged group whose income was much higher. This group represents a larger than average share of people with higher education, and is also characterized by preferences for books that are rational and technical.

The age gap between individuals under 30 and over 45 is an essential cultural differentiator. While among people over 45 an orientation towards the realistic and traditional 'classical' culture prevails, and they tend to combine cultural activities with an active interest in politics and in social matters, among young people, active participation in entertainment culture is combined with relatively little interest in political and social activities. The dominant position of the youth culture means a shift from more reflective cultural forms (reading books) to forms providing more emotional engagement (enjoyment of music and seeking thrilling experiences), not to mention the complicated practices of multimedia usage. The rising prestige of entertainment, *vis-à-vis* 'classical culture', among wealthy and technically innovative people who have little interest in the humanities and social matters may reveal a more general change in cultural orientations in present-day Estonia.

As the most general conclusion, we can say from looking at the present picture of cultural orientations in Estonia that from the hierarchical structure of cultural preferences embedded partly in national conservative traditions, partly in the ideological valorization of culture during the Soviet regime, the patterns of cultural consumption had moved towards the horizontal variety of preferences and lifestyles, described by Bourdieu as a field of legitimate cultural distinctions.

## Acknowledgements

This research was supported by a grant from the Estonian Science Foundation (5854) and by the targeted research financing program of the Estonian Ministry of Science and Education (grant 0180017s07).

## Notes

1  A – highly cultivated taste, characterized by the dominance of aesthetic, creative criteria over pragmatic and social criteria: high culture; B – cultural taste of the upper-middle class, oriented towards aesthetic values of high culture, but prefers 'solid', 'classical' and 'mainstream' to the search for the new and is characterized by the transfer of socially appropriate and generally recognized norms: upper-middle culture; C – lower-middle class taste, which is built on the 'pleasant', such criteria as closeness to life and morality: lower-middle culture; D – low vulgar

cultural taste that tends to see art as entertainment, offering excitement and sexual enjoyment: low culture; E – separate from the hierarchical scale, a distinct taste oriented to alternative culture or authentic heritage culture: quasi-folk, low culture.

2   We do not use the word 'culture' here in its social-anthropological meaning (as values, traditions, norms and rituals) but apply it in a more restricted sense as practices and relationships in the process of participation in the field of cultural production and consumption.

3   The empirical survey *Me. The World. The Media* was conducted by the University of Tartu in November 2005. The data were collected using self-fulfilling questionnaires combined with face-to face interviews. The national representative sample of population aged 15–74 was used (1,500 respondents, from those 1,000 were ethnic Estonians and 500 represented the Russian-speaking minority).

4   The formation of culture consumption index. Respondents were asked to evaluate the sufficiency of finances for different expenditures. Seven different types of expenditures were considered in forming the indices of culture consumption – journal and newspaper subscriptions, book purchases, sports, travel, entertainment and hobbies, studies and self-improvement, theater and concert visits. The index of wealth was defined from 0 to 14. Each answer of 'generally sufficient' added two points to the index; each answer of 'sometimes sufficient' added one point. The index of lack of means was defined from 0 to 7, showing the sum of the answers 'not sufficient'. The index of indifference was from 0 to 7, showing the sum of the answers 'not necessary'. The averages of the indices of different groups were compared (characteristics: financial wealth, lack of finance, consumption indifference), based on seven culture-related types of expenditures; the averages of the indices were compared among social-demographic groups.

# References

Bourdieu, P. (1984) *Distinction* (London, Routledge).
Bourdieu, P. (1992) *Language and Symbolic Power* (Cambridge, Polity Press).
Chan, T. W. & Goldthorpe, J. H. (2007) 'Social Status and Newspaper Readership', *American Journal of Sociology*, 112, 4.
Denzau, A. T. & North, D. C. (1994) 'Shared Mental Models: Ideologies and Institutions', *Kyklos*, 47.
Gans, H. J. (1999) *Popular Culture & High Culture. An Analysis and Evaluation of Taste* (New York, Basic Books).
Hion, E., Lauristin, M. & Vihalemm, P. (1988) *Meie muutuv elulaad* (Tallinn, Eesti Raamat).
Järve, M. (1985) *Kulturnaja dejatelnost naselenija* (Tallinn, Eesti Raamat).
Kalmus, V., Keller, M. & Kiisel, M. (2009) 'Emerging Consumer Types in a Transition Culture: Consumption Patterns of Generational and Ethnic Groups in Estonia', *Journal of Baltic Studies*, 40, 1.
Kalmus, V., Lauristin, M. & Pruulmann-Vengerfeldt, P. (eds) (2004) *Eesti elavik 21. sajandi algul: Ülevaade uurimuse Mina. Maailm. Meedia tulemustest* (Tartu, Tartu Ülikooli Kirjastus).
Kask, K. & Vellerand, L. (1980) *Inimesed teatrisaalis* (Tallinn, Perioodika).

Lõhmus, M. (2002) *Transformation of the Public Text in a Totalitarian System: A Socio-semiotic Study of Soviet Censorship Practices in Estonian Radio in the 1980s*, Annales Universitatis Turkuensis, Ser. B, Tom. 248, Humaniora (Turku, Turun Yliopisto).

Lõhmus, M. (2004) 'Effect of Meaning-breaker: Analysis of the Cartoon, "Just shit" (Priit Pärn 1987)', *Semiotica*, 150, pp. 257–82.

Lõhmus, M., Lauristin, M. & Salupere, R. (2004) 'Inimesed kultuuriväljal: aktiivsus ja eelistused', in Kalmus, V., Lauristin, M. & Pruulmann-Vengerfeldt, P. (eds) (2004).

Lõhmus, M., Lauristin, M. & Salupere, R. (2006) 'People in the Domain of Culture: Everyday Environment, Active Participation and Preferences', in Sudweeks, F., Hrachovec, H. & Ess, C. (eds) (2006).

Mühle, E. (ed.) (1997) *Vom Instrument der Partei zur 'vierten Gewalt': Die ostmitteleuropäische Presse als zeithistorische Quelle* (Marburg, Herder-Institut).

Narusk, A. (ed.) (1995) *Everyday Life and Radical Social Changes in Estonia* (Tallinn, Estonian Academy of Sciences).

Rannik, E. (ed.) (1985) *Perekond ja kultuur* (Tallinn, Eesti Raamat).

Rausell, P. & Carrasco, S. (1998) 'Preferences and Cultural Consumption', paper presented at the CEAPE Conference, Lisbon, 5–8 November.

Saar, A., Kivirähk, J. & Pärtlisaar, V. (1985) *Avalik arvamus 1984/1985. Aruanne* (Tallinn, Televisiooni- ja Raadiokomitee Informatsiooni- ja Arvutuskeskus), unpublished research report, manuscript in the Estonian Social Science Data Archive at the Faculty of Social Sciences, University of Tartu.

Sudweeks, F., Hrachovec, H. & Ess, C. (eds) (2006) *Cultural Attitudes towards Technology and Communication 2006. Proceedings of the Fifth International Conference* (Murdoch, Murdoch University).

Van Dijk, T. A. (1998) *Ideology: A Multidisciplinary Approach* (London, Thousand Oaks & New Delhi, Sage).

Vihalemm, P. & Lauristin, M. (1997) 'Political Control and Ideological Canonisation. The Estonian Press during the Soviet Period', in Mühle, E. (ed.) (1997).

Vihalemm, T. & Kalmus, V. (2009) 'Cultural Differentiation of the Russian Minority', *Journal of Baltic Studies*, 40, 1.

Virtanen, T. (2007) *Across and Beyond the Bounds of Taste. On Cultural Consumption Patterns in the European Union*, Series A, No. 11 (Turku, Turku School of Economics).

**APPENDIX 1** Structures of factors and clusters of cultural preferences (the shaded fields contain factor loads of profiling characteristics by each cluster)

| Cluster of cultural preferences | | I CLUSTER Active, versatile | II CLUSTER Traditional, pragmatic | III CLUSTER Entertainment, excitement-centered | IV CLUSTER Passive, indifferent | Total |
|---|---|---|---|---|---|---|
| | N | 411 | 532 | 387 | 145 | 1475 |
| Factor 1: artistic experience, openness to other cultures | 1. Good works of art make us better understand life and people** | 4.1 | 3.7 | 3.1 | 0.1 | 3.3 |
| | 2. Art allows us to perceive the divine essence of man and the harmony of the world** | 3.3 | 2.3 | 2.0 | 0.1 | 2.3 |
| | 3. I like art that knows no boundaries and lets me feel a part of the world culture** | 3.4 | 2.2 | 2.6 | 0.1 | 2.4 |
| | 4. Art expresses my deeply personal internal being** | 3.0 | 1.8 | 2.2 | 0.1 | 2.1 |
| | 5. Total freedom of the creative personality is the most important characteristic of art** | 3.4 | 2.9 | 2.8 | 0.1 | 2.7 |
| | 6. I like to discover and experience other cultures** | 3.9 | 3.1 | 3.1 | 0.1 | 3.0 |
| | 7. Books, theater, music and art play an essential role in the development of personality** | 4.0 | 4.1 | 3.7 | 0.1 | 3.6 |
| | 8. I recognize and can appreciate works of high artistic value** | 3.0 | 2.0 | 2.1 | 0.1 | 2.1 |
| Factor 2: entertainment, emotionality and excitement | 9. I have no specific preferences in culture and art; what I like depends on my mood and the company I am with** | 2.3 | 3.1 | 3.9 | 0.2 | 2.8 |
| | 10. I like to experience concerts, plays, books and films, not to argue about them** | 3.1 | 3.9 | 4.1 | 0.2 | 3.4 |
| | 11. A good book, film or theater performance has to be exciting and offer sharp experiences** | 2.6 | 3.9 | 4.1 | 0.3 | 3.2 |
| | 12. All lectures on culture are too serious; actually, culture is still an entertainment** | 1.8 | 2.5 | 3.1 | 0.1 | 2.2 |

*(continued)*

**APPENDIX 1** Continued

| | Cluster of cultural preferences | I CLUSTER Active, versatile | II CLUSTER Traditional, pragmatic | III CLUSTER Entertainment, excitement-centered | IV CLUSTER Passive-, indifferent | Total |
|---|---|---|---|---|---|---|
| | N | 411 | 532 | 387 | 145 | 1475 |
| | 13. Most of all I enjoy the excited mood of people and the lively atmosphere at cultural events** | 2.3 | 3.1 | 3.2 | 0.3 | 2.6 |
| | 14. Culture is the best entertainment** | 3.0 | 3.6 | 3.0 | 0.2 | 2.9 |
| | 15. My life would be poor and dull without films, books and music | 3.9 | 4.0 | 4.0 | 0.1 | 3.6 |
| Factor 3: traditions, mother tongue, patriotism | 16. For me, culture is primarily my mother tongue, traditions, and common cultural values that make us members of our ethnos** | 3.2 | 4.2 | 3.0 | 0.1 | 3.2 |
| | 17. Culture teaches people to live more ethically, in a more proper way** | 3.7 | 4.0 | 3.0 | 0.2 | 3.3 |
| | 18. Cultural activities give me the chance to spend time with other people and feel that something unites us** | 2.8 | 3.4 | 2.8 | 0.1 | 2.7 |
| | 19. I feel that folk culture and national heritage are especially close to me** | 2.9 | 3.1 | 1.9 | 0.1 | 2.4 |
| Factor 4: information and awareness | 20. I regularly follow radio and TV broadcasts, articles, and criticism and reviews concerning culture** | 2.8 | 2.4 | 2.0 | 0.1 | 2.2 |
| | 21. I try to follow all new and important phenomena in modern culture as much as I can** | 3.3 | 3.0 | 2.7 | 0.1 | 2.7 |
| Factor 5: interest in other cultures, applicability of culture, sociability | 22. My friends appreciate my taste and respect my opinions on works of art** | 2.6 | 2.0 | 2.8 | 0.1 | 2.2 |
| | 23. Generally, I am more interested in translations than in books by Estonian authors** | 1.9 | 1.9 | 2.9 | 0.1 | 2.0 |
| | 24. I like to watch films in original languages (or with subtitles), instead of dubbing or voice translation** | 2.3 | 2.2 | 3.6 | 0.1 | 2.4 |
| | 25. Artistic works can provide witty ideas that can be used in one's own works** | 2.6 | 2.6 | 3.0 | 0.1 | 2.4 |

*Notes*: Averages of ratings inside clusters on a scale of 0–5.

**Difference between the groups is statistically significant at $p < 0.01$.

**APPENDIX 2** Social and demographic background of cultural orientations (composition of cluster membership)

|  | I CLUSTER<br>Active, deep and versatile relationship with culture | II CLUSTER<br>Traditional, down-to-earth relationship with culture | III CLUSTER<br>Emotional tension and entertainment-centered relationship with culture | IV CLUSTER<br>Remote, passive relationship with culture | All respondents |
|---|---|---|---|---|---|
| Number | 411 | 532 | 387 | 145 | 1475 |
| % among all respondents | 28 | 36 | 26 | 10 | 100 |
| *Gender (% inside cluster)*** | | | | | |
| Men | 40 | 45 | 52 | 56 | 47 |
| Women | 60 | 55 | 48 | 44 | 53 |
| *Age (% inside cluster)*** | | | | | |
| 15–19 | 10 | 6 | 17 | 7 | 10 |
| 20–29 | 16 | 14 | 26 | 23 | 18 |
| 30–44 | 24 | 25 | 32 | 26 | 27 |
| 45–54 | 20 | 19 | 13 | 21 | 18 |
| 55–64 | 16 | 18 | 7 | 14 | 14 |
| 65–74 | 14 | 18 | 5 | 10 | 13 |
| *Education (% inside cluster)*** | | | | | |
| Primary | 14 | 19 | 24 | 24 | 20 |
| Secondary | 53 | 61 | 55 | 60 | 57 |
| Higher | 33 | 20 | 22 | 16 | 24 |
| *Ethnic groups (% inside cluster)*** | | | | | |
| Ethnic Estonians | 58 | 73 | 82 | 62 | 70 |
| Estonian Russians | 42 | 27 | 18 | 38 | 30 |
| *Income per family member (% inside cluster)** | | | | | |
| Up to 1500 – low | 14 | 14 | 16 | 16 | 15 |
| 1501–2500 | 21 | 23 | 17 | 21 | 21 |
| 2501–4000 – average | 32 | 36 | 27 | 33 | 33 |
| 4001–6000 | 17 | 17 | 19 | 18 | 18 |
| Above 6000 – high | 15 | 10 | 20 | 12 | 14 |
| *Type of residence (% inside cluster)** | | | | | |
| Capital city | 33 | 28 | 27 | 39 | 30 |
| Big city | 16 | 19 | 20 | 27 | 19 |
| Small city | 22 | 19 | 23 | 16 | 21 |
| Countryside | 29 | 34 | 30 | 19 | 30 |
| *Status (% inside cluster)*** | | | | | |
| Lower | 10 | 13 | 8 | 24 | 12 |
| Lower-middle | 18 | 21 | 17 | 20 | 19 |
| Middle | 35 | 35 | 36 | 31 | 35 |
| Upper-middle | 22 | 19 | 25 | 17 | 21 |
| Upper | 15 | 12 | 14 | 8 | 13 |

Notes: *Difference between the groups is statistically significant at $p < 0.5$.
**Difference between the groups is statistically significant at $p < 0.01$.

# CULTURAL DIFFERENTIATION OF THE RUSSIAN MINORITY

## Triin Vihalemm and Veronika Kalmus

The 'April events' in Tallinn in 2007 – when demonstrators, predominantly Russian youngsters, resisted the removal of the Soviet war monument, the Bronze Soldier, by assaulting police and committing acts of vandalism – upset the common understanding of the course of inter-ethnic integration in Estonia. According to the prevalent opinion in public discussions of inter-ethnic relations and the integration of the Russian population[1] into Estonian society, the problem of poor adaptation concerned only elderly and middle-aged people without command of the Estonian language. It was believed that the problem would be solved gradually in the course of generational replacement.[2]

A survey commissioned by the Office of the Minister for Population and Ethnic Affairs in Estonia in spring 2007 revealed that every second Estonian Russian considered the need to protest against the Estonian government policy towards non-Estonians to be the main reason why the April riots broke out (Saar 2007). The majority of Russians felt that ethnic Estonians had better opportunities for jobs and education and for participating in political and local community life (Saar 2007). They also believed that Estonians owe their better opportunities not to citizenship or knowledge of the national language, but to their ethnic origin (Hallik 2006). The removal of the Bronze Soldier was considered to be an attack against Russians' collective memory and a brutal demonstration of force (CCCS 2007). Russians' evaluations of the democratization of Estonia have become more negative compared with 2002 and 2005; also, their trust in state institutions has diminished. A large proportion (39%) of Russians now believe that the Integration Policy has failed and that it makes no sense to continue spending money on it (Saar 2007).

Studies show that ethnic Estonians consider inter-ethnic integration in most spheres satisfactory (Saar 2007). Among different aspects of integration, they judge language learning to be the most important. At the same time, only 28% of Estonians regard greater participation of Russians in Estonian politics and economy to be beneficial for the development of the country (Saar 2007). Furthermore, 26% of ethnic Estonians show a low level of tolerance towards Russians, measured on a social distance scale (Korts 2009). In this situation, it is very difficult to heal the broken relations between the Russian community and the state, and to (re)create a mutual understanding between the two ethno-linguistic groups. The Integration Strategy 2008–2013 in Estonia (Asari 2007) pays more attention to state identity and citizenship, including the latter's value for naturalized citizens and the problems connected with its acquisition. However, the experiences of other countries show that an emphasis on the civic dimension does not solve all problems. The riots by second and third generation Arab immigrants in the suburbs of Paris in October 2005 led to heavy criticism of French immigration and integration policy. Critics argued that the French civilizing mission, rooted in Republican idealism and the rigidly centralized government structure, had failed: 'The grand French idea of *égalité*, the equality of all citizens of the Republic, itself a by-product of France's colonial past, demonstrated its incompatibility with the twenty-first century' (Haddad & Balz 2006, p. 23).

Many Western European countries face challenges connected with inter-ethnic integration: how to diminish the (feeling of) exclusion of members of ethnic minority groups and build up social coherence. We think that the case of Estonia adds interesting arguments to international academic and other discussions on this topic, because integration in post-Soviet Estonia is an interactive process, where the members of both the ethnic majority and the minority face the challenge of developing strategies to overcome the Soviet (colonial) past and to resocialize into the new, transformational society, which has quickly and, in several aspects, imperfectly passed the first phases of marketization and democratization. Our aim is to analyze the cultural resources of the ethnic majority and the minority for coping with the situation, and to discuss whether and how it is possible to build social coherence in the society. We focus on the joint value and identity structures of three generations of the ethnic majority and the minority. Our interpretation focuses mainly on Estonia, but we have also carried out an empirical analysis of Latvian data to serve as a comparative background. Latvia is a suitable case for comparison since it has a similar ethnic situation and the integration policy has also concentrated on language learning. Moreover, the political and economic transformation has taken place according to an analogous pattern. We have developed a specific methodological approach: the analysis of joint factor structures of values and identities, which enables us to compare social groups and outline their differences.

In the first section, we give an overview of the historical background of inter-ethnic relations in Estonia and Latvia. Then we discuss our theoretical and methodological considerations. In the third section we present and discuss the results of the factor analyses. The essay ends with conclusions and general discussion.

## Background

Estonia is considered to be a successful post-Soviet transformational country due to the speed of the marketization process in the first decade of the post-Soviet period.[3] Democratization in Estonia has occasioned critical comments (for example, Lagerspetz 1999; Rose & Munro 2003). The ethnic aspect of democracy – more precisely the Citizenship Law, which restricted citizenship to individuals who were citizens in June 1940 and their descendants, and established the requirements of the knowledge of Estonian and passing a citizenship examination for naturalization – is relatively central to the criticism. Many scholars who have explored post-Soviet Estonian nation-building (for example, Kolstø 2002; Kymlicka 2000; Lagerspetz 2001; Lauristin & Heidmets 2002; Pettai & Hallik 2002; Smith 2003, among many others) have also discussed the question of whether Russians might mobilize to protest. Most of them have remained relatively skeptical about the possibility of mobilization for different reasons: 'social' citizenship, the lack of leaders, the specificity of the political 'market', etc. Nevertheless, the question remains as to whether ethnic opposition will strengthen in the future, when the third generation of Russians becomes socially more active.

Today's situation of the ethnic majority and minority in Estonia, their perceptions and practices have a complicated historical background. The period of Soviet control (1944–1991) can be seen as imperial colonization from the point of view of ethnic Estonians. It was characterized by harsh repressions (executions and deportations) of the Estonian elite and farmers in the 1940s, forced industrialization, compulsory learning and use of the Russian language, the rewriting of history, and the 'cleansing' from culture of everything 'ideologically suspicious'. Personal memories of the 'good old Estonian time', the desire for Western welfare and consumption opportunities, and the preservation of the Estonian language became central ideas in the resistance to Soviet colonialism. Russians who settled in Estonia mostly in the course of coerced immigration by Soviet authorities had extraterritorial status and the right to use their own language; also, they had Russian-language institutions (for example schools) throughout the country (Goble 1995, p. 125). Thus, language became an attribute of power during the Soviet era.

The Singing Revolution in Estonia and the establishment of the legal framework and new institutions were based on the idea of restoration. One of its main implications was that the Estonian Republic should be restored on the basis of the continuity of its citizenry in 1940. Soviet citizenship lost legitimacy and most Russians who had settled in Estonia after 1940 had to choose whether to adopt Russian citizenship or to apply for Estonian citizenship through naturalization. At the same time, radical political and economic restructuring was taking place, which meant that former structures (enterprises, trade unions, etc.) and, to some extent, the common space of communication dissolved. A liberal thought pattern, with strong emphasis on individual choices, rights and obligations, dominated in the Estonian public sphere (Lauristin & Vihalemm 2009). In line with the same individualistic-liberal pathos, the state program *Integration in Estonian Society 2000–2007* (IF 2000) and media texts dealing with the problem of integration of Russians emphasized acquisition of the national language (Estonian) as the main prerequisite for integration. Russians and other ethnic minorities faced a double challenge of self-determination: in terms of post-socialist transition and the new Estonian nation-state.

Due to the above-mentioned reasons, inter-ethnic relations in Estonia were tense at the beginning of transition. During the second decade of transition, however, Russians' valuations of the development of Estonia in various spheres became more positive. Mass protests and the accompanying social depression evolved as late as in April 2007, when Estonia was relatively stable politically and economically.

Analysts have argued that the reasons for tensions between the third-generation immigrant youngsters and the host society are weaknesses in education and training, high unemployment, and objective and subjective social exclusion. Several studies indicate that the lower social position of immigrants is reproduced in subsequent generations via family socialization (Inman et al. 2007; Tsolidis 2001), as well as institutionally (immigrant neighborhoods in cities and separate schools) (Haddad & Balz 2006; 'On Integrating Immigrants in Germany' 2006; Rumbaut 1997). There are very few studies dealing with objective inequality between ethnic Estonians and other ethnicities (examples are Kasearu & Trumm 2008; Leping & Toomet 2007; Pavelson & Luuk 2002). Several studies, however, have covered the topic of subjective inequality and exclusion (for example LICHR 2006; Saar 2007). As noted above, the subjective feeling of exclusion is very high among Russians in Estonia.

A specific feature of the post-Soviet condition in Estonia is the weakness of civil society: there are relatively few active voluntary associations and they do not form a significant counterpart to party politics (Lagerspetz et al. 2002). Lagerspetz argues that the consolidation of democracy has not only meant the disappearance of non-democratic alternatives, but also of every alternative to the elite-run representative democracy. He concludes that the government's ability to pursue consequent reform policies is based on the fact that the demands of the 'losers of transition', that is, Russians and economically less well-situated groups, are not reflected in institutional politics (Lagerspetz 2001).

In addition to the features inherited from the Soviet past, the context of the formation of inter-ethnic relations in Estonia is shaped by global influences. The advance of English-based mass culture has spread explosively rather than step by step in Estonia since the re-establishment of independence. Estonia has moved rapidly into global communication networks and open media spheres. For example, 65% of the 6–74 year-old population of Estonia, including almost every 10–24 year-old, uses the Internet and 49% of households have home access to the Internet (TNS Emor 2007). The use of foreign TV production is also rather widespread: about two-thirds of the Estonian population has access to global TV channels via cable or satellite (Vihalemm 2007). The Estonian transition culture is also characterized by the fast penetration of consumer culture (Slater 1997) and its values: consumption opportunities are becoming more and more important in constructing identity and social success (Keller & Vihalemm 2005). Self-positioning in the hierarchy of 'winners and losers' of transition is highly correlated with evaluation of one's consumption possibilities (Lauristin 2004). Thus, the domination of liberal ideology is reinforced by consumerism and the rapid advance of new media technology in Estonia (see also Runnel et al. 2009).

We assume that people have specific cultural resources, formed during the Soviet time and the post-Soviet period, which help them to interpret social changes and develop strategies for coping with the situation. In this analysis, we do not aim to distinguish 'purely' ethnic, linguistic or political features in the majority–minority relations. Rather, we are aiming for a relatively generalized and comparable overview of the cultural resources possessed by three generations of the main ethnic groups.

## Theoretical and Methodological Considerations

Our assumption is that people develop a system of values, beliefs and allegiances – symbolic cultural resources – which help them to interpret social changes and form their political preferences and viewpoints on questions of public policy. To frame our assumptions theoretically, we use the concepts of 'transition culture' and 'cultural templates' developed by Kennedy (2002) and Sztompka (2004). Kennedy uses the term 'transition culture' to signify the framework of values, beliefs, symbols and narratives through which actors interpret the process of transformation of political and economic systems and undertake actions in the new circumstances. Sztompka applies the term 'cultural templates', by which he means, similarly to Kennedy, collectively shared symbolic mental resources used by members of the society for filtering and interpreting the facts of change. Such symbolic resources are, nonetheless, relatively loosely defined and operationalized by Kennedy and Sztompka. In our analysis, we have narrowed down the concept of 'cultural templates' to denote the structures of values and self-identification which we assume to be related to certain interpretations and evaluations of social changes (see also Kalmus & Vihalemm 2006; Vihalemm & Kalmus 2008).

Our methodological assumption is that broad categories of self-identification and value orientations represent one part of the pool of ambiguous 'cultural templates'. The importance of values among cultural aspects of transition is explicit in the conceptions of Kennedy and Sztompka, as well as of many other theorists. Identities, also, are important tools for cognitive processing of cultural changes at the level of the individual. In times of transformation, collective identities become mass vehicles for a popular understanding of events: ideologies and symbols 'circulating' in the public sphere are embedded in identities (Castells 1997). According to Hall, identities are the names we give to the different ways we are positioned and position ourselves within the narratives of the past (Hall 1990). Therefore we have used mental structures encompassing values and identities in our analysis. By the term 'mental structure' we refer to relations and patterns of co-variation between values and identities, which are not rigid or inherently characteristic of social groups. Instead, we assume that such structures are flexible and change over time, depending on the social and cultural context.

We also proceed from the argument developed by Sztompka (2004) and Vogt (2004) that the cultural condition of post-Soviet transitional societies is characterized by the parallel existence of symbols, values and identities brought along by 'new' (Western) cultural flows, and 'old' (Soviet) traditions, values and identities. Members of the society who are faced with the challenge of coping with the social, economic and political changes may refer both to the 'old' and 'new' cultural pools. Moreover, both Vogt and Sztompka have noted that different social groups may use different symbols and narratives. Sztompka, in particular, has emphasized the differences between generations in transition culture. He argues that the bearers of cultural legacies are generations that were socialized and habituated in a particular Socialist cultural milieu. The young generation starting careers today has been basically insulated from the cultural impact of the communist system. 'They are the children of a new epoch, the carriers of a new culture inoculated against post communist trauma' (Sztompka 2004, p. 193).

In a similar vein, Czech sociologist Marada (2004) argues that people filter a shared experience of historical periods or events through their respective socio-economic classes, gender orientations, geographical locations, etc. Most importantly, however, historical events have a different socializing impact on different age cohorts. In relying on Mannheim's ([1928] 1952) conception of the socially constructed nature of generations, Marada suggests that a generation, in the sense of shared generational identity and self-consciousness, is formed 'when a formative historical experience coincides with a formative period of people's lives' (2004, p. 153).

Based on these considerations, we use age groups as the second socio-demographic variable in our analysis.

## Data

Our analysis is based on data from two representative population surveys. In Estonia, the survey *Me. The World. The Media* (*Mina. Maailm. Meedia*) was carried out in November 2005. The survey covered the Estonian population aged 15–74 with a total sample size of 1,475. A proportional model of the general population (by areas and urban/rural division) and multi-step probability random sampling was used. In addition, a quota was used to include a proportional number of ethnic Estonians and Estonian Russians in the sample. A self-administered questionnaire, together with a follow-up interview, was used.

Latvian data derive from the survey *Social Identity: Latvia*, carried out by the Baltic Institute of Social Sciences. This survey consisted of 1,005 face-to-face interviews conducted in spring 2006 among Latvian inhabitants aged 15–75. The sampling method was similar to the one used in Estonia.

By using aggregated survey data, we set for ourselves no ambitions to analyze generations in the Mannheimian sense of self-consciousness and self-reflection. Strictly speaking, we operated with three age groups: the youngest group aged 15–29 (born in 1976–1990), whose formative years, i.e. adolescence and early adulthood, coincided mostly or entirely with the period of transition; the middle group aged 30–49 (born in 1956–1975), who were either students or starting their working careers at the beginning of the transition; and the oldest group aged 50–75 (born in 1930–1955), who had already established their careers at the beginning of the transition.

## Method

Our analysis is based on the assumption that, on the individual level, one's social identities form an organic structure. For instance, geo-political allegiances are formed in inter-relationship with other social identities. We understand social identity in general as a process of systematic establishment and signification between individuals and/or collectives, distinguishing them in their social relations with other individuals and/or collectives (Jenkins 1996). We have operationalized the concept of identity by relying on the definition proposed by the social psychologist Tajfel: identity is a part of an individual's self-conception which derives from knowledge about one's belonging in social groups, together with the value and emotional meaning ascribed to the groups (Tajfel 1981). This definition has, in addition to our research, fed several empirical studies on the political and cultural identity of minority groups.

In our surveys, identity was measured by the question: 'Which groups do you feel a certain belonging to, so that you could say "we" about them and yourself?' The multi-variable question included different categories (see Appendices), from which a respondent could choose as many as he or she wanted to.

In order to maintain the possibility of comparative analysis in the diachronic perspective, we used the 25 value indicators (Rokeach's system of measurement) employed already in the Balticom value surveys of 1991–1995 [see Lauristin and Vihalemm (1997) and the Appendices for the list of indicators]. The values were measured on a five-point scale (from 'not important at all' to 'very important'). In following Rokeach (1973), we looked at single value concepts (words and expressions denoting values) as relatively independent items, which are not built into definite hierarchies, but can be related to each other in various dimensions or clusters. For the purpose of generalizing and interpreting our data, we use Schwartz's (1990) theory of motivational types and dimensions of values, in particular its central assumption according to which values with similar meanings are highly inter-correlated (Schwartz & Sagiv 1995).

We are aware that the survey method we used has several limitations. Primarily, we were able to use only a standardized list of indicators of self-identification and values; respondents, however, lacked the ability to explain how they interpreted those standard categories. We tried to compensate for this by our method of analysis. We used factor analysis (the principal components method with Varimax rotation) to reduce 25 single value concepts and 25 categories of self-identification to generalized mental structures, consisting of items with similar meanings. Factors, in binding together single indicators according to the logic of answering, represented meta-level thought patterns underlying respondents' self-categorization and values. Moreover, resulting factor scores could be used as indicators of the internalization of such meta-level thought patterns by different social groups.

To be able to analyze and compare different factor solutions according to their natural internal structure, we used the criterion of eigenvalues over one, not any fixed number of factors, in extraction.

In order to reveal mental structures encompassing both patterns of self-identification and value orientations, we carried out secondary factor analysis, i.e. we used the factor scores resulting from the factor analyses of categories of self-identification and value indicators as new variables for factor analysis. This method made it possible to determine which patterns of self-identification were related to which value orientations. Again, we used the criterion of eigenvalues over one to determine the number of factors. The results of the primary and secondary factor analyses are presented in the Appendices.

In this essay, we focus on the joint factors of values and identities. We do not aim to find out the culture-specificity in the structure of these mental phenomena: we realize that factor structures depend on the homogeneity of samples, the distribution of variables included in factor analysis, the method of rotation, etc. Rather, we use the joint factors as meso-level analytical tools for comparing the scope of inter-ethnic and inter-generational differences in internalization of certain values and identities in the two countries.

In interpreting and labeling the factors, we relied on the theories of value types and dimensions by Schwartz (1990) and Inglehart (1997), and the theories of individualization (structure-centredness *vs.* individual-centeredness). Also, we identified similar and comparable elements in the factor structures of the two countries and used the same concepts and phrases to indicate similarity (for example Global Orientation and Emancipation in Estonia, and Global Orientation and Challenge in Latvia). We used the word 're-creation' in the label of the joint factor when the value orientation functioned to maintain the identity component or when the identity factor supported the value orientation. In the case of negative factor loadings of value or identity components, we used either antonymous meanings in the labels of joint factors (for example, 'Salvation' was labeled as 'Secularism') or used the phrase 'resistance to' (when no unambiguous antonyms existed). It is important to note that the factor labels are tools for analysis, not essential terms.

## Results

*Mental structures in Estonia*

In the Estonian sample, the secondary factor analysis brought out five joint mental structures (see Appendix 1 for the details of identity and value components). Figures 1 and 2 display the levels of internalization of the joint mental structures among ethnic Estonians and Estonian Russians, and three generations of the two ethnic groups, respectively.

The first factor, *Spiritual Harmony and Community Solidarity*, has a collectivist basis: local community identity is linked with universalistic values (for example *equality*, *world of peace*, etc.). The prominent position of *salvation* gives spiritual light to this value and identity structure. Identification with high social position is negatively correlated with this factor. Thus, solidarity with community members and pursuit of spiritual harmony are opposed to upward mobility in this thought pattern. Referring to Sztompka (2004), this value and identity structure belongs to 'old' cultural templates, representing the mixed legacy of a religious world-view and Soviet ideology. According to several authors, the ethics of Russian Orthodoxy and Soviet ideology were actually similar, both characterized by ideals of community, unanimity and rejection of economic competition (see, for example, Chaplin 2004). We have shown elsewhere (Vihalemm & Kalmus 2008) that this mental structure is correlated with a negative valuation of social changes, a positive attitude towards the Soviet era

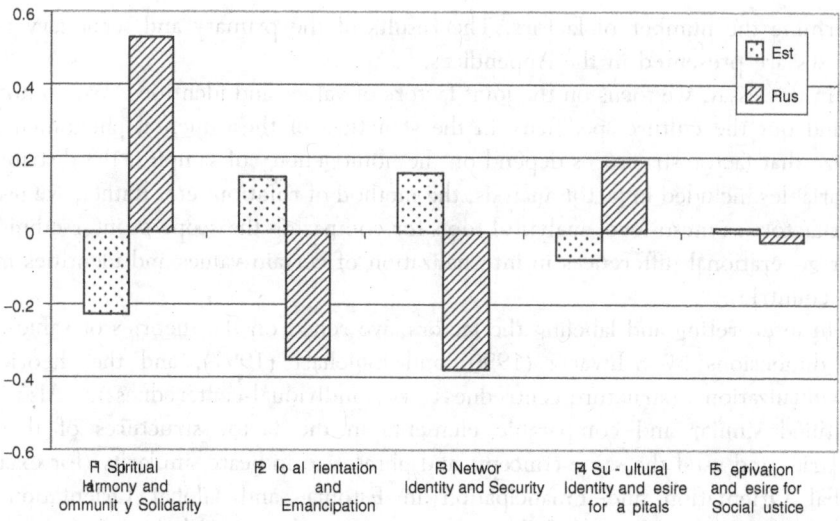

**FIGURE 1** Mental structures among ethnic Estonians and Estonian Russians (mean factor scores).

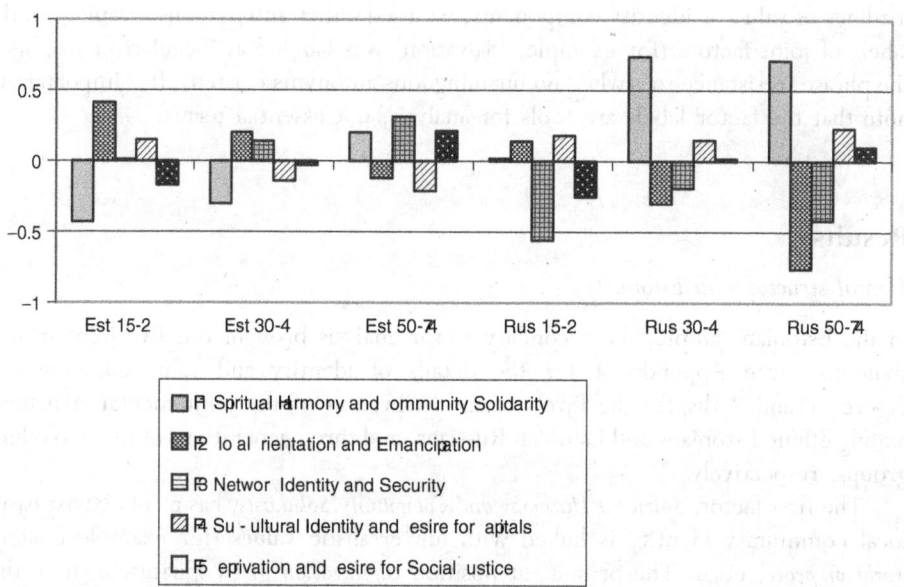

**FIGURE 2** Mental structures by age groups among ethnic Estonians and Estonian Russians (mean factor scores).

and a cognitive bond with the former Soviet Union. Thus, we may see this thought pattern as a reaction to the transition or as a certain mental encystation.

The mean factor score of this structure is significantly higher among Russian respondents (see Figure 1). This, in general, corresponds to more widespread religiosity among the Russian community: 33% of Russians *vs.* 15% of Estonians consider themselves religious (DJC 2005). Figure 2 shows that the thought pattern is especially characteristic of middle-aged and elderly Russians and – though to a significantly lesser degree – of the oldest age group of Estonians. Among the youngest and middle-aged Estonians, as well as the youngest Russians, this mental structure is much less common. Lõhmus and her colleagues also noted a trend towards spiritual values and aesthetic cultural orientation among Estonian Russians, especially among those with higher education, who might feel deprived of their previous position in the society (Lõhmus et al. 2009).

Nevertheless, the Orthodox Soviet world-view probably plays a crucial role in the historical–cultural memory of a large number of Estonian Russians. According to this, they may consider the transition in Estonia and its legitimizing ideologies unacceptable.

In this context, it is important to note that the relocation of the Bronze Soldier and the re-burial of the remains of Russian soldiers obviously affected Russians' religious and community values. In the ethics of Russian Orthodoxy, reburial is considered sacrilegious. Such an act is justified only under very exceptional circumstances (for example, the reburial of the Czar's family). The Estonian government did not take this into account in communicating the plan of the relocation of the monument and the reburial of the remains. The act also affected Russians' feelings of respect towards their relatives or compatriots who fought in World War II. For a number of people, those events represented a sense of imagined community, illustrated by an excerpt from a focus group interview: 'I never used to take flowers [to the Bronze Soldier] on May 9, but this time I went' (CCCS 2007).

In the second factor, labeled as *Global Orientation and Emancipation*, high valuation of personality development, close interpersonal relationships and hedonism were accompanied by supra-national and civic self-identification. This thought pattern probably represents emancipation from ethno-national allegiances and internalization of trans-national identity based on EU citizenship. This mental structure is significantly more widespread among ethnic Estonians (see Figure 1). It seems that the ethnic majority has internalized transnational identities more quickly. For Estonian Russians, the concept of being a European or Northern European, for instance, is vague (Vihalemm 2005).

In speaking about different generations, the structure of Global Orientation and Emancipation is significantly more widespread among the youngest and middle-aged Estonians, as well as among the youngest age group of Russians (see Figure 2). Qualitative studies conducted among young people in Estonia indicate that being European is related to better opportunities for self-realization without any hesitations and fears about the availability and achievability of these prospects. A quotation from a focus group illustrates this: 'Because we are in the EU now, there are more opportunities for all. All doors are open' (IRN 2006). We may say that this is one of the 'new' cultural templates formed alongside the geo-cultural opening-up of Estonia to the West. Elderly Estonians and Russians, as well as middle-aged Russians, have not internalized this cultural template.

The third factor, labeled as *Network Identity and Security*, is comprised of values that support physical and social security (for example, *health, clean environment, family security* and *national security*) and self-identification with a close network of family and friends. It is noteworthy that identification with one's own ethnic group also belongs to this thought pattern. Thus, ethnic belonging is strongly embedded in social networks.

The factor of *Network Identity and Security* differentiates Estonians and Russians most clearly: in general, as well as in all three age groups taken separately, this pattern is less common among Russians compared with Estonians (see Figures 1 and 2). Lower factor scores of this thought pattern are probably due to a drastic change in the social status of the Russian minority after the collapse of the Soviet Union. Studies indicate that Estonian Russians have, in general, less social capital than ethnic Estonians (Pruulmann-Vengerfeldt 2004).

In the Soviet time, Russians' social networks were often centered on formal organizations (for example, trade unions and work collectives). Those networks disappeared along with the dissolution or reorganization of Soviet enterprises. Among ethnic Estonians, informal social networks were more important in the Soviet time. According to an unofficial account, a network of friends, formed in student work brigades in the 1980s, stood behind many privatization transactions in Estonia at the beginning of the transition. Thus, Estonians could employ their social capital to adapt to transitional changes less painfully. Russians, on the contrary, may consider their social capital and network identity 'unusable' in today's Estonia and feel a lack of security. Other studies have also revealed that parents of children from the ethnic minority claim that they feel an inability to apply their own experience in the changed social environment in transmitting in-group values (Inman *et al.* 2007).

The common belief among Russians that ethnicity plays a decisive role in getting ahead in Estonian society is an explanation given to the situation, but this may also act as a barrier which prevents one from looking for new relationships and networks. For example, pupils of schools with Russian as the language of instruction participate less in various youth and other organizations compared with their peers from Estonian schools [the only exception is computer clubs and student governments (Toots *et al.* 2006, p. 72)].

The fact that Russians pay less attention to the reproduction of personalized social capital and networks may make them more receptive to a communitarian world-view, and vice versa. As shown above, the cultural template of Spiritual Harmony and Community Solidarity is more wide-spread among Estonian Russians than among Estonians. Other data support this thesis: for instance, 60% of Russian pupils (compared with 40% of Estonian pupils) engage in voluntary work, and 40% (compared with 30% of Estonian pupils) are ready to collect money for charity (Toots *et al.* 2006).

In the fourth factor, *Sub-Cultural Identity and Desire for Capitals*, self-identification on the basis of similar tastes, lifestyles, world-views etc. is connected with materialistic and power-related values (e.g. *wealth, comfortable life* and *power*). We assume that this value and identity structure has newly emerged from the opportunities and pleasures of identity construction offered by the fast-developing consumer culture and valuation of instrumental means necessary to afford it.

Among ethnic Estonians, this thought pattern is characteristic only of the youngest age group. Among the ethnic minority, however, this value and identity structure has a significantly higher factor score, being common to all three age groups of Russians (see Figures 1 and 2). It is possible that popular and consumer culture offered Estonian Russians a socio-culturally positive or neutral opportunity of self-identification at the time of the restoration of the Estonian Republic and social restructuring; therefore, signs of consumer culture and the means necessary to afford them are highly valued. Studies indicate that a consumerist orientation (measured by the index of consumerism comprised of indicators of different consumption practices and preferences) is significantly stronger among Estonian Russians than among Estonians (Kalmus et al. 2009); also, expensive brand-name clothes and accessories are relatively important in young people's self-representation (Keller & Kalmus forthcoming). The fact that young people who protested against the relocation of the Bronze Soldier in Tallinn mainly looted shops selling expensive brand-name goods can be interpreted as an extreme expression of this thought pattern.

In the fifth factor, *Deprivation and Desire for Social Justice*, the high valuation of *justice, wisdom* and *social recognition* is connected with the self-identification with people in low social and economic positions. This is the only mental structure which does not differentiate ethnic Estonians from Estonian Russians (see Figure 1). This thought pattern is significantly more characteristic of the older generation of both the ethnic majority and minority (Figure 2). We may say that it represents a nostalgic cultural format. The firm location of *justice* in this mental structure is in line with Vogt's idea of the utopian way of thinking characteristic of the Socialist belief system, which now may have changed into a mixture of nostalgia for Soviet-type egalitarianism and a need for recognition. Our interpretation of the thought pattern harmonizes with the fact that the index of the negative valuation of the Soviet time is significantly lower among 50–74 year-old respondents (DJC 2005).

*Mental structures in Latvia*

In the Latvian sample, five joint mental structures emerged in the secondary factor analysis (see Appendix 2 for the details of identity and value components). Figures 3 and 4 display the levels of internalization of the joint mental structures among

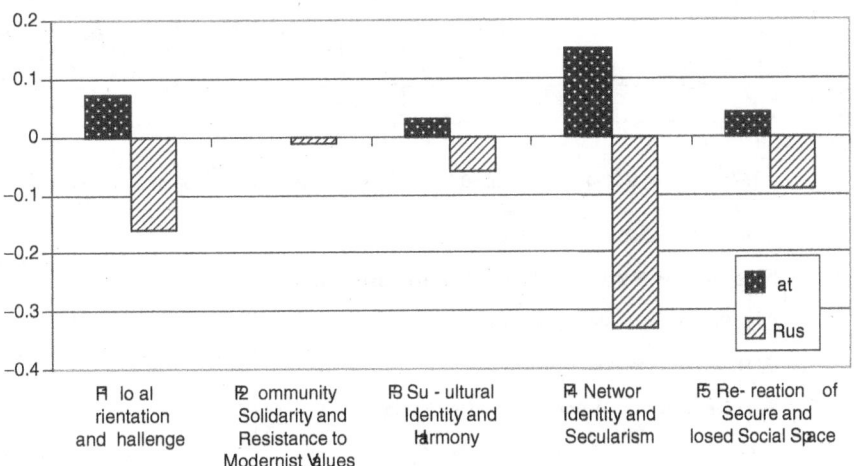

**FIGURE 3** Mental structures among Latvians and Latvian Russians (mean factor scores).

Latvians and Latvian Russians, and three generations of the two ethnic groups, respectively.

A key component of the first joint factor, *Global Orientation and Challenge*, is supra-national identity linked structurally with identification with successful people. The connection between a European or global orientation and the perception of social success can be illustrated by an excerpt from focus group interviews with Latvian Russians: 'To me, a European is someone who is normal and rich... well, not quite rich, but a normal person who makes a good living. There aren't many such people in Latvia' (Zepa 2006).

This identity structure correlates negatively with the values of physical security (*health* and *clean environment*), which means that those values are less important for people with a strong supra-national self-identification. Thus, unlike in Estonia, global orientation has elitist and risk-taking connotations in Latvia.

This thought pattern is significantly more widespread among ethnic Latvians than among Latvian Russians (Figure 3). Thus, both in Latvia and Estonia, the ethnic majority has more quickly adapted to the geo-cultural opening-up of the society and the opportunities for trans-national self-realization and self-identification that have emerged after joining the EU. Though trans-national identity could offer Russians a positive basis for self-identification (see, for example, Smith 1998), this strategy seems to be less common among the ethnic minority than among the majority. One of the reasons for this may be the fact that Estonian or Latvian citizens obtained EU citizenship automatically; however, only 52% of Estonian Russians and 56% of Latvian Russians are citizens of their respective countries (Lauristin 2008; MFARL 2007). Moreover, even Russians with EU citizenship have stated in focus group studies that they do not consider Estonia or Latvia as European countries in terms of the living

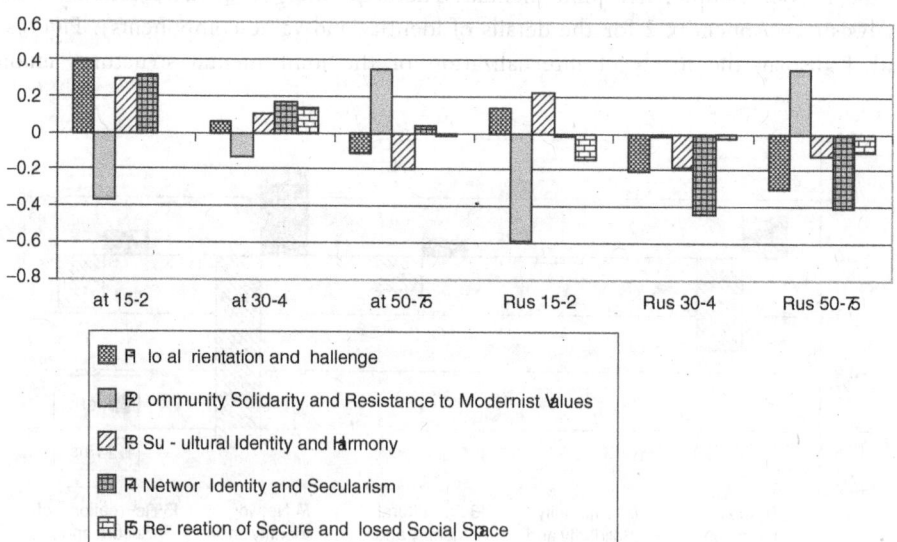

**FIGURE 4** Mental structures by age groups among Latvians and Latvian Russians (mean factor scores).

standard and attitudes towards ethnic minorities (Zepa 2006). Also, Russians tend to have somewhat fewer personal contacts with Western, especially Nordic, countries (for example, traveling and having relatives and friends in those countries), though the differences are diminishing (Vihalemm 2007).

The factor has significantly higher scores among the youngest age group of both ethnic Latvians and Latvian Russians. Among older age groups, the thought pattern is less common. While middle-aged Latvians are more similar to the youngest people, the middle age group of Russians is closer to the oldest respondents in respect to this factor (Figure 4).

In the second factor, *Community Solidarity and Resistance to Modernist Values*, local and civic identity is connected with lower valuation of materialist and modernist values, such as *wealth, comfortable life, technical development*, etc. Unlike in Estonia, local community identity in Latvia has no religious connotation. However, local identity in both countries is related to a more traditional world-view (spirituality in Estonia and the lesser importance of modernist values in Latvia). This thought pattern does not differentiate the ethnic minority from the majority (Figure 3). The factor has the highest scores among the oldest age group and the lowest scores among young people of both the minority and the majority (Figure 4). Thus, this mental structure represents a universal 'old' cultural template, differentiating generations on a statistically significant level regardless of ethnicity.

The third factor, *Sub-Cultural Identity and Harmony*, is comprised of sub-cultural identity and values supporting personal development and harmonious relationships between people (for example, *justice, honesty, true friendship, self-realization* and *wisdom*). This factor has a somewhat higher mean value among ethnic Latvians (Figure 3); the difference is not, however, statistically significant. Contrary to the second factor, this mental structure represents a 'new' cultural template, having significantly higher scores among the youngest age groups of both Latvians and Russians, and lower scores among the oldest people of both ethnic groups. Similarly to Factor 1, middle-aged Latvians are more similar to young people of their ethnicity while middle-aged Russians show a greater similarity to the generation of their parents (Figure 4).

The central component of the fourth factor, *Network Identity and Secularism*, is network identity connected with lower valuation of *salvation*. This mental structure differentiates the ethnic minority from the majority on a statistically significant level (Figure 3). Similarly to Russians in Estonia, Latvian Russians do not identify with close social networks as strongly as does the titular group. Statistically significant differences exist also between the three age groups of both the majority and the minority: the thought pattern is more characteristic of younger respondents (Figure 4). Among ethnic Latvians, inter-generational differentiation with regard to this 'new' cultural template has occurred relatively smoothly, while a harsh disruption in cultural reproduction has taken place between the youngest generation of Latvian Russians and their parents and grandparents.

The fifth joint factor, *Re-Creation of Secure and Closed Social Space*, involves two value factors and an identity component. One of the value factors represents seeking security and harmony (for example, *national security, world at peace* and *inner harmony*); another refers to a hedonistic orientation and intimate relationships (for example, *happiness, mature love* and *family security*). The identity component, due to its negative factor loading, means rejection of various 'others': wealthy as well as poor and unfortunate people, but also other ethnic groups. According to the logic of this thought pattern, such 'extreme others' would harm the security and harmony of one's social world. The factor has a somewhat higher mean value among Latvians, especially in the middle age group of the majority, and lower mean values among all three generations of Latvian Russians (Figures 3 and 4). The difference between the majority and the minority is statistically significant only on the level $p = 0.07$. Taken together with the difference in Network Identity and Secularism, this pattern, however, indicates that ethnic Latvians are somewhat more inclined to build a corporate social space closed to various 'others'.

## Conclusions and Discussion

On the most general level, we may conclude that the ethnic majority and minority in both countries differ in the degree to which they employ available cultural resources in response to macro-level social challenges. We can point out two main distinctions between ethnic Estonians/Latvians and the Russian minority.

Firstly, Russians in Estonia and Latvia show a relatively low score (compared with the titular groups) on the thought pattern, which favors reproduction of network identity and social capital. We may hypothesize that the post-Soviet transition and nation-building in Estonia and Latvia have diminished the opportunities for the reproduction of social capital among the ethnic minority, and that this has already become rooted in Russians' thought patterns: social capital is less valued, which, in turn, hinders its reproduction. Among the ethnic majority, on the contrary, the transition process may have strengthened a corporatist world-view. The radical reforms, which demolished old economic and political structures, created a situation where personal connections (such as friends from school) became essential. We have shown elsewhere that positive valuation of economic and political changes strongly correlates with the thought pattern fostering reproduction of social capital (Vihalemm & Kalmus 2008).

Secondly, global orientation is more represented among the titular groups in both countries. In Estonia, the discourse of 'return to Europe' was widely used at the beginning of the transition but, being intertwined with the discourse of national freedom (Feldman 2000; Lagerspetz 1999), it did not appeal to Russians. Mediated and immediate contacts may have also played an important role in forming the different levels of global orientation among the ethnic majority and minority. Though Internet penetration is relatively high both in Estonia and Latvia, the titular group in Estonia is more active in using it (DJC 2005; Vengerfeldt & Runnel 2004). Also, Estonians have traveled abroad more frequently than Russians (DJC 2005; P. Vihalemm 2007). The participation of Estonian schools in international pupils' exchange programs is also higher compared with schools with Russian as the language of instruction (Toots et al. 2006, p. 72).

Our second general conclusion is that the transition has polarized both ethnolinguistic communities in Estonia and Latvia; the break points on the generational time-lines are, however, located differently. The patterns of cultural continuity and disruption in Estonia and Latvia are similar to each other. Both in Estonia and Latvia, the youngest and the middle age groups of the ethnic majority have relatively similar thought patterns, while the oldest age group shows plainly different orientations. Among the ethnic minority, the oldest and middle-aged people tend to have thought patterns in common, while the youngest Russians have become clearly different from their parents and grandparents.

Among the youngest generation, 'new' cultural templates (*Global Orientation and Emancipation*, and *Sub-Cultural Identity and Desire for Capitals* in Estonia, and *Global Orientation and Challenge*, and *Sub-Cultural Identity and Harmony* in Latvia) are common to both ethno-linguistic groups. Russian youngsters in both countries, however, display lower scores on the thought pattern characteristic of Network Identity.

Several factors need to be taken into account to explain these phenomena. The youngest generation of both ethnic groups in Estonia and Latvia has been brought up under totally new societal conditions (a liberal ideology, an emerging consumer culture, an openness to the West, etc.). We suggest that these aspects of the environment of socialization have facilitated the internalization of 'new' cultural templates by the youngest age group and contributed to the homogenization of the thought patterns of the ethnic majority and minority youth in Estonia and Latvia. Along with this, a more drastic cultural disruption has taken place between the youngest Russians and their parents. Thus, society, especially globalizing popular and consumer culture, may have become more important as a socializing agent than family with regard to internalization of value and identity structures. This provides an additional explanation for the fact that Russian youngsters display lower scores on the thought pattern characteristic of Network Identity. As suggested above, Russians may consider their social capital 'unusable' in today's society. In addition, due to a disruption in primary socialization, Russian youth may feel a weaker sense of belonging to their proximate social networks (family, relatives, own ethnic group, etc.).

The middle age group of ethnic Estonians and Latvians has adapted very well to transitional changes and the 'new' culture. Based on longitudinal research in Estonia, a model of the generation of 'winners' (those who today are younger than 45) has been proposed (Titma 1999). At the beginning of the transition, this generation had graduated from universities or vocational schools and was in a good situation to take over emerging elite positions in economics and politics. Thus, the middle age group of ethnic Estonians and Latvians were able to develop a more competitive relationship with the previous generation, and adopted, similarly to the youngest generation, liberal meritocratic principles. Moreover, for a large part of the middle generation of ethnic Estonians and Latvians, their grandparents' narratives about the first period of independence (1918–1940) as the 'good old days' served as a powerful legitimizing tool for the transformation to a market economy and the 'return to the West'.

The middle age group of Russians in Estonia and Latvia lacked such a discourse of restoration. In Russia, Sovietization began one generation earlier, in the 1920s. The oldest age group of Russians, most of whom immigrated to Estonia or Latvia in the 1950s or 1960s, was already the second generation socialized into the Soviet culture. Thus, they were probably more inclined to reproduce the Soviet culture in the thought patterns of their children, the middle age group of Russians. Moreover, the double trauma from which the Russian community suffered has probably prevented them from going along with the 'new' culture as smoothly as did the middle generation of the ethnic majority.

Two of our findings have implications for future social scenarios and policies. Firstly, we may conclude that shared aspects of the environment of socialization, particularly the emerging consumer culture and openness to the West, have contributed to the homogenization of the mental structures of the ethnic majority and minority youth. The resulting cultural disruption between the young generation of Russians and their parents may either lead to sporadic public disputes or succumb to a pragmatic search for individual coping strategies (such as emigration). Also, on the basis of new cultural templates, a certain protest-identity, which uses signs and artifacts of global popular or consumer culture, may form. Research in other countries has revealed that specific sub-cultural items, such as pop songs, may be created in order to positively distinguish one's identity *vis-à-vis* the 'mainstream' society (Lee 2004; Sernhede 2006).

Secondly, we can state that the cultural templates, which favor reproduction of social capital and upward mobility, are far less widespread among the ethnic minority in Estonia and Latvia. Thus, reproduction of social deprivation among members of the minority group is already embedded in the process of cultural transmission. One possibility for Russians to become more 'regarded' might be through civic and community participation and 'non-personal' networks. However, civil society is weak in today's Estonia, as we discussed above (cf. Lagerspetz 2001). Thus, the potential for local and civic participation among the young generation of Russians may not be realized, or it may lead to further segregation rather than integration. Research carried out among ethnic minorities in Paris, France, concludes: 'rather than a patchwork of participative local democracy, the local minority associations can often be half-hearted antidotes to social disenfranchisement and, sometimes, actual mechanisms which maintain exclusion' (Kiwan 2005, p. 466). We suggest that the most critical aims of the new integration strategy should be working out the means for supporting the enhancement of social capital among the minority group, encouraging local and civic participation and voluntary associations among them, and preparing government officials to deal with them.

## Acknowledgements

The preparation of this article was supported by grants from the Estonian Ministry of Education and Science (0181774s01 and 0180017s07) and from the Estonian Science Foundation (5845 and 6968).

## Notes

1   Our analysis covers not only people with Russian ethnic or linguistic origin but also Ukrainians, Belorussians and other ethnicities. In Estonia there are about 406,700 people (30% of the population) whose mother tongue is Russian, among them about 351,200 are ethnic Russians (ESA 2001). In our study, ethnic groups were determined on the basis of language rather than ethnicity, because the number of non-ethnic Russians in the sample was too small for a separate analysis.

According to the results of previous empirical studies, however, it was not practicable to leave them out of the analysis. Immigrants to Estonia had experienced the Soviet civic assimilation several generations ago and, therefore, about one half of the Ukrainians and Belorussians in Estonia consider the Russian language their mother tongue. A significant part of the legislation of the Republic of Estonia is exclusionary in terms of language, not ethnicity, which brings into focus linguistic distinctiveness as a possible basis for collective identity. Indeed, integration monitoring and other studies have shown that, in Estonia, language is an important factor for interpreting minority–majority relationships and collective self-designations. Thus, in the context of this study it was optimal to use a sample representing the whole community of Russian-speakers in Estonia. We refer to the group as 'Russians' for the sake of brevity.

2   Relatively similar, language-centered views on inter-ethnic integration also predominated in Latvia. Ethnic problems became more significant in 2003 and 2004, when mass protests developed against education reform, according to which at least 60% of classes had to be taught in Latvian in grades 10–12 in public schools.

3   By 2008, economic growth in Estonia had slowed and, according to the evaluation of the World Bank, the reforms to improve the economic environment had stopped (*Postimees 2008*).

# References

Alexander, J. C., Eyerman, R., Giesen, B., Smelser, N. J. & Sztompka, P. (eds) (2004) *Cultural Trauma and Collective Identity* (Berkeley, CA, University of California Press).

Asari, E.-M. (2007) *Integration Strategy 2008–2013* (Tallinn, Office of the Minister for Population and Ethnic Affairs), available at: http://www.rahvastikuminister.ee/?id=10442, accessed 6 April 2008.

Castells, M. (1997) *The Information Age: Economy, Society, and Culture. The Power of Identity* (Oxford, Blackwell Publishers).

CCCS (2007) *The Bronze Soldier, The Media and Memory: Results of Focus Groups*, Working Paper (Tartu, The Center of Culture and Communication Studies of University of Tartu).

Chaplin, V. (2004) 'Orthodoxy and the Societal Ideal', in Marsh, C. (ed.) (2004).

DJC (2005) *Me. The World. The Media:* Survey database (Tartu, Department of Journalism and Communication, University of Tartu, The Research Center Faktum).

ESA (2001) *2000 Population and Housing Census: Citizenship, Nationality, Mother Tongue and Command of Foreign Languages* (Tallinn, Statistical Office of Estonia), available at: http://www.stat.ee/files/eva2003/RV200102.pdf, accessed 18 April 2008.

Feldman, G. (2000) 'Shifting the Perspective on Identity Discourse in Estonia', *Journal of Baltic Studies*, 31, 4.

Goble, P. (1995) 'Three Faces of Nationalism in the Former Soviet Union', in Kupchan, C. A. (ed.) (1995).

Haddad, Y. Y. & Balz, M. (2006) 'The October Riots in France: A Failed Immigration Policy or the Empire Strikes Back?', *International Migration*, 44, 2.

Hall, S. (1990) 'Cultural Identity and Diaspora', in Rutherford, J. (ed.) (1990).

Hallik, K. (2006) 'Multiple Citizenship and Self-Determination in Estonian Society', in LICHR (2006).

Heidmets, M. (ed.) (2008) *Estonian Human Development Report 2007* (Tallinn, Estonian Cooperation Assembly).

IF (2000) *Integration in Estonian Society 2000–2007* (Tallinn, Integration Foundation), available at: http://www.riik.ee/saks/ikomisjon/programm.htm, accessed 16 April 2008.

Inglehart, R. (1997) *Modernization and Postmodernization: Cultural, Economic, and Political Change in 43 Societies* (Princeton, NJ, Princeton University Press).

Inman, A. G., Howard, E. E. & Beaumont, R. L. (2007) 'Cultural Transmission: Influence of Contextual Factors in Asian Indian Immigrant Parents' Experiences', *Journal of Counseling Psychology*, 54, 1.

IRN (2006) *The Political Activity and Usage of Free Time among Youth in Tallinn*. Results of a qualitative study presented at the meeting of inter-universities Identity Research Network (Tallinn, Tallinn University).

Jenkins, R. (1996) *Social Identity* (Routledge, London).

Kalmus, V., Keller, M. & Kiisel, M. (2009) 'Emerging Consumer Types in Transition Culture: Consumption Patterns of Generational and Ethnic Groups in Estonia', *Journal of Baltic Studies*, 40, 1.

Kalmus, V., Lauristin, M. & Pruulmann-Vengerfeldt, P. (eds) (2004) *Eesti elavik 21. sajandi algul: Ülevaade uurimuse Mina. Maailm. Meedia tulemustest* [*Estonian Life-World at the Beginning of the 21st Century: Report of the Survey Me. The World. The Media*] (Tartu, Tartu University Press).

Kalmus, V. & Vihalemm, T. (2006) 'Distinct Mental Structures in Transitional Culture: An Empirical Analysis of Values and Identities in Estonia and Sweden', *Journal of Baltic Studies*, 37, 1.

Kasearu, K. & Trumm, A. (2008) 'The Socio-Economic Situation of Non-Estonians', in Heidmets, M. (ed.) (2008).

Keller, M. & Kalmus, V. (forthcoming) 'Between Consumerism and Protectionism: Attitudes towards Children, Consumption and the Media in Estonia', *Childhood: A Journal of Global Child Research*.

Keller, M. & Vihalemm, T. (2005) 'Coping with Consumer Culture: Elderly Urban Consumers in Post-Soviet Estonia', *Trames*, 9, 1.

Kennedy, M. D. (2002) *Cultural Formations of Post-Communism: Emancipation, Transition, Nation, and War* (Minneapolis & London, University of Minnesota Press).

Kiwan, N. (2005) 'Managing Marginalization: Young French–North Africans and Local Associations', *Modern & Contemporary France*, 13, 4.

Kolstø, P. (2002) *National Integration and Violent Conflict in Post-Soviet Societies: The Cases of Estonia and Moldova* (Lanham, Rowman & Littlefield Inc.).

Korts, K. (2009) 'Inter-Ethnic Attitudes of Ethnic Estonians and Russians', *Journal of Baltic Studies*, 40, 1.

Kupchan, C. A. (ed.) (1995) *Nationalism and Nationalities in the New Europe* (Ithaca, Cornell University Press).

Kymlicka, W. (2000) 'Eesti integratsioonipoliitika võrdlevas perspektiivis' ['Estonian Politics of Integration in Comparative Perspective'], in Laius, A., Proos, I. & Pettai, I. (eds) (2000).

Lagerspetz, M. (1999) 'Postsocialism as a Return: Notes on a Discursive Strategy', *East European Politics and Societies*, 13, 2.

Lagerspetz, M. (2001) 'Consolidation as Hegemonization: The Case of Estonia', *Journal of Baltic Studies*, 32, 4.

Lagerspetz, M., Rikmann, E. & Ruutsoo, R. (2002) 'The Structure and Resources of NGOs in Estonia', *Voluntas: International Journal of Voluntary and Nonprofit Organizations*, 13, 1.

Laius, A., Proos, I. & Pettai, I. (eds) (2000) *Integratsioonimaastik – ükskõiksusest koosmeeleni* [*Integration Landscape: From Indifference to Concordance*] (Tallinn, Jaan Tõnisson Institute).

Lauristin, M. (2004) 'Eesti ühiskonna kihistumine' ['Stratification of Estonian Society'], in Kalmus, V., Lauristin, M. & Pruulmann-Vengerfeldt, P. (eds) (2004).

Lauristin, M. (2008) 'Non-Estonians as Part of the Population and Citizenry of Estonia', in Heidmets, M. (ed.) (2008).

Lauristin, M. & Heidmets, M. (eds) (2002) *The Challenge of the Russian Minority: Emerging Multicultural Democracy in Estonia* (Tartu, Tartu University Press).

Lauristin, M. & Vihalemm, P. (2009) 'External and Internal Dimensions in Estonian Political Agenda during Different Periods of Transformation', *Journal of Baltic Studies*, 40, 1.

Lauristin, M., Vihalemm, P., Rosengren, K. E. & Weibull, L. (eds) (1997) *Return to the Western World: Cultural and Political Perspectives on the Estonian Post-Communist Transition* (Tartu, Tartu University Press).

Lauristin, M. & Vihalemm, T. (1997) 'Changing Value Systems: Civilizational Shift and Local Differences', in Lauristin, M., Vihalemm, P., Rosengren, K. E. & Weibull, L. (eds) (1997).

Lee, J. S. (2004) 'Linguistic Hybridization in K-Pop: Discourse of Self-Assertion and Resistance', *World Englishes*, 23, 3.

Leping, K.-O. & Toomet, O. (2007) *Ethnic Wage Gap and Political Break-Ups: Estonia during Political and Economic Transition* (Tartu, Tartu University Press).

LICHR (2006) *Estonia: Interethnic Relations and the Issue of Discrimination in Tallinn* (Tallinn, Legal Information Center for Human Rights).

Lõhmus, M., Lauristin, M. & Siirman, E. (2009) 'The Patterns of Cultural Attitudes and Preferences in Estonia', *Journal of Baltic Studies*, 40, 1.

Mannheim, K. ([1928] 1952) *Essays on the Sociology of Knowledge* (London, Routledge & Kegan Paul).

Marada, R. (2004) 'Social Construction of Youth and Formation of Generational Awareness after Socialism', in Mareš, P. et al. (eds) (2004).

Mareš, P. et al. (eds) (2004) *Society, Reproduction and Contemporary Challenges* (Brno, Barrister & Principal).

Marsh, C. (ed.) (2004) *Burden or Blessing? Russian Orthodoxy and the Construction of Civil Society and Democracy* (Boston, MA, Institute on Culture, Religion and World Affairs, Boston University).

MFARL (2007) *Policy/Civil Society* (Riga, Ministry of Foreign Affairs of the Republic of Latvia), available at: http://www.am.gov.lv/en/policy/4641/4642/4651/, accessed 17 April 2008.

'On Integrating Immigrants in Germany' (2006) *Population & Development Review*, 32, 3.

Pavelson, M. & Luuk, M. (2002) 'Non-Estonians on the Labour Market: A Change in the Economic Model and Differences in Social Capital', in Lauristin, M. & Heidmets, M. (eds) (2002).

Pettai, V. & Hallik, K. (2002) 'Understanding Process of Ethnic "Control": Segmentation, Dependency and Co-optation in Post-Communist Estonia', *Nations and Nationalism*, 8, 4.

*Postimees* (2008) 'Maailmapank: Eestis on reformid lõppenud' ['The World Bank: Reforms Have Stopped in Estonia'], 18 September, available at: http://www.postimees.ee/?id=34321, accessed 29 September 2008.

Pruulmann-Vengerfeldt, P. (2004) 'Kultuuriline, sotsiaalne ja majanduslik kapital: Eesti inimeste ressursid erinevates eluvaldkondades' ['Cultural, Social and Economic Capital: Estonian People's Resources in Different Spheres of Life'], in Kalmus, V., Lauristin, M. & Pruulmann-Vengerfeldt, P. (eds) (2004).

Rokeach, M. (1973) *The Nature of Human Values* (New York, Free Press).

Rose, R. & Munro, N. (2003) *Elections and Parties in New European Democracies* (Washington, DC, CQPress).

Rumbaut, R. (1997) 'Paradoxes (and Orthodoxies) of Assimilation', *Sociological Perspectives*, 40, 3.

Runnel, P., Pruulmann-Vengerfeldt, P. & Reinsalu, K. (2009) 'Estonian Tiger Leap from Post-Communism to the Information Society: From Policy to Practices', *Journal of Baltic Studies*, 40, 1.

Rutherford, J. (ed.) (1990) *Identity: Community, Culture, Difference* (London, Lawrence & Wishart).

Saar, A. (2007) *Rahvussuhted & integratsioonipoliitika väljakutsed pärast Pronkssõduri kriisi* [*Inter-Ethnic Relations & the Challenges for Integration Policy after the Crisis of the Bronze Soldier*]. Questionnaire by Lauristin, M., Vihalemm, T., Kallas, K. & Jakobson, V. Fieldwork by Saar Poll Ltd (Tallinn, Office of the Minister for Population and Ethnic Affairs), available at: http://www.rahvastikuminister.ee/upload/dokumendid/Integratsioonipoliitika_valjakutsed.pdf, accessed 25 August 2007.

Schwartz, S. H. (1990) 'Individualism–Collectivism: Critique and Proposed Refinements', *Journal of Cross-Cultural Psychology*, 21, 2.

Schwartz, S. H. & Sagiv, L. (1995) 'Identifying Culture-Specifics in the Content and Structure of Values', *Journal of Cross-Cultural Psychology*, 26, 1.

Sernhede, O. (2006) *Social Exclusion, Territoriality and Cultures of Resistance in the Post-Colonial City*. Unpublished paper presented at the 9th Nordic Youth Research Information Symposium at Södertörn University College, Stockholm.

Slater, D. (1997) *Consumer Culture and Modernity* (London, Routledge).

Smith, D. (1998) 'Russia, Estonia and Ethno-politics', *Journal of Baltic Studies*, 29, 1.

Smith, D. (2003) 'Minority Rights, Multiculturalism and EU Enlargement: The Case of Estonia', *Journal on Ethnopolitics and Minority Issues in Europe*, 1.

Sztompka, P. (2004) 'The Trauma of Social Change: A Case of Postcommunist Societies', in Alexander, J. C., Eyerman, R., Giesen, B., Smelser, N. J. & Sztompka, P. (eds) (2004).

Tajfel, H. (1981) *Human Groups and Social Categories* (Cambridge, Cambridge University Press).

Titma, M. (ed.) (1999) *Kolmekümneaastaste põlvkonna sotsiaalne portree* [*The Social Portrait of the Generation of 30-Year-Olds*] (Tallinn, Academy of Sciences Press).

TNS Emor (2007) *E-monitoring Survey March/May 2007* (Tallinn, TNS Emor).

Toots, A., Idnurm, T. & Ševeljova, M. (2006) *Noorte kodanikukultuur muutuvas ühiskonnas. Üle-Eestilise kodanikukasvatuse kordusuuringu lõppraport* [*Youth Civic Culture in the Changing Society. Final Report of Estonian Follow-Up Survey on Civic Education*], available at: http://www.oef.org.ee/_repository/File/raport%20IEA.2006.pdf, accessed 25 August 2007.

Tsolidis, G. (2001) 'The Role of the Maternal in Diasporic Cultural Reproduction – Australia, Canada and Greece', *Social Semiotics*, 11, 2.

Vengerfeldt, P. & Runnel, P. (2004) 'Uus meedia Eestis' ['New Media in Estonia'], in Vihalemm, P. (ed.) (2004).

Vihalemm, P. (ed.) (2004) *Meediasüsteem ja meediakasutus Eestis 1965–2004* [*Media System and Media Use in Estonia 1965–2004*] (Tartu, Tartu University Press).

Vihalemm, P. (2007) 'Changing Spatial Relations in the Baltic Region and the Role of the Media: An Estonian Perspective', *European Societies*, 9, 4.

Vihalemm, T. (2005) 'The Strategies of Identity Re-Construction in Post-Soviet Estonia', *Pro Ethnologia*, 19.

Vihalemm, T. & Kalmus, V. (2008) 'Mental Structures in Transition Culture: Differentiating Patterns of Identities and Values in Estonia', *East European Politics and Societies*, 22, 4.

Vogt, H. (2004) *Between Utopia and Disillusionment: A Narrative of the Political Transformation in Eastern Europe* (New York, Berghahn Books).

Zepa, B. (2006) 'The Changing Discourse of Minority Identities: Latvia', *Baltic Institute of Social Sciences: Publications*, available at: http://www.biss.soc.lv/?category=publikacijas&lang=en, accessed 31 July 2007.

**APPENDIX 1** Results of the primary and secondary factor analyses in Estonia

| | Joint factor | Factors of values and identities | Indicators |
|---|---|---|---|
| 1 | Spiritual Harmony and Community Solidarity | F2 Spiritual harmony 0.78 | Equality 0.66 |
| | | | World at peace 0.59 |
| | | | Salvation 0.58 |
| | | | World of beauty 0.57 |
| | | | Inner harmony 0.53 |
| | | | Freedom 0.41 |
| | | F4 Local community identity 0.54 | Other ethnic groups in Estonia 0.59 |
| | | | Neighbors 0.58 |
| | | | All people living in Estonia 0.48 |
| | | | Inhabitants of the same town/parish 0.48 |
| | | F6 Identification with high social position −0.48 | Wealthy people 0.78 |
| | | | Successful people 0.77 |
| 2 | Global Orientation and Emancipation | F1 Personal harmony 0.76 | Mature love 0.66 |
| | | | Happiness 0.66 |
| | | | Pleasant life 0.61 |
| | | | Self-realization 0.54 |
| | | | Self-respect 0.50 |
| | | | True friendship 0.48 |
| | | F3 Supra-national and civic identity 0.51 | Europeans 0.77 |
| | | | Humankind 0.72 |

(*continued*)

**APPENDIX 1** Continued

| Joint factor | Factors of values and identities | Indicators |
|---|---|---|
| | | People from Nordic countries 0.71 |
| | | People having the same citizenship 0.38 |
| 3  Network Identity and Security | F3 Environment and security 0.74 | Health 0.75 |
| | | Clean environment 0.65 |
| | | Technical development 0.49 |
| | | Family security 0.46 |
| | | Honesty 0.43 |
| | | National security 0.43 |
| | F2 Network identity 0.63 | Friends 0.66 |
| | | Family 0.65 |
| | | Workmates 0.63 |
| | | Class-, school- and course-mates 0.59 |
| | | Relatives, kin 0.54 |
| | | Own ethnic group 0.47 |
| 4  Sub-cultural Identity and Desire for Capitals | F4 Material well-being and self-establishment 0.73 | Wealth 0.69 |
| | | Comfortable life 0.66 |
| | | Power 0.60 |
| | | Exciting life 0.52 |
| | F1 Sub-cultural identity 0.45 | People with similar taste, preferences 0.76 |
| | | ...lifestyle 0.73 |
| | | ...world-views 0.71 |
| | | ...hobbies 0.66 |
| | | ...memories 0.66 |
| | | The same generation 0.39 |
| 5  Deprivation and Desire for Social Justice | F5 Social maturity and recognition 0.73 | Justice 0.62 |
| | | Wisdom 0.59 |
| | | Social recognition 0.51 |
| | F5 Identification with low social position 0.66 | Poor people 0.81 |
| | | People having no luck in life 0.80 |
| | | Ordinary working people 0.51 |

**APPENDIX 2** Results of the primary and secondary factor analyses in Latvia

| Joint factor | Factors of values and identities | Indicators |
|---|---|---|
| 1  Global Orientation and Challenge | F3 Supra-national and successful 0.77 | Europeans 0.77 |
| | | Humankind 0.71 |
| | | People from Nordic countries 0.65 |
| | | Successful people 0.47 |
| | F5 Physical security −0.66 | Health 0.79 |
| | | Clean environment 0.67 |

(continued)

**APPENDIX 2** Continued

| | Joint factor | Factors of values and identities | Indicators |
|---|---|---|---|
| 2 | Community Solidarity and Resistance to Modernist Values | F5 Local and civic identity 0.75 | People living in the same town/parish 0.66<br>Neighbors 0.59<br>All people living in Latvia 0.50<br>People having the same citizenship 0.38 |
| | | F2 Material well-being and self-establishment −0.61 | Wealth 0.68<br>Comfortable life 0.66<br>Technical development 0.64<br>Power 0.63<br>Exciting life 0.63<br>Social recognition 0.52 |
| 3 | Sub-cultural Identity and Harmony | F2 Sub-cultural identity 0.72 | People with similar lifestyle 0.71<br>...taste, preferences 0.69<br>...hobbies 0.63<br>...world-views 0.61<br>...memories 0.61<br>The same generation 0.39 |
| | | F1 Personal and social harmony 0.64 | Justice 0.71<br>Honesty 0.70<br>True friendship 0.70<br>Self-respect 0.68<br>Self-realization 0.51<br>Wisdom 0.50 |
| 4 | Network Identity and Secularism | F1 Network identity 0.73 | Relatives, kin 0.80<br>Family 0.79<br>Friends 0.65<br>Workmates 0.54<br>Own ethnic group 0.54<br>Class-, school- and course-mates 0.53 |
| | | F6 Salvation −0.72 | Salvation 0.75 |
| 5 | Re-creation of Secure and Closed Social Space | F4 The 'other' −0.72 | People having no luck in life 0.71<br>Poor people 0.68<br>Ordinary working people 0.48<br>Wealthy people 0.46<br>Other ethnic groups in Latvia 0.37 |
| | | F3 Social security and mental harmony 0.54 | National security 0.68<br>World at peace 0.65<br>World of beauty 0.61<br>Equality 0.54<br>Inner harmony 0.54<br>Freedom 0.49 |
| | | F4 Hedonism and intimacy 0.40 | Happiness 0.71<br>Mature love 0.64<br>Family security 0.62<br>Pleasant life 0.55 |

# INTER-ETHNIC ATTITUDES AND CONTACTS BETWEEN ETHNIC GROUPS IN ESTONIA

## Külliki Korts

### Introduction

The years 2007 and 2008 brought significant changes to the focus of discussions on Estonia's development, in both the public and academic spheres. A sharp fall in economic growth produced a 'cooling effect' and, for the first time after several years of carefree optimism in the face of the future, there arose feelings of uncertainty amongst a large part of the population.

In the political sphere, ethnic issues once again came to the fore. These had figured prominently on the political agenda in the early 1990s, but had been largely neglected thereafter, at least amongst the majority population. In 2006–2007, however, the Estonian Russian population displayed unexpectedly determined opposition to the government's decision to remove the Soviet War Memorial from the center of Tallinn. This culminated in the first violent riot Estonia had witnessed since independence in 1991. These events created a new wave of interest in the development of majority–minority relations and stimulated academic and political discussions regarding the success – or otherwise – of Estonia's integration policy.

In the academic sphere, inter-ethnic relations in Estonia have been a key topic of research ever since the early 1990s (see, for example, Evans 1998; Kolstø 1995; Laitin 1998; Pettai & Hallik 2002). Different studies have produced varying assessments of the possible consequences of the reversal of power relations between ethnic Estonians and the Russian-speaking population following Estonia's independence from the Soviet Union, and the ensuing citizenship and language politics of the new elites. In the early 1990s, rather negative assessments were advanced, both by researchers and by representatives of the majority and minority groups themselves (Kelley 2004, p. 95); a decade later, these had given way to arguments downplaying any possibility of overt ethnic tensions and highlighting trends towards 'pragmatic accommodation' (see, for example, Laitin 2005). Iris Pettai, in her survey-based analyses of inter-ethnic attitudes among ethnic Estonians and Estonian Russians, distinguished five types of 'tolerance': rejection/negation, passive tolerance, internalized toleration, active toleration, and social cohesion. Different sections of the population entered different 'phases' of tolerance at different times (Pettai 2000, 2002, 2005).

While all of these studies focus on inter-ethnic attitudes in Estonia at the group level, a more micro-level approach has been taken by David Laitin, who in his 1998 book argued that, against all odds, Estonian Russians showed signs of cultural 'accommodation' purely on rational and pragmatic grounds in reaction to the nationalizing tendencies of the Estonian state, as well as calculating Estonian economic success in comparison to Russia (Laitin 1998, p. 335, 2003, p. 199). His arguments were based on such markers as the tendency of Russian parents to send their children to Estonian-speaking kindergartens and schools.

At the political level, meanwhile, the government's integration policy gave far more emphasis to language learning and the acquisition of citizenship than it did to the question of inter-ethnic attitudes. The latter aspect is, however, of key significance for the minority population in their evaluation of the success of the integration process. Whereas the majority of ethnic Estonians see integration through an institutional prism, focusing on language acquisition, (Russian language) school reform, and the reintegration of marginal groups, for Russians the main goals are decreasing social inequality, an increase of tolerance and intercultural understanding, and participation in public life and recognition (Lauristin & Vihalemm 2008, p. 23). Similar differences in majority–minority standpoints, where minority populations adopt a more multicultural perspective, while the majority population expects adaptation to majority culture, have been found in other countries (see, for example, Brug & Verkuyten 2007, p. 127). At the same time, these findings challenge the optimistic perspective advanced by David Laitin, in that the signs of pragmatic accommodation to Estonian cultural and linguistic dominance by part of the minority population do not necessarily mean approval of the current model of integration.

Critics of Laitin's approach have also highlighted his neglect of the regional aspect in the Estonian minority question: namely, the fact that almost half of the Russophone population in Estonia lives in a linguistically homogenous (Russian speaking) region (Ponarin 2000, p. 1539) where adaptation to majority culture would be difficult even with great personal effort. On the other hand, Laitin has been criticized for underestimating the reaction of the majority population to the purportedly assimilationist aspirations of the Russophone population (Ponarin 2000, p. 1538) while prioritizing the issue of state language acquisition by the minority. According to a survey carried out in 2007, one third of ethnic Estonian respondents considered an increase in the participation of Estonian Russians in the political and economic spheres harmful (Lauristin & Kallas 2008, p. 57).

In addition to this, recent research into the identity patterns of Estonia's majority and minority populations has revealed the existence of linguistically separated majority and minority communication networks (Vihalemm 2007, p. 497). Vihalemm concluded that individuals' ethnic belonging is closely related to personal communication networks which are embedded in larger patterns of inter-group communication (Vihalemm 2007, p. 497; see also Vihalemm & Kalmus 2009).

In recent years, the symbolic value of language as a key aspect of ethnic belonging among the minority population has increased and may express itself in the kind of pragmatic resistance (Vihalemm 2007, pp. 490, 497) previously exhibited by ethnic Estonians in their language use during the Soviet period. This indicates that the acquisition of Estonian language by the minority population might not necessarily give rise to cultural adaptation or a swift change in inter-ethnic attitudes.

While there is ample research on inter-ethnic attitudes at the group level, as well as on the relationship between personal communication networks and ethnic identity, the relationship between personal communication patterns and attitudes towards the other group has been neglected. In what follows, the focus will be on the correlation between inter-ethnic attitudes and the level and nature of everyday contacts with the other group on an individual level. In the analysis, special attention is paid to the younger generation, for several reasons. Young people have been brought up entirely within the context of an independent Estonia, and have thus come of age under new societal conditions and a changed balance of majority–minority relations. Furthermore, they have been the core focus of an integration policy implemented through both the formal and the informal education system, which are amongst the few socializing agents that are to a certain extent controllable through state policy (Kalmus 2003, p. 668). Also, the surveys conducted after spring 2007 have shown that the April crisis has had a greater impact on the attitudes of the youngest generation from both ethnic groups (Korts & Vihalemm 2008, p. 111).

## Inter-group Attitudes and Contacts

Classic studies of inter-group attitudes and contacts have focused on the strong relationship between frequency of contact with members of the other group and positive attitudes towards the group (Hayes & Dowds 2006, p. 456; Mi'Ari 1999, p. 340; Tropp & Bianchi 2006, p. 533). According to different studies, this relationship is also influenced by various other factors, for example time-span, purpose and degree of intimacy of the interaction (Bochner 1982, p. 8), as well as the power relations between the respective groups (Allport 1954, p. 281; Amir 1982, p. 485; Saenger 1953, p. 217).

Newer studies have concluded, however, that the classic model of positive correlation between personal experience and attitudes applies only in the case of predominantly negative relations between ethnic groups. The last few decades have brought a change in this respect: in many European societies, the evaluation of diversity has become widely accepted, both in political and public discourse. Against this background, positive attitudes towards other ethnic groups do not necessarily presume the existence of positive communicative experience (Tropp & Bianchi 2006, p. 534). The Eurobarometer survey on the topic, conducted in 2007, affirmed this trend: cultural diversity was valued highly by a quarter of European inhabitants, with a considerably higher share among the populations of the older member states in comparison to the newcomers (Eurobarometer 127 2007, p. 6).

On the other hand, research in the field of inter-group relations has also shown that abstract openness and valuation of tolerance does not always express itself in a person's attitudes towards a particular majority or minority group. Readiness to communicate with another group can be strongly influenced by the evaluation of the other group's attitude towards 'Us' (the in-group) or to cultural diversity in general. In cases where the other group is not expected to respond in a similar, open way, or is perceived as responding negatively, this can have a negative influence on attitudes towards that particular group (Klineberg 1982, p. 53; Tropp & Bianchi 2006, p. 535). Similarly, among youngsters, the development of inter-ethnic relationships can be hindered by peer-pressure from more exclusionary-minded contemporaries (Baerveldt et al. 2007, p. 704).

Research into the patterns of ethnic relations among youngsters and in schools has established school as one of the major arenas for forming cross-ethnic friendships, especially in younger classes. Although at high school level ethnic communication networks in the class become dominant, cross-ethnic communication can be promoted through the development of groups with common interests (for example, sports). Where children from an ethnic minority form only a small proportion of the pupils in a school, they tend to have more frequent cross-ethnic friendships compared to situations where the group constitutes a larger part of the student body (Reynolds 2007, p. 387). In the Estonian case, these patterns are probably influenced by the fact that schools and most institutions providing extra-curricular activities are linguistically segregated, owing to the legacy of the Soviet period. However, the growing number of children with Russian as their mother tongue in schools with Estonian as the language of tuition might start to influence communication patterns. In her study of ethnic discourses among ethnic Estonian and Estonian Russian youth, Veronika Kalmus has discussed the influence of several agents on the development of attitudes among the young. Besides school and the media, a major role is also played by family and peers, and also lived experiences (Kalmus 2003, p. 668). Basing her research on pupils' essays and interviews, Kalmus concluded that youth attitudes are taken over from 'discursive communities' in the immediate environment, while more open attitudes are related to the positive experience of the other group (Kalmus 2003, p. 671).

The following study is based on both quantitative (survey) and qualitative data (pupils' essays). In the quantitative analysis, the focus is on the relationship between attitudes towards the other ethnic group and the level and nature of everyday contacts with the other group on an individual level in Estonia, also taking into account regional differences in ethnic composition of the population. While in Tallinn, ethnic Estonians and Russians both make up approximately half of the population, in the north-eastern towns of Narva and Kohtla-Järve there is a clear majority of ethnic Russians (97% and 78%, respectively). In the rest of Estonia, ethnic Russians are clearly in the minority position. In the analysis of pupils' essays, the focus is on experiences with other groups and references to general discourses upon which the pupils draw to substantiate their attitudinal positions.

The essay argues that ethnic relations in Estonia are characterized by the classic model of inter-group relations, where, against a background of generally dominating negative attitudes, more open attitudes towards the other group are strongly linked with higher levels of contact. Similarly, pupils' attitudes towards the other group are influenced by their personal experiences with members of the other group, which are weighed against dominating negative attitudes within one's own group.

## Data and Method

The quantitative part of this analysis is drawn from the survey 'Ethnic Relations and Challenges to the Integration Policy after the Bronze Soldier Crisis'. Carried out in June 2007, it targeted the 15–74 age-group, and is representative of the whole of the Estonian population. Attitudes towards the other ethnic group on a personal level have been measured through a modified version of the classic Bogardus 'social-distance recording method',[1] which includes five statements of self-declared readiness for regular contact with the other ethnic groups at different levels of proximity: (1) live in the same house with Russians/Estonians; (2) be a member together with Russians/Estonians in a club/society; (3) work in an enterprise with a Russian/Estonian as a superior; (4) be the patient of a Russian/Estonian doctor; and (5) have a Russian/Estonian in the close family-circle through marriage. The values were measured on a five-point scale (0 – completely positively, it would not bother me at all ... 4 – it would bother me very much) which were combined into an index of ethnic tolerance, ranging from 0 to 20. Respondents were divided into three groups of tolerance, with scores of 0–3 indicating the highest level of tolerance; 4–10 average tolerance; and 11–20 (i.e. replying negatively to at least four out of five statements) the lowest tolerance.

On top of this survey, a qualitative study of inter-ethnic attitudes and contacts among the younger age-group was conducted. This analysis is based on essays written by ethnic Estonian and Estonian Russian 11th graders (aged 16–17) on the topic 'My good and bad experiences with Russians/Estonians' in November 2007. A total of 107 pupils from ten schools with Estonian as the language of tuition and 127 pupils from eight schools with Russian as the language of tuition participated,[2] from Tallinn, Kohtla-Järve, Narva, Sillamäe and several smaller towns. In the analysis the focus is on experiences with other groups and references to general discourses upon which the pupils draw to substantiate their different attitudinal positions.

## Contacts between Groups and Social Distance

Measured according to the social distance scale (see Table 1), one quarter of ethnic Estonians are characterized by a high level of tolerance and just as many show a low level of readiness to accept Russians into their social space, with half of the population falling between these extremes. Among the Estonian Russians, the majority shows a high level of tolerance; attitudes towards ethnic Estonians are related to the general evaluation of the social–political development in Estonia, with the evaluations being systematically more positive among the group with higher levels of tolerance towards ethnic Estonians.

Age, which usually plays a significant role in the context of value and attitude research, with younger generations showing greater adherence, for example, to valorizing openness and diversity, has no effect in the case of inter-ethnic relations in

**TABLE 1** Distribution of groups of with different levels of tolerance towards the other ethnic group among Estonians and Estonian Russians, by region and age-group and educational level

|  |  | Highest tolerance | Average tolerance | Lowest tolerance |
|---|---|---|---|---|
| *Total* | | | | |
| Estonians | | 28 | 45 | 26 |
| Russians | | 55 | 40 | 5 |
| *Age* | | | | |
| Estonians | 15–24 | 25 | 44 | 31 |
| | 25–39 | 34 | 45 | 21 |
| | 40–54 | 27 | 48 | 25 |
| | 55–74 | 26 | 45 | 29 |
| Russians | 15–24 | 48 | 44 | 8 |
| | 25–39 | 60 | 34 | 6 |
| | 40–54 | 55 | 42 | 3 |
| | 55–74 | 55 | 42 | 4 |
| *Education* | | | | |
| Estonian | Elementary education | 21 | 53 | 25 |
| | High school | 30 | 42 | 27 |
| | Higher education | 29 | 45 | 25 |
| Russian | Elementary education | 33 | 54 | 12 |
| | High school | 59 | 37 | 4 |
| | Higher education | 61 | 36 | 3 |
| *Region* | | | | |
| Estonians | Tallinn | 20 | 40 | 40 |
| | Narva, Kohtla-Järve* | 55 | 22 | 22 |
| | Rest of Estonia | 30 | 48 | 22 |
| Russians | Tallinn | 51 | 43 | 6 |
| | Narva, Kohtla-Järve | 54 | 39 | 6 |
| | Rest of Estonia | 61 | 36 | 3 |

*Note*: This group is constituted by nine respondents only, thus cannot be considered representative.

Estonia – one can even see a slight growth of intolerance among the youngest age group, both among ethnic Estonians, and on a smaller scale, also among ethnic Russians. In the case of ethnic Estonians, educational level has no significant effect, though it is relevant in the case of Estonian Russians, where the level of tolerance is higher in more educated groups.

The strongest factor influencing attitudes seems to be the region: there are considerable differences between the capital city and the rest of Estonia, as amongst the ethnic Estonian inhabitants of Tallinn, the level of intolerance is considerably higher than in the rest of the country. The same phenomenon is evident among all age groups in Tallinn, including the youngest generation. This can be explained by the demographic situation – in Tallinn both groups are of almost equal sizes, while in the rest of the country the dominance of one group is undisputed with Russians dominating in the north-eastern part, and ethnic Estonians in the rest, hence the majority–minority patterns are more strongly established. The same pattern is reflected also in the case of Estonian Russians, although on a considerably lower level.

If we compare the frequency of everyday contact amongst groups with different levels of tolerance, we find a pattern of higher frequency of contact among people with higher levels of tolerance, which is stronger amongst Estonian Russians

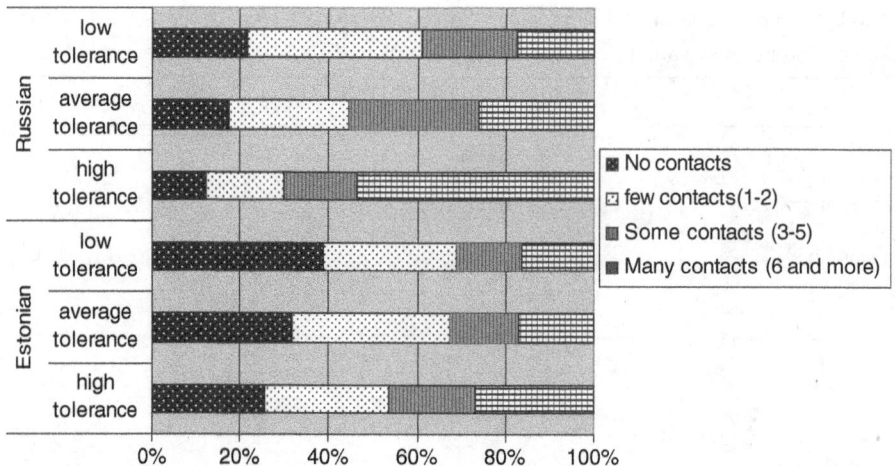

**FIGURE 1** Frequency of contact among ethnic Estonians and Estonian Russians with different levels of tolerance towards the other group.

**TABLE 2** Nature of contacts between ethnic Estonians and Estonian Russians (%)*

|  | All of Estonia | | Tallinn | |
| --- | --- | --- | --- | --- |
|  | Estonian | Russian | Estonian | Russian |
| ...at work | 37 | 47 | 53 | 53 |
| ...in the shops, shopping centre | 20 | 51 | 36 | 58 |
| ...on the street, in the park | 18 | 29 | 19 | 25 |
| ...in my house, courtyard | 17 | 35 | 33 | 42 |
| ...in public transport | 13 | 28 | 22 | 30 |
| ...among acquaintances | 8 | 28 | 25 | 24 |
| ...among friends | 4 | 15 | 6 | 11 |
| ...among family or relatives | 3 | 10 | 5 | 6 |
| ...at a bar, café | 2 | 9 | 4 | 8 |
| ...at a society/voluntary organization | 0 | 3 | 0 | 2 |

Note: *Survey question: Please recall all the encounters with Russians and other people speaking Russian during the last week.

(see Figure 1). This, however, does not allow us to assume the directionality of the correlation: the relationship between contacts and attitudes can be mutually reinforcing, as people with higher tolerance are in all likelihood more prone to make (or admit to) contacts with the-out-group.

Nor does the frequency of contacts reveal the nature and time-span of encounters. According to the survey data, contacts between ethnic Estonians and Estonian Russians are dominated by either instrumental work-related contacts (both colleagues and clients) or by brief contacts in the service sector or on the street-level (see Table 2). Although a third of ethnic Estonians (half in Tallinn) and half of Estonian Russians encounter people of other ethnicity at work, this rarely translates into social contacts in the private sphere. Rather, the number of friends or acquaintances among the other ethnic group with whom people keep frequent contact is very small, something which is also the case in Tallinn.

These data thus support the findings by Triin Vihalemm (2007) that personal networks in Estonia have remained strongly ethnically divided. How such communicative separation is perceived and interpreted by ethnic Estonian and Estonian Russian youngsters, whose school environment is even more deeply ethnically segregated than the adult work environment, will be analyzed in the rest of the essay.

## Inter-ethnic Attitudes among Ethnic Estonian and Estonian Russian Youngsters

The following qualitative analysis focuses on the ways in which inter-ethnic attitudes of young people are shaped by different patterns of interactions. Although the title of the essay emphasized pupils' experiences, most essays included explicit or implicit attitudinal discourses. For the purpose of analysis, the essays were divided into three groups with different attitudinal positions: (1) those that expressed prevalently open, positive attitudes towards the other group; (2) those with overtly negative attitudes; (3) those with ambivalent attitudes, with both positive and negative aspects brought out. Each group is then analyzed further according to typical experiences with the other group, as well as with reference to general discourses upon which the pupils draw to substantiate their attitudinal positions.

*Estonian discourses*

*Affirmative, tolerant attitude.* This attitudinal position could be found in almost half of the essays. It supports the understanding that in relationships, one's nationality is not important; people should be valued as individuals. Negative experiences (for example, with aggressive gangs of Russian youngsters) are treated as exceptions.

> You cannot categorize people as if Estonians are friendly and Russians arrogant... Every nation is made up of all kinds of people. (Estonian female, Tallinn)

The discourse is characterized by a general appreciation of cultural diversity as well as a strong interest in the Russian language and an admission that Estonians should be more tolerant.

> I consider [Russians] very interesting people who make Estonia more colorful. (Estonian female, Tapa)

More than of half of the youngsters with prevalently positive attitudes claim to have many friends among both ethnic groups and emphasize positive experiences. Russians are described as 'warm, kind and friendly'. A positive attitude expresses itself through a strong personal conviction based on a coherent world-view, which is supported by personal experience, even if this is in discord with prevalent attitudes in the peer-group.

> When we live in Estonia it is inevitable that we have contacts with Russians and Russian language. Though some people can find it unpleasant, I do not see a problem. My experiences with Russians have been mostly positive. (Estonian male, Tallinn)

*Ambivalent attitude.* Ambivalent attitudes towards Estonian Russians, which could be found in almost one third of the essays, are based on conflicting experiences. Positive experiences are most commonly related to interactions with classmates or childhood friends; negative encounters have occurred mostly in shops or on public transport (due to language barriers), or with gangs of aggressive Russian youngsters.

> My experiences with Russians are good. I have some friends who are not fully Russians or just speak Estonian. I don't see a difference in socializing with people, whether Russians or not. To talk of Russians in general, my opinion is a bit lower... Most buses are defaced with Russian vulgarities, also abandoned houses... And the Russians who shout, bawl and vandalize on the streets... If Russians live in Estonia, they should know Estonian. For me this is the only thing they should learn. If I see in the shops or bus Russians who don't know a word of Estonian, I am a bit sad. (Estonian female, Tallinn)

The crucial aspect shaping the attitude towards concrete persons is the acquisition of Estonian language, which functions as the symbolic marker of respect for the Estonian state and ethnic Estonians. Estonian Russians who have learned to speak the Estonian language or are trying hard to learn it are regarded highly. At the same time, most negative experiences are related to instances where the person was not able to speak Estonian in shops or another service context, or was being reprimanded for not being able to communicate in Russian.

> There are also bad experiences. In my childhood an elderly lady attacked me angrily because I did not speak Russian. Most of the elderly, who reprove about something, are Russians. (Estonian female, Tallinn)

A lack of knowledge of the Estonian language is regarded as arrogance or disrespect for the Estonian state or hindering the communication between the two nationalities.

> ...As we live in the same country, it would be normal that everybody speaks Estonian. It is possible to get by only with Russian, but a common language would unite the two nationalities. (Estonian female, Tallinn)

Besides language skills, the evaluation of Russians is dependent on their ability to suppress characteristics that are defined as typically 'Russian' and adjust to the Estonian-defined behavioral code.

> ...I don't regard my own friends as Russians. They are just friends. I know there are Russians who are not behaving like hooligans on the street, but when I see Russians, the so-called bad Russians come to mind first.... (Estonian female, Tallinn)

Most of the young people characterized by this attitude have either some or considerable personal experience with Estonian Russians. Good experiences with long-term relationships are pitted against negative occurrences of street-level contact and the generally negative attitude perceived among one's peers, with neither part of the experience gaining prevalence in shaping the attitude.

*Negative attitude.* While the attitudinal positions analyzed above were based on reflections of one's own lived experiences, the overtly negative attitudes are often expressed blatantly and with no further substantiation:

> I do not like Russians in general and nothing can change my mind. (Estonian male, Tallinn)

The attitudinal discourse is based on a fear of lack of respect from the minority's side towards the Estonian state, ethnic Estonians and the Estonian language. In this regard, suspicion seems to have been reinforced by the April crisis.

> I have friends who have told that at their school Russians refused to learn the Estonian anthem, reasoning that 'why do we need the anthem of the morons'. I consider it strange, if they don't like it here, why don't they go to their wonderful Russians in Russia, but they are here and only complain that they are treated wrongly . . . . (Estonian male, Tallinn)

As is the case with the ambivalent attitudinal discourse, Russians are ascribed certain behavioral characteristics: loudness, aggressiveness and violence. Despite admittance of some experiences with 'normal', 'good' Russians (classmates, acquaintances), encounters with aggressive gangs of Russian youngsters are emphasized to support their own suspicion. The discourse also includes frequent references to the prevalence of Russians in the criminal news, as well as historical injustices ('occupants'). Often, the attitude has been reinforced in the context of immediate family.

> My own parents hate Russians and throughout my whole life they've impressed upon me that Russians are bad. (Estonian male, Tallinn)

The negative attitudinal position, which could be found in around one quarter of the essays, is more typical of young boys living in Tallinn.

*Russian discourses*

*Open, affirmative attitude.* Compared to those of ethnic Estonians, the essays of Russian youngsters express prevalently positive attitudes towards their ethnic Estonian peers. However, the aspects emphasized as valuable in inter-ethnic interaction vary to a certain extent according to the frequency and nature of contact. Russian youngsters whose experiences with ethnic Estonians are infrequent value these encounters (accidental, at sport competitions, festivals, etc.) highly, as they have helped them to get over the psychological barrier connected with using the Estonian language.

> I communicated with Estonians twice. First time [it happened] in the street when somebody asked what time it was. Second time I was fishing, and needed to use

all my language skills. I learned many new words from this dialogue. (Russian male, Tallinn)

They express the wish to have more contacts with ethnic Estonians, primarily to practice Estonian language.

Communication with Estonians has one big advantage – the Russians can practice Estonian language. (Russian female, Maardu)

The discourse is based on generally open attitudes towards cultural variety, emphasizing the importance of good relations between ethnic groups sharing the country. This approach is typical to youngsters from the north-eastern part of the county, but prevalent also among Tallinn youth who have rare contacts with their ethnic Estonian peers.

Those who estimate themselves to have more manifold experiences with ethnic Estonians – through participation in sports teams, pupil exchanges, or at work – emphasize inter-ethnic friendships that have developed from these encounters, while practicing language is of secondary importance. The attitude is based on the belief that ethnic belonging is not important in personal relationships and should not be influenced by politics; both ethnic Estonians and Estonian Russians should reassess their attitudes and overcome prejudices.

For me, all people are the same. I have only good experiences with Estonians. Estonians are simple people, cheerful, kind-hearted... I think that it is good to communicate with other people, it is useful also for broadening your mind. We should not forget that Estonians are also human beings; many Russians should change their attitudes. (Russian female, Sillamäe)

Young Russians who claim to have many friends among both Russians and ethnic Estonians also emphasize the importance of cultural variety and the primacy of personality over ethnic belonging. The encounters with ethnic Estonians have occurred in similar circumstances – practicing sports, in work places, or on pupil exchanges. However, a significant feature that differentiates this group from the others is the frequent reference to a strong personal attachment to Estonia (through friends and family), and the intention to remain living here.

I like to live in Estonia. We have friends from many nationalities: Russians, Estonians and others. With Estonians we have good relations. I do sports in a club where there are both Estonians and Russians, we have friendly relations... We can always find common language, it is not as big a problem as it seems. All Russians should integrate into the society, but keep their own culture. (Russian male, Tallinn)

One's own openness is pitted against the perceived distrustful attitude towards ethnic Estonians dominant among one's own peers.

Many Russians who live in Estonia think that Estonians are bad people. I do not agree with that. I was born in Estonia and live here. I have both Estonian and Russian acquaintances, and many Estonians are nice people. Among Estonians there are bad people, but this goes for each nationality. (Russian male, Tallinn)

If the persons with negative attitudes from both sides use the April crisis in 2007 as a confirmation of their previously held suspicions, within this discourse the crisis is discussed as an event that hurt both sides and which should be overcome.

> None of the political problems have marred our friendship. When there were 'Bronze Soldier nights' in the town, we were all together at my place and went through these events together. It was like a test of friendship for us, because some of my acquaintances do not want to communicate with Russians after that night. (Russian female, Tallinn)

*Ambivalent attitudes.* As is the case with ethnic Estonians, an ambivalent position towards the other group among Estonian Russians is shaped by contradictory experiences: a general perception of ethnic Estonians' reticence towards Russians, supported by personal experience of arrogant behavior on the part of many ethnic Estonians on the one hand, and amiable relationships with a small number of ethnic Estonians on the other. Also, the question of language plays a significant role. While it is recognized that knowledge of the Estonian language is important for living and working in the country, it is argued that the role of Russian should be greater, and that it should be possible to get by with Russian in shops and similar places. Encounters with ethnic Estonians are also interpreted through this lens:

> Some people who live here are not interested in communicating with Estonians, and vice versa. I am Russian, but I have both Estonian and Russian friends... While talking to Estonians I make mistakes, but they don't mind... Good experiences with Estonians are those when they understand that I am Russian and they try to communicate in Russian. ... Estonians do not understand that Russians are also human beings, like Estonians. They have no right not to understand us. (Russian male, Maardu)

Encounters are perceived as positive when ethnic Estonians encourage and help people to speak Estonian; they are negative when people pretend not to understand Russian or reprimand Russians for not knowing Estonian well enough. Estonians are described as 'close' and 'difficult to understand'. A crucial aspect is a perceived feeling of disrespect from the part of ethnic Estonians that mars ethnic relations:

> Sometimes they see in me a bad Russian, but I try not to take notice. (Russian female, Tallinn)

An ambivalent attitude is characteristic of Russian pupils with little or occasional contact with ethnic Estonians, both in Tallinn and the Ida-Virumaa region.

*Negative attitude.* This attitudinal discourse uses two types of arguments. Negative attitudes towards Estonians are fuelled by the perceived disrespect ethnic Estonians express towards Russians (for example, in Internet forums):

> Now some think that living here, we have no rights to argue over anything, that we are just guests, we have no rights... And also, I am interested in why, coming to the shop and trying to buy something, I am not answered in my mother

tongue. 40% of the people are Russians, it would be logical to teach Russian to all Estonians. (Russian female, Tallinn)

Also historical references are made to conflicts between Estonians and Russians, where the April events are used:

In my opinion, Estonian politics does not want to see Russians in Estonia. Estonians were against the bronze monument that was dedicated to Russian soldiers who saved the whole world from fascism. But historical facts show that Estonians have taken up arms against Russians... Deep in my soul I do not respect Estonians, though I understand that young people are not guilty of the great mistakes that have left a dark spot on Estonia. I have read opinions of Estonians in the forums and seen different opinions. For example, that Russians should know Estonian language and respect Estonian culture. I don't understand how anyone can respect Estonian culture, if they are like fascists, who pull down monuments.... (Russian male, Kohtla-Järve)

Both types of arguments are similar to those used by their ethnic Estonian peers. Overall, however, the expression of overtly negative attitudes is very rare among Estonian Russians.

## Discussion: Patterns of Interethnic Contacts and Attitudes among Estonian Youth

Pupils' descriptions of their encounters with the other ethnic group show a relationship between personal experience and attitudes among young people, though this is often reinforcing: those who value intercultural communication are more prone to establish such contacts, while youngsters who hold negative attitudes try to avoid contacts. Those with strong personal convictions, either ethnocentric or tolerant, tend to rationalize those experiences which conflict with their pre-established worldview. At the same time, unanticipated positive or negative experiences can change the attitudes of those with less firm beliefs. The different interpretations of the April crisis constitute a noteworthy example of this tendency.

Previous research has pointed to a rather high level of ethnic segregation of personal and family networks in Estonia (for example, Vihalemm 2007). Compared to societies with a comprehensive educational system, the linguistically separated school system in Estonia does not support the creation of contacts across ethnic boundaries, but rather works in reverse. This leads to a situation where for many youngsters, the majority of relations occur in the form of casual contacts on the streets, which in that age-group tends to include a relatively high level of small-scale violence; or in the service sector where relations are often perceived as negative due to linguistic misunderstanding. This may be one of the reasons for higher levels of ethnic tension amongst the younger age group. The significant exception is constituted by the small, though growing number of minority children in schools with Estonian as the language of tuition. However, rather than building bridges between two linguistic communities, the school system tends to assimilate them into ethnic Estonian peer networks. As the pupil essays show, their ethnic Estonian classmates also tend to highly value their loss of characteristic features dubbed as 'Russian', including accent and certain behavioral features.

Ethnic attitudes among Estonian Russians are (with a few exceptions) predominantly positive. The dominant attitudes vary less according to region, but rather on the level of experience of communication with ethnic Estonian youth, or ethnic Estonians in general. Those with limited experience tend to value those contacts rather instrumentally, compared to their Russian peers with more frequent contact who emphasize the emotional aspects of friendships with their ethnic Estonian peers.

Similarly to other countries where youth friendship networks have been studied (see for example, Reynolds 2007), the most significant arena for establishing long-term contacts across ethnic borders for young people lies in the (seasonal) work environment, sports groups and other leisure-time activities. In the Estonian case, however, multiethnic sports and hobby clubs are rather exceptional, as most extra-curricula activities (except in areas with a considerable ethnic Estonian majority) tend to be monolingual and children in general choose other-language groups only in extraordinary circumstances, for example when there is no particular sports/hobby group in their mother tongue. Whereas amongst adults, inter-ethnic contacts at work do not have a strong effect on networks in the personal sphere, the best tool for increasing ethnic overlapping of friendship networks among youth would be a comprehensive educational system. For the time being, this is not politically feasible, due both to opposition from a majority of the Russian-speaking population and to a lack of preparedness in the educational system. However, even minor adjustments in the arrangement of extra-curricula activities could have a significant effect in this regard.

For ethnic Estonian youth, the acquisition of Estonian language is one of the key markers of respect on the part of the minority population (expressed both in appreciation of acquaintances who have learned the language and reprimands for those who do not). For Estonian Russian youngsters, Estonian language has considerably less symbolic value, but is rather viewed as a pragmatic necessity.

Explicitly hostile attitudes towards the other ethnic group are characteristic of young people whose self-declared personal experience with the other group is (voluntarily) either lacking or consists of only casual street-level contacts. In line with the findings of Kalmus (2003), this can be assumed to reflect dominant discourses within the family or other immediate peer groups, which are further mutually reinforced through ethnocentric attitudes in Internet forums. Conversely, the lack of respect among ethnic Estonians towards Russian as the mother tongue of many inhabitants of Estonia is increasing the symbolic value of Russian among a part of the Estonian Russian population.

## Conclusion

This essay has focused on inter-ethnic attitudes in Estonia at the individual level, and their relationship to personal communication patterns. For the majority of ethnic Estonians, contacts with other groups tend to remain in the public sphere, either at work or through casual relations in the service sector or public transport. In the private sphere, the contacts remain rather scarce. Of crucial significance to intergroup relations is the widespread perception (or fear) of lack of respect from the other side characteristic to both ethnic Estonians and Estonian Russians, which was further reinforced by the Bronze Soldier crisis in April–May 2007. Among the youth, these attitudes, based on both media coverage and discourses among the family and peers, are either taken over directly, reinforced by a few negative encounters or weighed against one's own contrasting experiences. For ethnic Estonians, knowledge of the Estonian language by the minority population constitutes one of the key symbolic elements showing respect towards their new motherland. Among the majority of ethnic Estonian youngsters this expresses itself through the rather ethnocentric appreciation shown towards their Russian peers (often classmates) who have become 'impossible to tell apart' from ethnic Estonians both in terms of (lack of) accent and behavior. For the Estonian Russian youth, although appreciation by their ethnic Estonian peers for their efforts to learn the Estonian language is highly significant, the language itself is mostly of instrumental importance as a necessary tool for succeeding in Estonian society. Despite better knowledge of the language by Russian youth due to increased language learning at school, this has not functioned as a mechanism of cultural adaptation as predicted by David Laitin. For many, encounters with ethnic Estonians are often viewed as primarily instrumental to language acquisition rather than cultural acquaintance, even if in the long run these can lead to better cultural understanding. At the same time, the symbolic value of Russian in the eyes of young Estonian Russians has increased and attempts on the part of ethnic Estonians to use Russian are interpreted as signs of ethnic tolerance.

While in the case of societies where the evaluation of diversity is more widely accepted among the population, ethnic overlapping of personal networks is not a presumption for maintaining harmonious ethnic relations, the Estonian case showed the continuation of the classical model at least among the majority population. Personal attitudes towards the other group are strongly influenced by the evaluation of the other group's attitude towards the in-group, which are usually positive in cases with a high level of personal experience and negative if this experience is mediated.

## Acknowledgement

The research has been partly supported by grants from the Estonian Ministry of Education and Science (0181774s01 and 0180017s07).

## Notes

1. Bogardus' scale (1928) included seven statements for 'expressing racial reaction': (1) marriage; (2) friends in one's social club; (3) neighbors; (4) members of the same occupation; (5) fellow citizens; (6) allowing such persons to enter one's country as visitors only; and (7) excluding from the country (Bogardus 1928, p. 24).
2. The students were expected to write in their mother tongue in order to have equal ease in expression. However, most of the teachers in schools with Russian language tuition asked their pupils to write the essay in Estonian.

# References

Allport, G. W. (1954) *The Nature of Prejudice* (Cambridge, MA, Addison-Wesley).
Amir, Y., Ben-Ari, R., Bizman, A. & Rivner, M. (1982) 'Objective versus Subjective Aspects of Interpersonal Relations between Jews and Arabs', *Journal of Conflict Resolution*, 26, 3, pp. 485–506.
Baerveldt, C., Zijlstra, B., de Wolf, M., Van Rossem, R. & Van Duijn, M. A. J. (2007) 'Ethnic Boundaries in High School Students' Networks in Flanders and the Netherlands', *International Sociology*, 22, 6, pp. 701–20.
Barany, Z. & Moser, R. G. (eds) (2005) *Ethnic Politics After Communism* (Ithaca & London, Cornell University Press).
Bochner, S. (1982) 'The Social Psychology of Cross-Cultural Relations', in Bochner, S. (ed.) (1982), pp. 5–44.
Bochner, S. (ed.) (1982) *Cultures in Contact, Studies in Cross-Cultural Interaction*, International Series in Experimental Social Psychology, Vol. 1 (Oxford, Pergamon Press).
Bogardus, E. S. (1928) *Immigration and Race Attitudes* (Boston & New York, D.C., Heath and Company).
Brug, P. & Verkuyten, M. (2007) 'Dealing with Cultural Diversity. The Endorsement of Societal Models among Ethnic Minority and Majority Youth in the Netherlands', *Youth & Society*, 39, 1, pp. 112–31.
Eurobarometer Flash 127 (2007) *Intercultural Dialogue in Europe*, November, available at: http://ec.europa.eu/public_opinion/flash/fl_217_sum_en.pdf, accessed 28 May 2008.
Evans, G. (1998) 'Ethnic Schism and the Consolidation of Post-Communist Democracies: The Case of Estonia', *Communist and Post-Communist Studies*, 31, 1, pp. 57–74.
Hallik, K. (ed.) (2002) *Integration in Estonian Society: Monitoring 2002* (Tallinn, Institute of International and Social Studies and Integration Foundation).
Hayes, B. & Dowds, L. (2006) 'Social Contact, Cultural Marginality or Economic Self-Interest? Attitudes towards Immigrants in Northern Ireland', *Journal of Ethnic and Migration Studies*, 32, April, pp. 455–76.
Heidmets, M. (ed.) (2008) *Estonian Human Development Report 2007* (Tallinn, Eesti Koostöö Kogu).
Kalmus, V. (2003) 'Is Interethnic Integration Possible in Estonia?: Ethno-political Discourse of Two Ethnic Groups', *Discourse & Society*, 14, 6, pp. 667–9.
Kelley, J. G. (2004) *Ethnic Politics in Europe. The Power of Norms and Incentives* (Princeton & Oxford, Princeton University Press).
Klineberg, O. (1982) 'Contact between Ethnic Groups: A Historical Perspective of Some Aspects of Theory and Research Cultures in Contact', in Bochner, S. (ed.) (1982), pp. 45–55.
Kolstø, P. (1995) *Russians in the Former Soviet Republics* (Bloomington & Indianapolis, Indiana University Press).
Korts, K. & Vihalemm, T. (2008) 'Rahvustevahelised suhted, kontaktid ja meie-tunne' ['Interethnic Relations, Contacts and Us-Feeling'], *Integratsiooni monitooring 2008* [*Integration Monitoring 2008*], available at: http://www.rahvastikuminister.ee/public/Rahvustevahelised_suhted_kontaktid_ja_meie_tunne.pdf, accessed 26 November 2008.

Laitin, D. (1998) *Identity in Formation: The Russian-speaking Populations in the Near Abroad* (Ithaca, NY, Cornell University Press).
Laitin, D. (2005) 'Culture Shift in a Postcommunist State', in Barany, Z. & Moser, R. G. (eds) (2005), pp. 46–77.
Laitin, D. D. (2003) 'Three Models of Integration and the Estonian/Russian Reality', *Journal of Baltic Studies*, 34, 2, pp. 197–222.
Lauristin, M. & Kallas, T. (2008) 'The Participation of Non-Estonians in Estonian Social Life and Politics', in Heidmets, M. (ed.) (2008), pp. 55–63.
Lauristin, M. & Vetik, R. (eds) (2000) *Integration in Estonian Society: Monitoring 2000* (Tallinn, Institute of International and Social Studies and Integration Foundation).
Lauristin, M. & Vihalemm, T. (2008) *RIP 2008–2013. Vajadus ja teostatavusuuringu lõpparuanne. I osa: Sissejuhatus* (Tartu, Praxis, Tartu Ülikool, Balti Uuringute Instituut, Hill & Knowlton, Geomedia), p. 23, available at: http://www.rahvastikuminister.ee/public/I_osa.pdf, accessed 28 May 2008.
Mi'Ari, M. (1999) 'Attitudes of Palestinians toward normalization with Israel', *Journal of Peace Research*, 36, 30, pp. 339–48.
Pavelson, M., Proos, I., Pettai, I., Kruusvall, J., Hallik, K. & Vetik, R. (2005) *Integration of Estonian Society: Monitoring 2005* (Tallinn, Institute of International and Social Studies and Integration Foundation).
Pettai, I. (2000) 'Tolerance of Estonians and Non-Estonians', in Lauristin, M. & Vetik, R. (eds) (2000), pp. 6–10.
Pettai, I. (2002) 'Estonians and Non-Estonians: A Typology of Tolerance', in Hallik, K. (ed.) (2002), pp. 14–21.
Pettai, I. (2005) 'Tolerance in Ethnic Relations in Estonia', in Pavelson, M., Proos, I., Pettai, I., Kruusvall, J., Hallik, K. & Vetik, R. (eds) (2005), pp. 36–46.
Pettai, V. & Hallik, K. (2002) 'Understanding Processes of Ethnic Control: Segmentation, Dependency and Co-optation in Post-Communist Estonia', *Nations and Nationalism*, 8, 40, pp. 505–29.
Ponarin, E. (2000) 'The Prospects of Assimilation of the Russophone Populations in Estonia and Ukraine: A Reaction to David Laitin's Research', *Europe-Asia Studies*, 52, 8, pp. 1535–41.
Reynolds, T. (2007) 'Friendship Networks, Social Capital and Ethnic Identity: Researching the Perspectives of Caribbean Young People in Britain', *Journal of Youth Studies*, 10, 4, pp. 383–98.
Saenger, G. (1953) *The Social Psychology of Prejudice* (New York, Harper and Brothers).
Tropp, L. R. & Bianchi, R. A. (2006) 'Valuing Diversity and Interest in Intergroup Contact', *Journal of Social Issues*, 62, 3, pp. 533–51.
Vihalemm, T. (2007) 'Crystallizing and Emancipating Identities in Post-Communist Estonia', *Nationalities Papers*, 35, 3, pp. 477–502.
Vihalemm, T. & Kalmus, V. (2009) 'Cultural Differentiation of the Russian Minority. Mental Structures in Estonia and Latvia', *Journal of Baltic Studies*, 40, 1.

# THE BRONZE SOLDIER: IDENTITY THREAT AND MAINTENANCE IN ESTONIA

# Martin Ehala

The relocation of the monument to those killed in WWII, located in the center of Tallinn, on 27 April 2007 triggered the first large-scale ethnic riots in Estonia since 1980, when a punk rock concert mobilized ethnic Estonian youth to riot against Russification. Unlike in 1980, the rioters in 2007 were predominantly Russian speakers.

The monument, the 'Bronze Soldier', was erected in 1947 by the Soviet authorities, and was ritually used in Soviet identity politics. However, it escaped the removal that befell many Soviet statues in Estonia during the collapse of the Soviet Union. Although the issue was usually raised prior to elections, no serious attempts were made to remove the monument until 2006.

The crucial question in this context is why the presence of a statue that had been accepted for 15 years suddenly became such an annoyance that it needed to be relocated, and why the relocation of a statue which for years had been visited by a decreasing number of elderly war veterans suddenly incited young people to commit acts of vandalism on the streets of Tallinn.

The answers to these questions require an analysis of the shifts and changes in ethnic identities in Estonia that have occurred during the last 15 years. These shifts are a response to the transition of Estonia from a post-Soviet country to an EU member state, as well as to the growing prominence of Russia in world affairs during the last eight years. Thus, the tension around the monument reflected the threat to identity that changed social circumstances have caused in both major ethnic groups in Estonia.

## The Context of the Relocation of the Bronze Soldier

The relocation of a statue of both cultural and historical significance is certainly a statement. As such it can be seen as a communicative act governed by the principles of pragmatics (Austin 1961; Habermas 1979). According to these principles, the meaning of each communicative act depends on both the message and its context. The context involves the time and place of the utterance, as well as the sequence of previous utterances by communicators. To understand the specific meaning of this event, therefore, contextual factors need to be taken into account.

Revolutionary changes in a society often trigger the removal of monuments which carry the messages of the overthrown ideology and symbolize the domination patterns of the past. In the case of Estonia, the twentieth century was synonymous with radical changes of power, almost all of which were accompanied by the removal or destruction of ideologically charged monuments. Thus, after Estonian independence was recognized in 1920 by the signing of the Tartu Peace Treaty, the monument to Peter the Great in the center of Tallinn was removed. The myth goes that its bronze was used to mint the smallest Estonian coin, the one cent piece.

To commemorate the fallen in the 1918–1920 War of Independence, around 200 monuments were erected throughout Estonia, usually financed by local communities. In 1940, after the annexation of Estonia, most of these monuments were destroyed by the Soviet authorities. During WWII, when Estonia was occupied by Nazi Germany, many of them were restored, but not for long. After the end of the war, the Soviet regime destroyed them again. Most of these monuments were finally re-erected after the collapse of the Soviet Union.

The Bronze Soldier in Tallinn has been subject to a somewhat similar fate. In April 1945, several fallen Red Army soldiers were reburied on Tõnismägi and a simple wooden memorial was placed on the square. On the 8 May 1946, two schoolgirls, Ageeda Paavel and Aili Jürgenson, demolished it in revenge for the demolition of the monuments of the Independence War. Ageeda Paavel recalls:

> Our beloved monuments started to disappear one after another. They had to be paid back somehow and the so-called Liberators' Monument on Tõnismägi was picked. It was situated in the square of the current 'bronze man' on the side facing the church. It was about a meter high wooden pyramid, which was only about 20 centimeters in diameter; it was of a plain blue color and its top was decorated by a red tin pentagon. ... Juhan [Juhan Kuusk] gave us the explosives and instructions. There was nothing really difficult about it. (Kaasik 2006, p. 21)

A year later, on 22 September 1947, on the third anniversary of the re-instatement of Red Army control over Tallinn, the Bronze Soldier was unveiled in the same place in Tõnismägi, where it remained for a long period of time, and became the most representative war memorial in the city (Figure 1). It was actively used as a site for Soviet rituals until the Singing Revolution in the late 1980s.

The area around the monument was modified after the Soviet Army left Estonia in 1994 in order to reduce its ideological weight. The hollow for the eternal flame was removed, and the central position of the monument on the square was reduced by replacing the direct access paths to the monument with a diagonal sidewalk across the

**FIGURE 1** The WWII monument in Tõnismägi in 1999 (fragment). *Photo*: Peter Van den Bossche.

square and by planting new trees to close the square. The commemorative text on the statue (*Eternal glory for the heroes who have fallen for the liberation and sovereignty of our country* [*Igavene au langenud kangelastele, kes on langanud meie maa vabastamise ja sõltumatuse eest*]) was replaced by a more neutral one (*For the fallen in the Second World War* [*Teises maailmasõjas hukkunutele*]) (Smith 2008; Tamm & Halla 2008, p. 43).

There were also several suggestions to redesign the entire memorial, including a design competition held in 1995. The preliminary plan suggested that the existing monument should be balanced by a seven-meter-high steel cross symbolizing Christian values and counterbalancing Soviet power; a black granite pedestal uniting the fallen of all backgrounds, a black granite colonnade separating the adversaries and an oak symbolizing Estonian national identity were also to be added (Kaasik 2006, p. 17).

However, these plans never materialized. The Bronze Soldier remained at its original location for another ten years and attracted little discussion about its redesign or removal. The issue caught the public's attention again in 2004 and the dispute led to the statue's relocation to a site approximately two kilometers away in the Tallinn Military Cemetery in April 2007.

At least partly, the spark for this discussion was provided by the removal of yet another WWII monument. This monument, now commonly known as the Lihula monument, due to its location, was devoted to the men who fought against

Bolshevism from 1940 to 1945, and to the restoration of Estonian independence. The monument was created in 2002 and portrayed an armed soldier in German uniform. It was first erected in Pärnu, but was removed even before its official opening because of its obvious Nazi resemblances. In August 2004 it was re-erected in Lihula and stood for about two weeks (Brüggemann & Kasekamp 2008). It was decisively removed by the Estonian government in September 2004, without notice to the owners of the statue or to the public. The crudeness of this act shocked even those who agreed, in principle, that the symbolic language of the monument was improper.

After this removal, the parallel with the Bronze Soldier in a Soviet uniform became salient and an increasing number of people started to see its presence in the center of Tallinn as an injustice. A number of spontaneous acts of vandalism against Soviet WWII monuments in Estonia took place after the removal of the Lihula monument. Half a year later, on the eve of 9 May 2005, Russian Victory Day, red paint was thrown over the Bronze Soldier. From then until its relocation, the monument became the focal point for identity battles in Estonia.

This was the immediate context of the relocation of the statue, but wider societal, international and global trends also contributed to the setting. Ruutsoo (2008, pp. 117–8) outlines five such factors: (1) the re-emergence of a bipolar understanding of the world as a place of antagonistic struggles after 9/11; (2) the crisis of liberal multiculturalism in Europe; (3) the re-emergence of historicist arguments in international politics, particularly the rebirth of imperialist rhetoric in Russia; (4) the neo-conservative turn in Estonian politics as a response to the emerging New Cold War, in which Estonia stands in the front line; and (5) attempts to remedy the lack of solidarity in Estonian society by nationalism.

As the descriptions of the chain of events that directly resulted in removal of the statue and its subsequent relocation are easily attainable (see Brüggemann & Kasekamp 2008; Lehti *et al.* 2008; Poleschuk 2007; Smith 2008), I will only provide a short account here.

In late 2006, in connection with the approaching parliamentary elections, the liberal party *Reformierakond* (Reform Party) promised to relocate the statue before the next victory day, 9 May 2007. This move helped to give the party and their leader unprecedented popularity among a wide range of Estonians, and as a result they won the elections in March 2007: they became the largest party in the parliament with 28% of the seats and the leading party in the new governmental coalition. Thus, the promise demanded fulfillment.

In the early hours of 26 April, without notice, the monument and its surrounding area was covered by a large tent and surrounded by a fence. According to officials, there were no plans to remove the statue at that point; the intention was simply to carry out the necessary archaeological work for the exhumation of the remains of the buried. Nevertheless, a large crowd of mostly Russophones gathered around the fence that evening. There was shouting – 'Shame' and 'Fascists' – and empty bottles were thrown at the police. Later in the evening, the police ordered the protesters to leave and pushed them out of the immediate area into the surrounding streets. The angry crowd started to attack property in the surrounding streets, breaking shop windows and smashing the interiors, looting, and turning over cars. At first, the police failed to respond to the vandalism, but as the night passed, a large number of arrests were made to gain control of the situation.

Arguably, such a large outbreak of vandalism was not expected by the government, which met for an emergency meeting the same night and decided to remove the statue immediately. This was done early the following morning. Although order was restored and the following day was peaceful, the unrest continued for another two nights and, to some extent, also spread to other cities with large Russophone communities. The removal of the statue also elicited a fierce response from political leaders and the public in Russia, cyber attacks on important Estonian websites and a week-long blockade of the Estonian Embassy in Moscow by the Russian youth organization *Nashi*. A drastic decline in Russian oil transit through Estonia and a boycott of Estonian goods in Russia followed soon thereafter. It is ironic that this economic setback was triggered by the identity politics of the same party (*Reformierakond*), which for years had pursued a pragmatic libertarian politics aimed, first and foremost, at economic prosperity.

As the unrest faded, the statue was re-erected in the military cemetery and, on 8 May, the Estonian government and members of the diplomatic corps held a ceremony at the new location, laying a wreath for the fallen in WWII. This was the first time that Estonian officials had ever paid homage to the monument. Thousands of Russophones commemorated the end of the war the next day, covering almost the entire area with flowers. The fact that the strong emotional response to the removal of the statue by Russophones caught the government and the public by surprise indicates a lack of understanding of the complex set of social meanings that the statue embodied. These meanings are crucial in analyzing the psychology of the conflict.

## Social Meaning Construction around the Bronze Soldier

According to Pierre Bourdieu (1991), a well-functioning society is based on the use of symbolic power which stems from a shared and consensual understanding of justice. Justice is presented as an ideology that explains the existing status and power differences among the social and ethnic groups belonging to this society. Ideologies, in turn, contain narratives that assign the categories of pride, shame and guilt to different groups within the society (Lawler 2006). If the current social situation is perceived to be just, people are ready to accept the places in the social hierarchy that the ideology ascribes to them. In this way, the dominant ideology legitimizes the power and status relations between the subgroups in the society.

Identity construction is tightly connected to ideological debates in society. There are continuously emerging alternative ideologies to the dominant position within a society, but usually their social base is weak and they do not attract wider societal attention (see Hogg & Reid 2006). If, however, an ideology gains support among several subgroups in a society, this invariably creates tension and opposition in the groups benefiting from the dominant ideology.

In contemporary Estonia, the center of the ideological debate is the interpretation of the events of WWII. Symbolically, the interpretation found its expression in the statue of the Bronze Soldier. Since it is a monument with ambiguous aesthetics, it could be imbued with a number of meanings, some of which were directly oppositional. Even though the confrontational meanings were supported only by small fractions of the society, the symbolic acts that these meanings provoked emotionally touched a very large part of society, for whom the statue had a much broader and less ambiguous meaning. Thus, this ambiguity allowed groups to use the monument as a tool of social mobilization. The range of possible meanings of the monument may be summarized as follows.

(1) The layer of meaning of the Bronze Soldier that is shared, or at least openly espoused, by the largest segment of the population in Estonia derives from its commemoration of the fallen in WWII. This most neutral of meanings has provided for some degree of common ground uniting different ethnic groups, and perhaps explains why, in 2006, 29% of Estonians as well as virtually all Russophones were opposed to the idea of moving the monument. A further 18% of Estonians were undecided at this time, meaning that around 67% of Estonia's overall population wanted the monument to be left in its original location (BNS 2006).

(2) The second layer of meaning of the Bronze Soldier is associated with victory in what is known in Russian culture as the Great Patriotic War, i.e. the part of WWII in which the Russian nation was involved. In contemporary Russia, this victory is a central part of national identity, and constitutes an important source of pride and self esteem. It would be reasonable to assume that, for the vast majority of Russophones in Estonia, this meaning is emotionally significant. However, since Estonia had almost no control over the course of WWII, this emotional significance is understandably not shared by most Estonians, except perhaps for the Estonian veterans of the war who fought in the Red Army.

Even though Estonians may not attach significance to the celebration of victory in the Great Patriotic War, the major contribution of the Soviet Union to the destruction of the Nazis is internationally recognized. Thus, it is perfectly legitimate to celebrate the victory on 9 May in Estonia, a day later than the rest of the World celebrates the end of WWII in Europe (WWII did not end for the US and the UK until the defeat of the Japanese in August 1945), and the importance of the Bronze Soldier in these celebrations cannot be disputed. Altogether, one-third of the Estonian population may have a strong attachment to the Bronze Soldier as a symbol of victory.

(3) For a fraction of Russian radicals, the Bronze Soldier presented the opportunity to signify 'the liberation' of Tallinn and the rest of Estonia from the German occupation during WWII. This is stressed by naming the monument the statue of the 'Liberator' and by celebrating 22 September, the day the Red Army regained control over Tallinn, as the Day of Liberation. This layer of meaning is in strict conflict with the official historical narrative of Estonia, and consequently with the ideological bases of contemporary Estonia.

By depicting the Bronze Soldier as the 'Liberator', the Soviet period in the history of Estonia is implicitly redefined as freedom, whereby the Russophone community in Estonia would be given high status as the liberators of Estonians. Thus, the acceptance of this narrative would set the stage for a radical status revision between the two ethnic groups in Estonia. While the status of Russophones in Estonia is open to renegotiation, it is obvious that if claims for higher status are based on this historical narrative, they will hardly be accepted by Estonians.

It may be assumed that this layer of meaning has resonance among the segments of the Russophone community which have clear negative attitudes towards Estonia, and which still identify themselves as Soviet people and/or inhabitants of the (former) Soviet Estonia. According to Vihalemm and Masso (2007, p. 83), around 25% of Russophones choose this identification *certainly* or *sometimes*. Differently from some other ex-Soviet republics, where this identification is associated with mild Soviet nostalgia, Vihalemm and Masso argue that it expresses a protest identity in Estonia.

(4) As a response to the meaning construction of the Bronze Soldier as 'the Liberator', radical Estonian nationalists started to construct an opposing meaning, namely that it was a symbol of Soviet occupation. This meaning was latent until 2004, manifesting itself only occasionally, but without serious emotional resonance. However, the more vivid Russian activists' use of Soviet and Stalinist symbolism in their celebrations became, the more the monument began to irritate Estonians. Still, for quite a long time demonstrations by small radical groups were tolerated quite calmly.

The balance was tipped on 9 May 2006, when two Estonian right-wing nationalists went to the statue while the Russophone Victory Day celebrations were taking place. The Estonian nationalists carried the Estonian national flag and a banner emphasizing Soviet occupation. To prevent clashes, the police removed the two activists. The event was broadcast by the national media. This humiliation created a strong emotional reaction among Estonians and some politicians promised to remove this symbol of occupation from the center of Tallinn. As the removal of the monument was turned into an election campaign promise, active meaning construction of the monument as a symbol of Soviet occupation occurred in the Estonian media.

In this way the semiotic ambiguity of the monument led to an ideological dialogue between the Russophone and Estonian radical activists. If the statue had had an exclusive meaning pertaining to Soviet oppression, its removal would have been justified and it would not have affected more than the most radical fractions of the Russophone community in Estonia, perhaps 7.5% of all Russophones. Yet, the symbol was emotionally significant for the majority of the Russophone community because of its commemorative and celebratory meanings, meanings that are legitimate and humane in nature. For them, the relocation of the monument was perceived as a grave injustice.

Thus, the rich context and the puzzle of meanings of the monument make it clear why its removal created such a discrepant response in the Russophone community (and in Russia as well), but they do not explain why the whole issue suddenly gained prominence in Estonia after ten or more years of relative silence, when it appeared that the controversial history was conveniently being forgotten. To understand this unexpected turn we need to take into account the identity dynamics in Estonia during the last 15 years.

## Identity Dynamics in Estonia

According to Todd (2005), a social identity shift is a crucial factor for the success of institutional change. She argues that new institutions are able to create new dynamics of behavior only if the change in institutions is accompanied by changing self-perceptions. Often the identity categories have their own inertia, which is out of phase with structural changes, meaning that imposed political changes and changes in social practices may (initially) fail to bring about changes in the categories of collective identities. On other occasions, subtle shifts in identity content may gradually change the cultural substratum of the identity, which makes the path to radical category change possible.

In multi-ethnic societies these changes may make a difference in who is included or excluded, respected or disrespected, and eventually whether inter-ethnic relations are harmonious or conflictual. This means that the negotiation of intergroup boundaries is one central function of identity dynamics. On the other hand, as Hornsey and Hogg (2000, p. 143) claim, 'intergroup relations are almost by definition a matter of subgroup relations within a superordinate identity group'. Thus it is not only the nature and permeability of lateral boundaries between groups, but also the consolidation of groups under superordinate identity categories, or the dissolution of these categories in favor of lower level groups that shape identity dynamics.

A prime example of consolidation is the emergence of a nation from linguistically and culturally diverse dialects. This new superordinate collective identity unites linguistically and culturally diverse subgroups into one integrated whole, where the previous top-level collective identities are re-analyzed as sub-level collective identities. Thus, consolidation accommodates diversity within the new unity. It reduces its cognitive prominence, but does not erase it.

If the groups are not able to coalesce, and neither is assimilating, their co-existence in one society may become problematic, which in turn could lead to the dissolution of the superordinate identity category. The dissolution of Soviet and Yugoslavian identities as pan-ethnic identities is a good example of this process. Changes in the level of the strongest emotional attachment are also a part of identity dynamics.

Todd (2005) has presented a typology of changes in collective identity categories that may occur in different settings of social practice. As it is useful to analyze the identity dynamics in Estonia using this typology, I will briefly outline these types below.

Reaffirmation is a process that is likely to occur when there is a match between practices and identity categories. This means giving open support to the existing identity categories by making them more salient, distinct and oppositional. Usually one of the groups reaffirms its identity in order to promote change, while the other is opposed to it. Basically, reaffirmation means no change.

Conversion is a process by which an old identity category is abandoned altogether and a completely new identity is assumed. This is quite a radical category change which can happen only after most of the content of the old identity has been gradually eroded and/or replaced by new meanings. Todd (2005) gives the change in South African white identities as an example of conversion.

Assimilation is a process of partial identity change. Some of the meanings fade, some oppositions are rearranged, and some elements from the periphery are centralized. These shifts and changes in identity allow actors to succeed in new circumstances, while they retain continuity with their old identity. As assimilation would in inter-ethnic encounters mean mostly abandoning one's heritage identity in favor of the more rewarding majority identity, in this essay I will use the term integration instead to denote this type of identity change.

All three of these processes create coherence between social practices and identity categories. The next three types create and express ambiguity between social practices and identities.

Privatization is a process by which all macro-social elements of one's identity, including nationality, class, political affiliations and status are marginalized, and only the part of identity which manifests itself in the private sphere is retained. Privatization occurs when institutional change has made the old oppositional categories irrelevant or inapplicable, but the new categories imposed by the new practices cannot be accepted. Todd (2005) refers to identity changes under totalitarianism as a prime example of privatization.

Adaptation is an identity change that basically requires that new practices which come with a new social order are accepted, but are kept separate from one's old identity. Adaptation also means that the new values and meanings that come with new practices are not truly accepted. Adaptation is a kind of double life that was very common for Estonians under Soviet rule: while people cooperated with the authorities, they did not accept its value system. Adaptation made it easy to mobilize for social change when *perestroika* allowed for greater liberties.

Ritual approbation occurs when new practices are made to fit the old systems of meaning, through which they affect each other and mutually make the inherent tensions between them apparent. It is a group-based strategy which is often used officially when nations modernize, but still maintain pre-existing traditions.

These types of identity change are taken as the basis for analyzing the identity dynamics in Estonia during the past 15 years.

## *The first half of the 1990s: reaffirmation and privatization*

The ideological cornerstone for re-establishing Estonian independence was the consensual recognition of the existence and illegitimacy of the Molotov–Ribbentrop Pact of 1939. From this, it followed that Estonia did not join the Soviet Union in accordance with its free will but was illegally annexed. This recognition also reversed the status of ethnic groups in Estonia: the Russophone community, which enjoyed the highest status in Soviet Estonia, was assigned immigrant status, because its presence was attributed to an illicit colonization. This institutional change also forced changes in identity categorizations.

In 1993 as many as 59% of Estonian Russophones still considered themselves to be representatives of Soviet culture. At the same time, identification with Russian ethnic identity started to rise: from 85% in 1992 to 92% in 1993 (Kirch & Kirch 1995, p. 53). If we take the results of the independence plebiscite on 3 March 1991 (see Taagepera 1993) as an indirect indicator, it suggests that the 40% of Russophones who voted against Estonian independence were carriers of a reaffirmative identity. The 30% of nonvoters gives an approximation of the size of the group with a privatized identity. This means that the 30% of the Russophones that did vote for Estonian independence were carriers of integrative and adaptive identities. The size of the group with integrative identity configuration can be further estimated from the number of those who had knowledge of Estonian – around 13%. This leaves the number of pursuers of adaptive identity at around 17%. This means that on the eve of Estonian independence, a large proportion of Russophones held a reaffirmative identity and had the hope that Estonia would have two official state languages, with all permanent inhabitants receiving Estonian citizenship.

Yet, the illusions of two state languages and automatic citizenship faded rather quickly, and this had an effect on identity dynamics as well. As the Russophone Estonian journalist Lilia Sokolinskaja later recalled, at the beginning of the 1990s: 'Estonia turned all of its anger towards the Soviet regime against local Russians, making them responsible for all the troubles' (Sokolinskaja 2000, p. 7). This tendency was aggravated by the ethnic policies of Estonia in the first half of the 1990s, which had the goal of restoring the kind of predominantly Estonian nation-state that had existed prior to Soviet annexation. Estonians hoped that Russians would return to their ethnic homeland, and this process was actively supported. There were plans to adopt a very strict citizenship policy, which would have assigned the status of illegal immigrant to all non-Estonians who had settled in Estonia during the Soviet time period.

Even though this aggressive political rhetoric did not materialize in its entirety, a large proportion of Russophones were, nevertheless, pushed out of state-level politics, which caused their withdrawal from the public sphere in more general terms. At this point, for the majority of Russophones in Estonia, identity privatization was the most natural response to the status reversal.

This trend was reflected by shifts in the value systems of Estonians and Russophones in Estonia. During 1991–1993, the categories pertaining to having positions of power and self-realization fell in the value hierarchy for Russophones, but rose in the hierarchy for Estonians (Vihalemm 1997a, p. 33). At the same time, the importance of family, friends and a comfortable life rose in the value hierarchy of Russophones (Vihalemm 1997a, p. 35). A significant difference between Estonians and Russophones was the importance of national history as a part of their identity: while for the Estonians history played a significant part, for Russophones this feature was rather suppressed: only four out of ten mentioned history as a significant part of their identity (Valk 1997, p. 97).

Another important factor in the identity of Estonians was concern over the survival of the Estonian nation, and this concern was directly associated with the presence of Russophones in Estonia: as late as 1999, more than four years after the Soviet army withdrawal from Estonia, 63% of Estonians considered Russophones to be a national threat (Pettai 2000, p. 95). This threat induced a defensive attitude against Russophones, which is reflected in the parliamentary election results in 1992: the nationalist forces won the elections by a large margin, whereas the three electoral coalitions that included moderate politicians favoring milder treatment of Russophones got only 35% of the votes. For the majority of Estonians the main identity dynamic during the collapse of the Soviet Union was reaffirmation, which was directed towards increasing their collective self-assurance in Estonia. This strategy was constructive at the time of the destruction of the Soviet Union, and made possible quick and radical reforms that enabled the Estonian economy to achieve rapid growth. However, it started to hinder societal development quite soon after independence was restored.

Some easing of the attitudes and values of Estonians took place in the mid-1990s, when it became apparent that the Russian community would remain in Estonia permanently. The majority of Estonians came to understand the need to integrate the Russophone community into the society: 26% gave their full support to the idea, and 40% agreed that it might be necessary: 'for Estonians this signified weariness of emotional confrontation, and a wish to be more pragmatic' (Pettai 2000, p. 98). Reaffirmative identity declined among Russians, too. According to Kirch and Kirch (1995, p. 47), around 28% of Russophones showed high ethnocentrism in 1993, implying that around two-thirds of the Russophone community might have had a more pragmatic attitude towards inter-ethnic relations.

*The late 1990s: honeymoon of integration*

The second half of the 1990s appears to have been the most optimistic period of inter-ethnic attitudes in post-Soviet Estonia. By the end of the century, Estonians had become much more tolerant towards Russophones: one-third were willing to actively support integration, and one-third had come to see the Russian-speaking minority as having cultural value. Iris Pettai (2000) considered this a new trend in inter-ethnic relations in Estonia. There were significant changes among Russophones as well. Self-identification as an Estonian citizen and/or member of Estonian society had increased significantly: 47% of Russophones declared that they believed this to be the case (Vihalemm & Masso 2002, p. 188), while a third of Russophones expressed a desire to increase contacts with Estonians and find new friends among them (Proos 2000, p. 113).

With respect to job possibilities, Russophones were in a somewhat weaker position, although ethnic distribution among different job types corresponded quite closely to the ethnic structure of Estonia. Thus, economic inequality was not perceived as having direct and unjust ethnic causes. There was also some homogenization of values: a large proportion of Russophones had come to share the view, common among Estonians, that a good education and hard work were a guarantee of one's well-being in Estonia (Vihalemm 1997a, p. 37).

The recognition that knowledge of the Estonian language provided social capital had risen considerably. While in 1990, only 30% of Russophones in Estonia considered knowledge of Estonian necessary, by 1995 the proportion had risen to 82% (Vihalemm 1997b, p. 249). The significant rise was characterized by the number of those who had acquired a knowledge of Estonian: in 1993, only 13% of Russophones reported that they spoke Estonian fluently or very well, but in 1999 the proportion was 29%. During the same period, the number of those who did not know Estonian at all fell from 42% to 33% (Proos 2000, p. 107). Thus, in 1999, 67% of Russophones knew Estonian at least at a satisfactory level, while in 1993 only 43% were at that level. Even if these self-reported data do not reflect actual knowledge with perfect accuracy, the data certainly show a broad consensus among Russophones that knowledge of Estonian was necessary.

Noticeably, the value of Estonian citizenship had grown in the eyes of Russophones by 1999. While in 1993 48% wished to obtain Estonian citizenship, in 1999 this was the case for 71% of those polled. The proportion of those Russophones who had actually obtained Estonian citizenship was 29% of the community (Pettai 2000, p. 82). One could claim that, by the turn of the century, the majority of Russophones had accepted the existence of the Estonian state and wished to contribute to its sustainability. This positive attitude did not include Estonian politics, though: 70% of the Russophone community was not interested in the political life of Estonia (Proos 2000, p. 123).

Identity dynamics at the end of the century were characterized by a trend towards increasing similarities in the values, attitudes and practices between some subgroups of Estonians and Russophones. According to Todd (2005), such shifts point to integrative identity dynamics, i.e. to the erosion of some values that are incompatible with current practices and to the emergence of some new shared values between the groups. Quite significantly, this trend was supported by the emergence of the consumerist information society in Estonia (Lauristin & Vihalemm 2004) towards the end of the century.

The data presented above indicate that such integrative shifts in identities may have characterized about one-quarter to one-third of both major ethnic groups in Estonia by the end of the twentieth century. This integrative trend was also supported by the media: group-based portrayals of the ethnic communities were abandoned in favor of more person-centered approaches (Tammpuu 2000, p. 5).

In the Estonian media communication sphere, the construction of reaffirming identity configurations decreased significantly during this period. Opinions that Russians were not a part of Estonia, were disloyal and should return to their historic homeland had disappeared from official political statements by the turn of the century, but these opinions were still voiced occasionally in readers' letters to newspapers (Tammpuu 2000, p. 3). According to Kruusvall (2000, p. 15), there might have been around 15–20% of Estonians who still wished to maintain this confrontation, which clearly points to a reaffirming of identity dynamics.

These trends also occurred in the local Russian press, where reaffirming identity construction was weak and unsystematic. The chances of it becoming popular among the majority of Russophones were rated rather low (Jakobson 2002; Vihalemm & Masso 2002). This does not mean that integrative identity processes involved the whole Russophone community. It rather shows that the Russophone community was internally fragmented, a fact that has been stressed by many researchers (see Laitin 1998; Smith 1998; Vihalemm 1999). Thus, among the Russophone population, integrative identity shifts were taking place only for a limited number of subgroups, whereas others opted for identity privatization or adaptation.

This latter identity dynamic could be associated with having Russian citizenship. Statistically, those Russian citizens living permanently in Estonia were characterized by a weak interest in events in Estonia, poor knowledge of Estonian, low tolerance towards multiculturalism and doubtful attitudes towards the sustainability of Estonia in the future. By the end of the century, the number of Russian citizens permanently living in Estonia was 18% of the Russophone community; and there was roughly the same number who supported the opinion that Russians should compete with Estonians for political power within Estonia (Pettai 2000, p. 93).

*2000–2004: Integration on the basis of consumerist individualism*

Good economic growth and widening international communication at the beginning of the twenty-first century promoted the consumerist value system of the Western world in Estonia. According to Kalmus and Vihalemm (2004), this trend particularly influenced the values and attitudes of the younger generation. Much more than the elderly and middle aged, the young were oriented towards pursuing an interesting life and self-fulfillment. Material wealth was a widely desired goal not only for the younger generation. It seemed to be a deficit value, desired more by those who did not have it, i.e. by the poorer segments of society, and by Russophones than by Estonians, a fact that might reflect their weaker economic standing in Estonia. While in the first half of the 1990s Russophones valued power and self-realization less than Estonians, by 2003 these differences had disappeared (Kalmus & Vihalemm 2004, p. 39). This change indicates that Russophones had started to seek the same goals as Estonians: material wealth and an interesting life.

These shifts in values may also indicate the weakening of the privatization tendency in the identities of Russophones and an increase in integrative changes. For Estonians, changes in the value hierarchy were smaller, but the increase in the importance of individualism, personal fulfillment and consumerism meant that the old reaffirming identity trend had lost some of its appeal. According to Laitin (2003), two parallel processes were taking place: Russophones were integrating into Estonian society, while Estonians and Russophones were both integrating into Europe. Thus, shifts were taking place in the identities of both groups and these shifts introduced some common features for both, such as individualism and consumerism. Also, some older values, such as ethnic traditions, started to erode. In this way the changes in the first years of the twenty-first century started to create a basis for a common higher level identity that could be shared by both ethnic groups.

As membership in the EU and NATO became a real possibility, the sense of security increased among Estonians. By 2004, only 11% considered the use of the Russian language, and 16% considered the large number of Russians in Estonia as dangerous for the future of the Estonian culture and nation. Many more considered new immigrants, the extensive use of English and the weakening of their national identity as possible dangers (Kruusvall 2005, p. 48) – an indication that the signs of globalization were starting to be seen as possible threats to the Estonian way of life.

In national conservative circles, these new dangers motivated attempts to strengthen national identity: some organizations were born, such as 'The Society for the Protection of the Estonian Language' (1999) and 'The Estonian Club' (2003). A goal was set in the 'Strategy for the Development of the Estonian Language' (2004) that the state should initiate and finance a program that would promote Estonian national identity. The dangers of weakening ethnic identity were also noticed in the conservative circles of the Russophone community, where they were fueled by the first signs of what could be seen as a cascade of assimilation. According to Laitin (2003, p. 210), as many as 25% of Russophone parents expressed a wish to choose an Estonian medium school for their children, and 72% of Russophone ninth-graders wanted their prospective children to be educated at least partly in Estonian in the future.

However, the attempts to create ethnic mobilization did not resonate with the public mood, either in the Estonian or Russian community: support for conservative ethnic ideology and groups was very low. The society was involved in achieving economic goals, joining the EU was on the agenda, and the ideology of success was widely supported. Far more than the issues of identity, social inequality problems touched the nerve of the society. This was well reflected in the discourse of 'two Estonias', of the rich and of the poor, in 2002, and in the ensuing attempts to reach a national covenant to overcome the division.

## 2004–2007: identity threat

According to Hornsey and Hogg (2000), the identity threat caused by obscuring boundary features and low entitativity is a common cause for inter-ethnic conflicts in situations where the conflicting groups have a common superordinate identity category. Intergroup conflict is, in this situation, the most effective path, because it leads to the sharpening of ethnic boundaries and to the clarification of the group identity prototype.

As argued by Saarts (2008), the Bronze Soldier chain of events was an ethnic counter-reaction to forceful Europeanization in the last decade, when Estonia struggled to meet European standards in multiculturalism and political correctness in order to achieve EU membership. Also, as some authors (Lobjakas 2008; Loone 2008; Saarts 2008) note, EU and NATO membership provided the sense of security that enabled the Estonian majority to reinforce its values in the society in such an outright manner as the relocation of the war memorial. However, in 2004, the ethnic situation was far too relaxed for anything of this scale to happen. Yet, as the analysis below shows, it was precisely the feeling of the threat of weakening ethnic identity and the blurring of boundaries between Estonians and Russophones that motivated small right-wing groups on both sides to look for measures to increase ethnic mobilization.

The conflict surrounding the Lihula monument can be seen as an attempt to reinforce Estonian identity and pride; however, it did not create momentum or gain any significant popularity. It was just another attempt at identity politics, in which various political entrepreneurs hoped to mobilize the masses to gain power and influence. However, the monument was a nuisance for the government and its careless removal in August 2004 created significant resistance. In a public poll on the most important events of 2004, the removal of the Lihula monument was placed third, after joining NATO and the EU.

After the removal of the Lihula monument, the fact that the Bronze Soldier still stood in the center of Tallinn created a sense of injustice among many conservative Estonians. This injustice was the basis for the emergence of an 'eye-for-an-eye' type of discourse against the Bronze Soldier. This discourse, in turn, provided a good rationale for the mobilization of conservative Russophones in defense of the monument.

These developments were catalyzed by Russian identity politics, which had taken the victory in the Great Patriotic War as one of its core elements, particularly in connection with its 50th anniversary. Russian identity politics had also significantly influenced the identity of Estonian Russophones: at the beginning of the 1990s, history was not seen as an important part of the identity of Estonian Russophones, mainly because the communists' crimes were a public issue at that time. This trend changed and the victory became the backbone of Russian national pride.

The more important the Bronze Soldier became for the Russophone community, the more eagerly Estonian conservative circles demanded its removal. However, public opinion was still quite indifferent and indecisive. To change this, it was necessary to have a blow struck against the pride of Estonians. To achieve this, two Estonian national activists went to the gathering of Russophones at the Bronze Soldier on 9 May 2006 with a banner and national flag. As one of them, Jüri Böhm, later admitted, their goal was to let the flag be desecrated in order to awaken an Estonian nation that had been numbed by the welfare society (Liiv 2007). The Russophone activists used a similar rhetoric. For example, one of their leaflets stated that the Estonian elite 'aim to tear away Estonian Russians from their Russian roots, to break their emotional ties to their historic homeland... Russians are being made into well-fed slaves of the nationalist elite' (Põld 2008).

Even though activist groups on both sides were relatively small, their identity dialogue was amplified in the media to a considerable extent. A paradoxical situation emerged in which marginal groups in the society were able to bring about quite significant changes in the values and attitudes of the majority (see Hogg & Reid 2006). In Estonian politics, this was decisive in determining the choice of actions that followed.

The relocation of the Bronze Soldier fulfilled the goals of the ethnic activists: reaffirmation of the old identity distinctions and meanings increased. By comparing different identity orientations among Estonians and Russophones in 2002 (Pettai 2002) and in the summer of 2007 (Lauristin 2008), it becomes apparent that there has been a shift towards the sharpening of the ethnic opposition between Estonians and Russophones. While in 2002 about 19% of Estonians followed the reaffirmative pattern of identity, after the relocation of the statue the proportion rose to 23%. The number of Estonians manifesting integrative attitudes had decreased from 53% to 36%. The proportion of those who accepted the presence of Russophones, but did not want to have contacts with them had risen considerably, in 2002, 28% were in this category and as many as 40% in 2007 (Lauristin 2008; Pettai 2002). This segment of society can be associated with the adaptive pattern of identity; they accept the multicultural practices of Europe, but would certainly prefer a mono-ethnic state. If the inter-ethnic tension grew, this group would most likely turn towards open reaffirmation of their ethnic Estonian identity.

Among Russophones, the number of those manifesting integrative attitudes and values has dropped from 46% (Pettai 2002) to 27% (Lauristin 2008). The number of those who cooperate on pragmatic grounds, but are disillusioned has risen from 20% (Pettai 2002) to 33% (Lauristin 2008). This segment can be associated with the adaptive identity. According to Belobrovtsev (2008, p. 123), the Russophones 'who previously had sincerely believed in Estonian democracy and justice, have been deeply hurt' by the government action and the reactions of large sections of Estonians to the 'Bronze night' (the common name for the Russophone unrest). As the following year did not normalize the situation, but made it even worse, Belobrovtsev (2008) predicts that in the near future, this will lead to the emigration of Russophone specialists. Similarly, it is possible that this group will turn towards the reaffirmative identity. The possibility of the mobilization of Russophones to an oppositional position towards Estonians is stressed by a number of researchers, such as Lobjakas (2008) and Vetik (2008).

It is evident that among Russophones, the number of supporters of the reaffirmative identity has also risen since the Bronze Soldier relocation. However, it is not easy to estimate the size of this group. According to Pettai (2002), in 2002, 21% of Russophones could be categorized as non-tolerant and 14% as discrepant. Both of these categories could indicate a reaffirmative identity configuration. However, it is more likely that, for elderly people, these characteristics indicate a privatized identity. Thus, it would be sensible to differentiate these identity groups on the basis of age. In the first category, 80% of the respondents were younger than 60, while in the second category only 41% were. These two subgroups together would make a total of 22% of the Russophone population manifesting the reaffirmative identity. This would leave the 12% of the discrepant and non-tolerant elderly Russophones as bearers of the privatized type of identity. Using the same method to examine the 2007 data (Lauristin 2008) would give us a 28% share in the reaffirmative identity and a 12% share in the privatized identity.

The identity dynamics in Estonia from the 1990s to 2007, discussed in this essay, are summarized in Figure 2. Each line in the diagram indicates a period that ends with the year indicated. However, as the surveys that the data are based on were not conducted in exactly the years indicated, but during the whole period, the data characterize the period, not the exact year indicated. I also note that, as the analysis is based on indirect features matched with particular identity trends, the percentages in the summary diagram are rough estimations of the size of different identity groups. Thus the summary diagram is a hypothesis that is grounded on empirical data, not an exact result of surveys specially conducted to specify these identity classes.

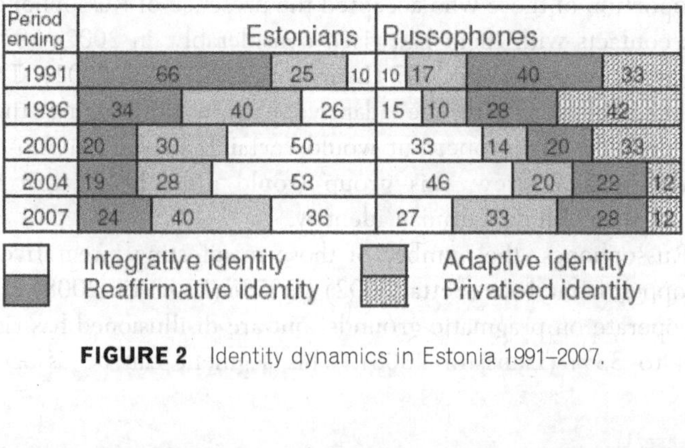

| Period ending | Estonians | | | | Russophones | | | |
|---|---|---|---|---|---|---|---|---|
| 1991 | 66 | | 25 | 10 | 10 | 17 | 40 | 33 |
| 1996 | 34 | 40 | 26 | | 15 | 10 | 28 | 42 |
| 2000 | 20 | 30 | 50 | | 33 | 14 | 20 | 33 |
| 2004 | 19 | 28 | 53 | | 46 | | 20 | 22 | 12 |
| 2007 | 24 | 40 | 36 | | 27 | 33 | 28 | 12 |

Integrative identity — Adaptive identity
Reaffirmative identity — Privatised identity

**FIGURE 2** Identity dynamics in Estonia 1991–2007.

Despite these cautions, the overall pattern of identity dynamics should be a close approximation of the actual developments.

## Discussion: Search for a New Equilibrium

Hornsey and Hogg (2000, p. 148) stress that 'emphasizing a superordinate identity without acknowledging subgroup differences can be threatening to the distinctiveness of the subgroup identities'. The developments during the last ten years indicate that this might well have been the case in Estonia. The speedy integration process with the EU, the over-stressing of specific European values and the emergence of post-modern fluid consumerist identities created insecurity among Estonians, while the over-stressing of Estonian civic identity and values created the same insecurity in the Russophone community. Instead of reinforcing the sense of superordinate identity, this created a negative reaction. To avoid such backlashes, Hornsey and Hogg (2000, p. 149) suggest that, in certain critical dimensions, acknowledgment of subgroup identities and the preservation of differences within the context of an abstractly defined superordinate identity would enhance integrative identity dynamics and strengthen the superordinate identity category.

Such a need is also apparent in Estonia. It is understandable that the Estonian Russophone community strives for positive self-esteem, as does any other ethnic group. Partially, the ideological struggle around the Bronze Soldier can be seen as an attempt by Russophones to claim a higher status and level of self-esteem. As this discourse has a zero sum structure, i.e. more positive self-esteem for Russophones could only be achieved by some lowering of the status of Estonian self-esteem, the removal of the Bronze Soldier was a bold statement that such identity politics would be considered unacceptable by the Estonian majority.

The question remains as to what the response of the Russophone community will be towards this development. The latest research shows that the time may be ripe for a collective demand for some societal recognition and higher status for Russophones in Estonian society. According to Lauristin (2008), two-thirds of Estonian Russophones have adjusted well or quite well to the life and demands of Estonia since the collapse of the Soviet Union. Many have learned the Estonian language and gained citizenship, but this has not brought about a rise in their status within Estonian society. According to Vihalemm (2008), the values of self-attainment, power and success have risen considerably in the value hierarchy of Russophones and are at present higher than the same values in the hierarchy of Estonians. Recall that in the early 1990s, these values were higher in the hierarchy of Estonians and, by the turn of the century, had roughly equal standing.

This means that the period of identity privatization that occurred after the collapse of the Soviet Union is over. Quite a large number of Russophones went through an integrative shift in their identities and wanted to be culturally recognized in Estonia. However, the removal of the Bronze Soldier was a powerful sign of rejection of one of those claims.

Whether this means a new round of identity privatization for Estonian Russophones or whether they will still opt for identity reaffirmation on the same ideological premises, depends to a great extent on whether it is possible to find an alternative ideology for the improvement of the self-esteem and status of the Russophone community in Estonia that will also be acceptable to the majority of ethnic Estonians. Certainly there are some attempts at this being made (see Ehala 2008; Vetik 2008) and the context has changed considerably since the Georgian war – but only time will tell how all this will affect identity dynamics in Estonia.

## References

Austin, J. (1961) *How to Do Things with Words: The William James Lectures Delivered at Harvard University in 1955* [edited by J. O. Urmson] (Oxford, Clarendon).

Belobrovtsev, V. (2008) 'Kuidas me kaotasime integratsiooni', *Vikerkaar*, 23, 4–5, pp. 121–8.

BNS (2006) 'Eestlased ei poolda pronkssõduri omaalgatuslikku kõrvaldamist', *Postimees*, 23 May, available at: http://www.postimees.ee/270506/esileht/siseuudised/202804.php, accessed 15 April 2008.

Bourdieu, P. (1991) *Language and Symbolic Power* (Cambridge, Polity Press).

Brüggemann, K. & Kasekamp, A. (2008) 'The Politics of History and the "War of Monuments" in Estonia', *Nationalities Papers*, 36, 3.

Burke, P. J. (eds) (2006) *Contemporary Social Psychological Theories* (Stanford, Stanford University Press).

Ehala, M. (2008) 'The Birth of the Russian-speaking Minority in Estonia', *Eurozine*, available at: http://www.eurozine.com/articles/2008-09-11-ehala-en.html, accessed 8 December 2008 [translation of 'Venekeelse põhisvähemuse sünd'], *Vikerkaar*, 4–5, pp. 93–104].

Habermas, J. (1979) 'What is Universal Pragmatics?', in Habermas, J. (ed.) (1979), pp. 1–68.

Habermas, J. (1979) *Communication and the Evolution of Society* (Boston, Beacon Press).

Hogg, M. A. & Reid, S. A. (2006) 'Social Categorization and Human Communication: The Social Identity Perceptive and Group Norms', *Communication Theory*, 16, 1, pp. 7–30.

Hornsey, M. J. & Hogg, M. A. (2000) 'Assimilation and Diversity: An Integrative Model of Subgroup Relations', *Personality and Social Psychology Review*, 4, 2, pp. 143–56.

Jakobson, V. (2002) 'Civic, Political and Ethno-cultural Collective Identities Constructed in the Russian Press of Estonia since 1947', in Lauristin, M. & Heidmets, M. (eds) (2002), pp. 175–84.

Järve, P. (ed.) (1997) *Vene noored Eestis: sotsioloogiline mosaiik* (Tallinn, Avita).

Kaasik, P. (2006) *Common Grave for and a Memorial to Red Army Soldiers on Tõnismägi, Tallinn. Historical Statement.* Manuscript, available at: http://www.valitsus.ee/brf/failid/statement_red_army_memorial.pdf, accessed 9 April 2008.

Kalmus, V. & Vihalemm, T. (2004) 'Eesti siirdekultuuri väärtused', *Eesti elavik 21. sajandi algul: ülevaade uurimuse mina: maailm: meedia tulemustest. Studia Societatis et Communicationis*, 1, pp. 31–44.

Kirch, M. & Kirch, A. (1995) 'Ethnic Relations: Estonians and Non-Estonians', *Nationalities Papers*, 23, 1, pp. 43–59.

Kruusvall, J. (2000) 'Integratsioonist arusaamine Eesti ühiskonnas', *Integratsioon Eesti ühiskonnas: Monitoring 2000* (Tallinn, MEIS), pp. 14–21.

Kruusvall, J. (2005) 'Hinnangud lõimumise edukusele, tulevikuohud ja tõrjuva suhtumise ilmingud', *Uuringu 'Integratsiooni monitoring 2005' aruanne* (Tallinn, TLÜ Rahvusvaheliste ja Sotsiaaluuringute Instituut), pp. 43–59.

Laitin, D. (1998) *Identity in Formation: The Russian-Speaking Populations in the Near Abroad* (Ithaca & London, Cornell University Press).

Laitin, D. (2003) 'Three Models of Integration and the Estonian/Russian Reality', *Journal of Baltic Studies*, 34, 2, pp. 197–222.

Laius, A., Proos, I. & Pettai, I. (eds) (2000) *Integratsioonimaastik – ükskõiksusest koosmeeleni* (Tallinn, Jaan Tõnissoni Instituut).

Lauristin, M. (2008) 'Eesti ühiskonna valmisolek integratsiooniks', *Eesti inimarengu aruanne 2007* (Tallinn, Eesti Koostöö Kogu), pp. 81–6.

Lauristin, M. & Heidmets, M. (eds) (2002) *The Challenge of the Russian Minority: Emerging Multicultural Democracy in Estonia* (Tartu, Tartu Ülikooli Kirjastus).

Lauristin, M. & Vetik, R. (eds) (2000) *Integratsioon Eesti ühiskonnas. Monitooring 2000* (Tallinn, TPÜ Rahvusvaheliste ja Sotsiaaluuringute Instituut).

Lauristin, M. & Vihalemm, P. (2004) 'Sissejuhatus : uurimuse mina : maailm : meedia metodoloogiast ja tähendusest', *Eesti elavik 21. sajandi algul: ülevaade uurimuse mina: maailm: meedia tulemustest. Studia Societatis et Communicationis*, 1, pp. 23–8.

Lawler, E. J. (2006) 'The Affect Theory of Social Exchange', in Burke, P. J. (eds) (2006), pp. 137–64.

Lehti, M., Jutila, M. & Jokisipilä, M. (2008) 'Never Ending Second World War: Public Performances of National Dignity and the Drama of the Bronze Soldier', *Journal of Baltic Studies*, 39, 4.

Liiv, U. E. (2007) *Pronksöö: vene mäss Tallinnas*. Documentary movie.

Lobjakas, A. (2008) 'Huntington ja kartulikoored', *Vikerkaar*, 23, 4–5, pp. 128–34.

Loone, O. (2008) 'Tänu kellele pole meil kodusõda?', *Vikerkaar*, 23, 4–5, pp 139–45.

Petersoo, P. & Tamm, M. (eds) (2008) *Monumentaalne konflikt: mälu, poliitika ja identiteet tänapäeva Eestis* (Tallinn, Varrak).

Pettai, I. (2000) 'Eestlaste ja mitte-eestlaste integratsiooniparadigma', in Laius, A., Proos, I. & Pettai, I. (eds) (2000), pp. 70–106.

Pettai, I. (2002) 'Eestlaste ja mitte-eestlaste sallivustüpoloogia', *Integratsioon Eesti ühiskonnas. Monitooring 2002* (Tallinn, MEIS, TPÜRASI), pp. 25–41.

Põld, T. (2008) 'Pronksööl juhtunule eelnes aktiivne ässitustöö', *Postimees*, 28 January, available at: http://www.postimees.ee/290108/esileht/siseuudised/308632.php, accessed 23 September 2008.

Poleschuk, V. (2007) 'War of Monuments: A Chronological Review', in Poleschuk, V. (ed.) (2007), pp. 10–23.

Poleschuk, V. (ed.) (2007) *Bronze Soldier: April Crisis* (Tallinn, Inimõiguste Teabekeskus).

Proos, I. (2000) 'Eesti keele tähendus mitte-eestlaste integratsioonis', in Laius, A., Proos, I. & Pettai, I. (eds) (2000), pp. 107–34.

Ruutsoo, R. (2008) 'Järelaitav demokraatia Eestis: saavutused ja väljavaated', *Vikerkaar*, 23, 4–5, 1, pp. 11–120.

Saarts, T. (2008) 'Pronksiöö – sundeuroopastamise läbikukkumine ja rahvusliku kaitsedemokraatia sünd', *Vikerkaar*, 23, 4–5, pp. 105–10.

Smith, D. J. (1998) 'Russia, Estonia and the Search for a Stable Ethno-Politics', *Journal of Baltic Studies*, 29, 1, pp. 3–18.

Smith, D. J. (2008) '"Woe from Stones": Commemoration, Identity Politics and Estonia's "War of Monuments"', *Journal of Baltic Studies*, 39, 4.

Sokolinskaja, L. (2000) 'Intervjuu Lidia Sokolinskajaga', in Laius, A., Proos, I. & Pettai, I. (eds) (2000), pp. 7–9.

Taagepera, R. (1993) *Estonia. Return to Independence* (Boulder, Westview Press).

Tamm, M. & Halla, S. (2008) 'Ajalugu, poliitika ja identiteet', in Petersoo, P. & Tamm, M. (eds) (2008), pp. 18–51.

Tammpuu, T. (2000) 'Sallivus ja rahvussuhted eestikeelses ajakirjanduses', in Lauristin, M. & Vetik, R. (eds) (2000), pp. 1–5.

Todd, J. (2005) 'Social Transformation, Collective Categories, and Identity Change', *Theory and Society*, 34, 4, pp. 429–63.

Valk, A. (1997) 'Eestlaste ja venelaste ajaloolisest identiteedist', in Järve, P. (ed.) (1997) *Vene noored Eestis: sotsioloogiline mosaiik* (Tallinn, Avita), pp. 93–8.

Vetik, R. (2008) 'Etniline domineerimine Eestis', in Petersoo, P. & Tamm, M. (eds) (2008), pp. 112–26.

Vihalemm, T. (1997a) 'Vene vähemuse väärtusorientatsioonid, referents-rühmad ja igapäevastrateegiad Eesti ühiskonnas 1991–1995', in Järve, P. (ed.) (1997), pp. 27–46.

Vihalemm, T. (1997b) 'Vene elanikkonna eesti keele oskus, kasutamine ja hoiakud selle omandamise suhtes 1990–1995', in Järve, P. (ed.) (1997), pp. 245–54.

Vihalemm, T. (1999) 'Group Identity Formation Processes among Russian-Speaking Settlers of Estonia: A View from a Linguistic Perspective', *Journal of Baltic Studies*, 30, 1, pp. 18–39.

Vihalemm, T. (2008) 'Kultuurierinevused: identiteet ja väärtused', *Eesti inimarengu aruanne 2007* (Tallinn, Eesti Koostöö Kogu), pp. 67–72.

Vihalemm, T. & Masso, A. (2002) 'Patterns of Self-Identification among the Younger Generation of Russians', in Lauristin, M. & Heidmets, M. (eds) (2002), pp. 185–98.

Vihalemm, T. & Masso, A. (2007) '(Re)construction of Collective Identities After the Dissolution of the Soviet Union: The Case of Estonia', *Nationalities Papers*, 35, 1, pp. 71–91c.

# Index

Page numbers in *Italics* represent tables.
Page numbers in **Bold** represent figures.

activism 40, **42**
activism indices 39
activists 139, 147
adaptation: identity 141, 147
advertising 57
aestheticization 53
age: and attitudes 120-1; and consumption 55-6, 58-9, *58*; and cultural preferences 86; generational differences 106-7; and historical events 97; and identity 148; and mental structures **100, 104**; and sustainable consumption *58*; and values 120-1, *see also* generations
April crisis 125, 127, 128
April riots 17, 92, 116, 133, *see also* Bronze Soldier
art exhibitions 74
Aslund, A. 3
assimilation: identity 141, 146
attitudes 120-1; affirmative 125; ambivalent 124, 127; distrustful 126; inter-ethnic 123-8, 128-9; inter-group 118-20, 121-3; negative 125, 127-8; and personal experience 128; regional 121

Baltic independence 7-8
beliefs 96; ideological 76; normative 85; popular 4

book preferences 79-80, **80**, 83
Bourdieu, P. 75-6
brand valuation 57, *58*, 59, *59*, 62, 64, 103
Bronze night 148
Bronze Soldier 92, 133; crisis 22; and Europeanization 146; eye-for-an-eye discourse 146-7; and identity distinctions 147, 148; as Liberator 138-9; meaning of 138; relocation 101, 134-7, 147, *see also* April crisis *and* April riots

censorship 74
Centre Party 20
change 29; assessments of 1; external factors 2-5; information technology-related 32; infrastructural 43-4; internal factors 2-5; meaning of 29, 96; technological 28
children of freedom 65
Citizens' Committees 7-8
citizens' movement 7, 8
citizenship 10-11, 93, 94, 117, 142, 144; European 104-5; Russian 144-5
Citizenship Law 95
civic organizations 13-14
civic society 20, 35
civil society 3, 95, 108
class society 76

Coalition Party 11
commemoration 138, 139
communication 38, 39, 41, 117-18, 119
communicative act 134
communitarian world-view 102
community: discursive 119; imagined 101; solidarity with 66, 99, 105
community engagement 36-7
competition 3-4; political 20
competitiveness 31, 41-2
computerization 12, 33
computers training 34
Constitutional Assembly 8
consultation websites 35-6
consumer literacy 68
consumer types 60-5, *61*; socio-demographic groupings *62*
consumerism 13, 18, 44; and age 58-9, *58*; by consumer types **60**; and education 63, 65; and ethnicity 59-60, *59*; index of 57; as phenomenon 53; as self-expression 55; and sustainability 53-5; Western 53; and young people 58, *see also* culture, consumer
consumerist individualism 145-6
contacts: inter-ethnic 143; inter-group 118-20, 121-3, 128-30
conversion: identity 140
cooling effect 116
Council of Europe 8
country people 67
creative activities 78, 81
cultural accommodation 117
cultural activities 76-7, 78, **79**, 80, 81
cultural adaptation 130
cultural beliefs 76-7, **78**
cultural consumption 73, 76, 83-5, **84**
cultural cosmopolitanism 82-3
cultural hobbies 77
cultural orientations 80; active and versatile 81-2; entertainment-centered 82-3; and ethnicity 85; excitement-centered 82-3; pragmatic 82; social and demographic backgrounds *91*; traditional 82
cultural pools 96-7
cultural preferences 73, 76, **84**, 85, *89-90*; Soviet period 85
cultural resistance 75
cultural resources 77, 96, 106
cultural templates 67, 96, 105, 107, 108
culture: and age 86; classical 85; consumer 51, 52-3, 65, 66, 95, 102-3, 107; diversity of 118, 123; as a field 75-7, 85; high 73-4, 85; indifferent attitudes 83; interest in 80; low 73-4, 85; majority 117; mass 73-4, 95; media 66; normative meaning of 73-5; popular 107; public opinion 74; as socializing agent 107; Soviet 107-8, 141-2; spiritual value 75, 85; transition *see* transition culture; Western popular 74

deficit economy 74
democracy 4, 34, 41-2; alternatives to 95; consolidating 2-3; consumerist 44; deficit of 14; Internet 44, 45; new 3; participatory 11, 34, 45; and technology 28, 35
democratic forum 36
democratic practices 33-7
democratic space 36
democratization 94
deprivation 103
development agenda 4, 54
development planning 18
discursive communities 119
discursive learning 5
disrespect 127
diversity 118, 120-1
domestic agencies 12-15
dumping 54

e-services 38, 39, 41, 43
e-state 29, 31-2, 35

e-voting 35, 45
eco-labels 58, 59
economic crisis 22
economic development 16, 17-18
economic efficiency 10
economic growth 1
economic reforms 8-11
economic restructuring 42
economic stabilization 11-12
education 41-2; and consumerism 63, 65; and cultural orientation 82; and ethnic communication 119; and information technology 32; linguistically separated 128; minority 16-17
*Eesti Keskerakond* 20
*égalité* 93
elections 9, 14-15, 16
electronic tax office 43
elites 5, 13, 14, 20
emancipation 101
engagement 35
entertainment 38, 39, 41, 74, 81, 82-3, 85, 86
environmental responsibility 53-4
environmentalism 54, 55
equality 10
The Estonian Club 145
Estonian crisis 15
Estonian Development Fund 18
Estonian nationalists 139, 147
Estonias: two 14
ethnic belonging 101-2
ethnic groups: and consumerism 59-60, *59*; and consumption 55-6, 59-60, *59*; cultural orientations 85; cultural resources 106; cultural templates 108; identity 145-6, 146; inequality 92; inter-group attitudes 118-20; inter-group contacts 118-20, 120-3; inter-group relations 140; mental structures **100**; network identity 106; social status 141; and sustainable consumption *59*; tolerance of *121*, 143, see also Russian-speaking minority
ethnic minority policy 4, 12, 16-17
ethnic mobilization 146
ethnic opposition 95
ethnic policies 10, 142
ethnic tolerance index 120
European Union (EU): accession 1, 12, 12-15, 21; impact of 3; integration into 145; membership 1, 12, 15-16, 55, 145, 146
Europeanization 146
exclusion 95
experts 2
external aid 10
external factors 2-5, 18, 21

friendships 126

generations 92, 97, *see also* age
Global Competitiveness Report 31
global orientation 101, 104, 106
government *19*
Great Patriotic War 138
green consumerists 60, 63-4, 67
green ethic 67
green goods 55

health care 21
hedonism 101; alternative 68
hedonistic ethic 55
history 79; national 142
human rights agenda 4
humor 75

ideal preferences 76
identities 96; ethnic 133; social 97; subgroup 149; transnational 101
identity 98; and age 148; change of 141; collective 140; construction of 137; in media communication 144; national 145-6; network 101-2, 105, 107; protest 108; social 140; sub-cultural 102;

superordinate 140, 149; weakening 145-6, 146
identity battles 136
identity categories 140
identity dynamics 140-9, **148**
identity groups 140, 148
identity patterns 117-18
identity threat 146-9
ideological control 74-5
incomes 83-5
indifferent type consumers 60, 63-4
individualism 13, 145-6
individuals 29, 43; choices 73; turn to 53-4
information: study-related 38, 39, 41
information and communication technology (ICT) 28-9; indicators 30-2; political agenda 32-3
information society 13, 33; public understanding 43
Information Society (IS) policies 29
Institute of Memory 16
integration 16-17, 20, 21, 147; and consumerism 145-6; and enlargement discourses 21; honeymoon of 143-5; institutional 117; and language 94, 117; public image 17; recommendations 108; Russian-speaking minority 92
integration policy 12, 92, 117
Integration Strategy 93
interest groups 3-4
internal factors 2-5, 20, 21
international agencies 3, 9-10, 11; and minority integration 16-17
international monetary agencies 3, 9
Internet: banking 31; individual practices 37-41; non-users 39; use of 30, **30**, 31, 44, 95, 106; user typologies 37, 38, *40*, **42**
Internetization 28-9, 37
irony 75

jobs 143

justice 8, 10, 103, 137

*kaasamine* 35
knowledge transfer 10
Kohtla-Järve 119
*kolkhoz* mentality 67

Laitin, D. 117
language 117, 124, 126, 143-4; games 75; and respect 129, 130; Russian 127; segregated activities 119, 129; in Soviet period 94; symbolic value 118, 129, 130
Latvia 93, 103-6
lavish type consumers 60, 64, 67
leaders 3-4
learning process 21-2
liberalism 4, 13, 18; shock therapy 11
Liberators' Monument 134
lifestyle: dimensions of 78-9; family-centered 82; homogeneity of 52
lifestyle research 76
Lihula monument 135-6, 146
Lisbon Review 31
Lisbon strategy 17
littering 54
Look at the World 34

Maastricht criteria 12
Mägi, E. 32-3
marketization 14
mass movements 7, 11
material resources 83
meaning: constructing 137-9
media 39-41, 66, 144
memory: collective 92; historical 4
mental structures 96, 99-103, **100**, 108; and age **100**, **104**; Latvia 103-6
Meri, L. 12
military threat 9
minority protection 3, 16
modernity 54, 65
Molotov-Ribbentrop Pact 141

monuments 134, 135-6, **135**, 146, *see also* Bronze Soldier
mutual mediation 21

narratives 52, 96, 137
Narva 119
national anthem 125
national awakening 44
national currency 8
national movements 7
naturalization 17, 94
nature 79; relationship with 60, 62, 63, 64, 65; and society 68
networks: communication 119; friendship 129; overlapping 130
North Atlantic Treaty Organization (NATO): accession 1, 12; membership 145, 146
novels 74

online activities 31
online forum 43
online practices 37
online voting 35, 45
organized irresponsibility 54
Osale.ee 36-7, 45
*osalus* 35

Paris riots 93
participation 44; civic 7; e-participation 35-6; ladder of 36; local 37, 39-41; new media 39, **42**; online 33-7; political 29; pseudo-participation 36; Russian-speaking minority 93; token 45; traditional 39, **41**, **42**
participation indices 37
passivity 40, **42**, 44; cultural 83
personality 126
petition signing 45
poetry 75
policy agenda 4-5, 6
policy documents 32, 33, 42, 43
policy-making 36
political agenda 5-18, 22, 29, 32-3

political class 13
political expression 75
political parties: and capitalist elite 20; center-left 11, *19*; center-right 9, 11, 13, *19*; populist 15
politics 86; extraordinary 8-11; identity 133, 147; professionalization 13; reform 9, 11, 14
Popular Front 7
post-materialism 53, 62, 64
post-revolutionary generation 65
power 102, 142; imbalance of 36; symbolic 137
pragmatic accommodation 116
pragmatics: principles of 134
pressure groups 22
Principles of Estonian Information Policy 33
privatization: identity 141-3, 145, 148, 149
privatization schemes 10
*Pro Patria* party 15
protestant ethic 63
public accountability 14
public opinion: culture 74; information society 43; integration policy 17; reform policies 11, 14; transition policies 15
puritan ethic 55, 67

Rate.ee 44
reaffirmation: identity 140, 141-3, 147, 148, 149
reburial 101
recognition 117
recycling 63, 66
Reform Party 18, 136, 137
*Reformierakond* 18, 136, 137
religiosity 100-1
*Res Publica* 15
resistance 118
respect 129, 130
restitution 7-8, 10
restoration 94, 107

restraint 55
ritual approbation 141
romantic ethic 55, 68
Russian behavior 124, 125
Russian factor 9
Russian-speaking minority 2, 12; attitudes towards 123-5, 143; attitudes towards Estonians 125-8; and Bronze Soldier 147; and consumer culture 102-3; consumption patterns 56, 59, 66; contact with ethnic Estonians 120-3, *122*, **122**; cultural accommodation 117; cultural orientation 85; cultural templates 108; integration 92; Latvia 104-6; mental structures **100**; as national threat 142; network identity 106; participation 93; policy towards 16-17; power relations 116; regional dispersal 117; religiosity 100-1; riots 136-7; self-esteem 149, 150; social networks 102, 105; social status 139, 149, 150; Soviet culture 107-8, 141-2; sustainable consumption 66; value hierarchy 149; young people 123-8, *see also* ethnic groups
Rüütel, A. 14

*säästev tarbimine* 67
salvation 99, 105
saving consumption 67
saving practices 60
saving type consumers 60, 62-3, 67
scarcities 52, 53
school *see* education
secularism 105
security 101-2, 104-6, 145, 149
self-conception 98
self-expression 55, 75, 81
self-identification 96, 98, 101, 104
self-improvement 79
self-perceptions 140
self-realization 78, 104, 142
shock therapy 11

Singing Revolution 7-8, 75, 94
single application users 38, 39, 41
small-scale users 38, 39, 41
social coherence 93
social diseases 1
social distance 120-3
social exclusion 66
social mobilization 138
social movements 7
social networking 44
social networks 102
social status 81-2; ethnic groups 141; immigrants 95; Russian-speaking minority 139, 149, 150
social-distance recording method 120
socialization 44, 74, 108
socializing 78, 124
socializing agents 107
The Society for the Protection of the Estonian Language 145
Soviet heritage 67
Soviet period 94; cultural attitudes 85; environmental problems 54; as freedom 138-9; identity politics 133, 147; positive attitude towards 99-100
Soviet War Memorial *see* Bronze Soldier
spiral of silence 11
spiritual harmony 99-101
status symbols 65, 82
step-by-step approach 7-8
strategic planning 18
survey data 37, 56-7, 77, 97-9
sustainability 53-5
sustainable consumption 51, 54; and age *58*; by consumer types **60**; and ethnicity *59*; index of 58; Russian-speaking minority 66
sustainable development 53
symbolic consumption 53
symbolic differentiation 75
symbolic goods 53
symbols 52, 96, 137; commemorative 139; cultural consumption 76;

normative 75; old and new 55; Soviet occupation 139

Tallinn 119, 121, 133, 138-9
*Täna Otsustan Mina* (TOM) 33, 36, 37
taste 73, 74, 76, 85
technical hobbies 78
technological determinism 43
technological revolution 28
teenagers 59, 64
Terk, E. 18
theater 74, 75
Tiger Leap Program 13, 28, 32, 35
time 76
tokenisms 36
tolerance 117, 120, 123-4; of ethnic groups *121*, 143
tolerance groups 120
Tõnismägi 134, **135**
top-down logic 34, 43
transformation 1, 2; agenda 7; and consumer culture 52-3
transition: alienation phase 33-4; concepts of 5; conditions of 2; and environmentalism 54-5; external factors 18; and information and communication technology (ICT) 32-3; inter-ethnic relations 95; internal factors 20; losers 13, 14, 21, 21-2, 95; periodization of 5-18; post-revolutionary phase 33-4; studies of 29, 37; triple 20; winners 13, 14, 20, 21-2, 95, 107; and young people 65
transition culture 4-5, 13, 51-2, 95, 96; generations in 97; as mediation field 21-2
transition indicators 8

uncertainty 116

value systems 142
values 52, 96; and age 65; commodity 75; cultural 4; hierarchy 145, 149; inter-group 144; materialistic 63, 64, 76, 102; modernist 33, 105; national 82; post-materialist 62, 64; power-related 102; self-expression 22; Soviet 55; spiritual 85, 101; survival 22; universalistic 99
vandalism 136, 137
versatile user 38, 39, 41
Virtanen, T. 76

War of Independence 134
Washington consensus 8
wealth 63, 84, 102, 105, 145
web portal 33
well-being 33, 83-4
West 3, 93
Westernization 14
work 38, 39, 41; contacts at 122-3
World Bank 9, 21
World War Two 137-8

young people 44, 45, 52, 64; and consumption 55-6, 58; cultural templates 107; entertainment 86; ethnic relations 119, 120, 128; European identity 101; friendship networks 129; as green consumerists 64; inter-ethnic attitudes 118, 123-9; intolerance 121; and nature 65; network identity 107; peer pressure 119; and politics 86; pro-environmental behaviour 56; self-identification 65; self-representation 103; and sustainability 68; third-generation immigrant 95; tolerance 123-4; and transition 65